Turning Segmented Lamps

Ralph S. Buckland

Schiffer Publishing Ltd

4880 Lower Valley Road, Atglen, Pennsylvania 19310

Dedication

This book is dedicated to Kathy, my wife, for a lifetime of support and love. A special thanks to editor, Jesse Marth; my daughter, Kim Mead; and daughter-in-law, Dinah Thornton-Buckland.

Other Schiffer Books on Related Subjects:

Turning Natural Edge Bowls, 978-0-7643-3562-4, $19.99

Segmented Wood Turning, 978-0-7643-1601-X, $14.95

Copyright © 2011 by Ralph S. Buckland

Library of Congress Control Number: 2011922267

All rights reserved. No part of this work may be reproduced or used in any form or by any means—graphic, electronic, or mechanical, including photocopying or information storage and retrieval systems—without written permission from the publisher.

The scanning, uploading and distribution of this book or any part thereof via the Internet or via any other means without the permission of the publisher is illegal and punishable by law. Please purchase only authorized editions and do not participate in or encourage the electronic piracy of copyrighted materials.

"Schiffer," "Schiffer Publishing Ltd. & Design," and the "Design of pen and inkwell" are registered trademarks of Schiffer Publishing Ltd.

Designed by Mark David Bowyer
Type set in Futura Lt BT / Minion Pro

ISBN: 978-0-7643-3795-6
Printed in China

Schiffer Books are available at special discounts for bulk purchases for sales promotions or premiums. Special editions, including personalized covers, corporate imprints, and excerpts can be created in large quantities for special needs. For more information contact the publisher:

Published by Schiffer Publishing Ltd.
4880 Lower Valley Road
Atglen, PA 19310
Phone: (610) 593-1777; Fax: (610) 593-2002
E-mail: Info@schifferbooks.com

For the largest selection of fine reference books on this and related subjects,
please visit our website at
www.schifferbooks.com
We are always looking for people to write books on new and related subjects. If you have an idea for a book please contact us at the above address.

This book may be purchased from the publisher.
Include $5.00 for shipping.
Please try your bookstore first.
You may write for a free catalog.

In Europe, Schiffer books are distributed by
Bushwood Books
6 Marksbury Ave.
Kew Gardens
Surrey TW9 4JF England
Phone: 44 (0) 20 8392 8585; Fax: 44 (0) 20 8392 9876
E-mail: info@bushwoodbooks.co.uk
Website: www.bushwoodbooks.co.uk

Contents

Preface 4
I: Introduction and Basic Segmented Turning 5
II: Topic Section: Processes and Techniques 18
III: Segmented Lamp Projects
    Confetti Lamp 41
    Bloodwood and Birdseye Maple Confetti Lamp 41
    Tulip Wood and Purpleheart Confetti Lamp 42
    Dot Lamp 43
    Barrel Lamp 46
    Rope and Lace Lamp 48
    Rope Weave Lamp 51
    Navajo Deer Lamp 53
    Flower on the Wall Lamp 59
    Trunk Lamp 64
    Walnut Nut Lamp 69
    There's a Spider on That Post, Grandpa! 73
    Kokopelli Lamp 78
    Lady Bug Stump Lamp 82
    Pink Ivory Lamp 85
    Sunbonnet Sue Lamp 91
    A Bad Day in the Shop 100
    The Quilted Milk Can Lamp 112
    The Pagoda Lamp 120

Preface

Segmented turning involves cutting a piece of wood into smaller pieces called segments. Using this process, an infinite number of designs are possible. Most segmented turners never use stains but instead use a variety of colored and textured woods in their creations.

For lamps, segments are usually 3/4" or less in thickness and are assembled in rings. The diameter of the ring is determined by the diameter of the lamp at any given point. The rings are then stacked, one on top of the other, varying in size as they go up.

Larger segments, called staves, are also used in segmented turning. The process of building these staves is similar to barrel and drum construction. Both types of segments, rings and staves, are discussed in detail throughout the book.

Turning Segmented Lamps is organized in three sections. I suggest reading through the entire book before starting on any projects. You may answer a lot of your own questions as you read through each section.

The first chapter is an introduction to the basics of segmented turning. Chapter 2 presents several specific processes and techniques used in the lamp projects included in the book. You will also find some handy resources in this section. Finally, chapter 3 walks step-by-step through 18 different lamp projects. Throughout the book you will find large schematic diagrams of the projects, which I hope you will find valuable to your segmented turning work.

As with any woodworking endeavor I encourage you to proceed with safety as your number one priority. Equally important, I hope this guide to turning segmented lamps offers you hours of enjoyment in your wood shop and helps you produce expertly hand crafted pieces.

—Ralph Buckland

I: Introduction and Basic Segmented Turning

Tools for the Job

Here is a quick look at some of the basic woodworking tools needed for turning segmented lamps:

- Table saw
- Power miter saw or radial arm saw
- Disk sander
- A press (see the chapter 2)
- Hose or pipe clamp (2 to 11"—found in plumbing department)
- Band saw
- Table scroll saw (jig saw)
- Drill press
- Lathe
- Faceplate for lathe (you need at least 2)
- Five basic lathe tools (see chapter 2)
- Workbench
- Electric hand drill
- Orbital sander
- Router
- A variety of basic woodworking hand tools.

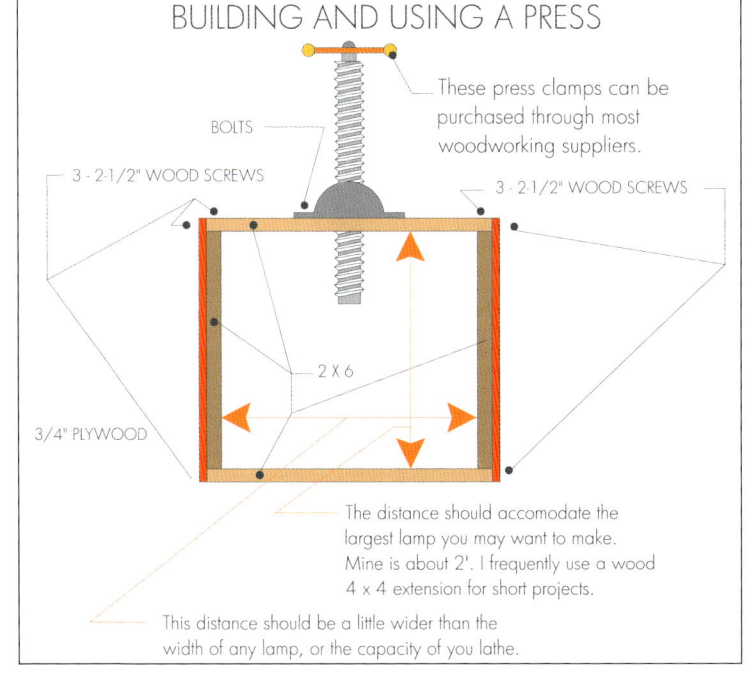

When making any of the lamps in this book, you will find that the ring sizes, their dimensions, and segment angles are all described in detail in the schematic drawing for each lamp.

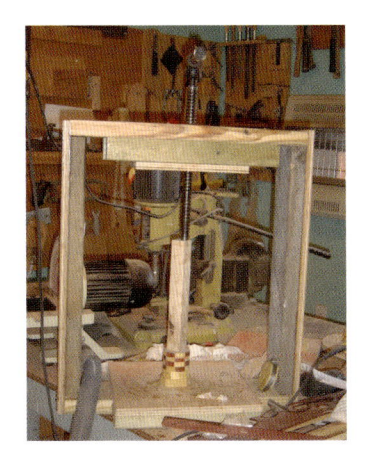

Fig. 1: This press is made with a screw from an old vice.

Diag. 1

Starting your first segmented lamp will require a press to keep your segmented rings flat while it is being glued. Commercial threading devices are available but usually they are about 1/2" in diameter and don't work very well. The press shown in Fig. 1 and Diag. 1 uses a thread from an old vice. This thread is encased in a cast iron square, which makes it stronger vertically and works much better. I often use a block between the threaded shaft and the project I'm working on.

Some rings are open in the center, by that I mean there is a hole in the center. Most of the rings in this book are open. The others are closed, meaning there is no hole in the center (see Fig. 2). The above press can be used for open and closed rings.

Fig. 2: The small ring is a closed ring and the large ring is an open ring.

A second option in press construction is a bolt press (see Fig. 3). This press can only be used to clamp open rings, which is great for lamps since most of the rings are open, not solid all the way to the center.

Fig. 3: Bolt presses attached to a plywood table.

To work more efficiently, and speed up the drying time, I have five bolt presses. To make these bolt presses, use a 5/8" diameter bolt, 4 to 6" long. First, drill a 3/4" hole in a plywood table top (see Fig. 4). Slide your bolt from the bottom up: through the table, then through the ring or rings that are being pressed, and finally through a round disk of plywood. Use a large washer and nut on top.

Fig. 4: This bolt press uses the table as its base. Use wax paper (not shown) below and above the ring to prevent gluing the ring to the table or the press.

If you have a more expensive table top, you may not want to drill holes in it; instead, you can use two plywood disks and a bolt (see Fig. 5).

Fig. 5: Press made with two plywood disks and a bolt.

Introduction and Basic Segmented Turning

Once your press is made, and you have decided on the ring size and determined the necessary angle for the segments, you are ready to start cutting. Diagram 1A shows the top view of a radial arm saw or a miter box looking down. You should cut enough segments to complete one full trial ring. The lamps in this book typically require a ring of 16 segments, but in a few cases eight segments are required for a smaller diameter ring. If the joints do not fit exactly make the necessary fine adjustment to the angle of the saw blade. Make another trial ring if necessary after the adjustment. Once you have completed this process, don't change the angle of your saw until you have finished all the desired segments for the particular project.

When cutting the length of your segment, use a fine mark on the fence to indicate how long the segments should be. Also you can use a block of wood as a stopping point, this wood should be clamped to the fence. Sometimes I'll screw my stop block to the actual table of the radial arm saw. Most of the time, however, I use a power miter box for cutting the segments to length. But this task can be accomplished by using a table saw or radial arm saw.

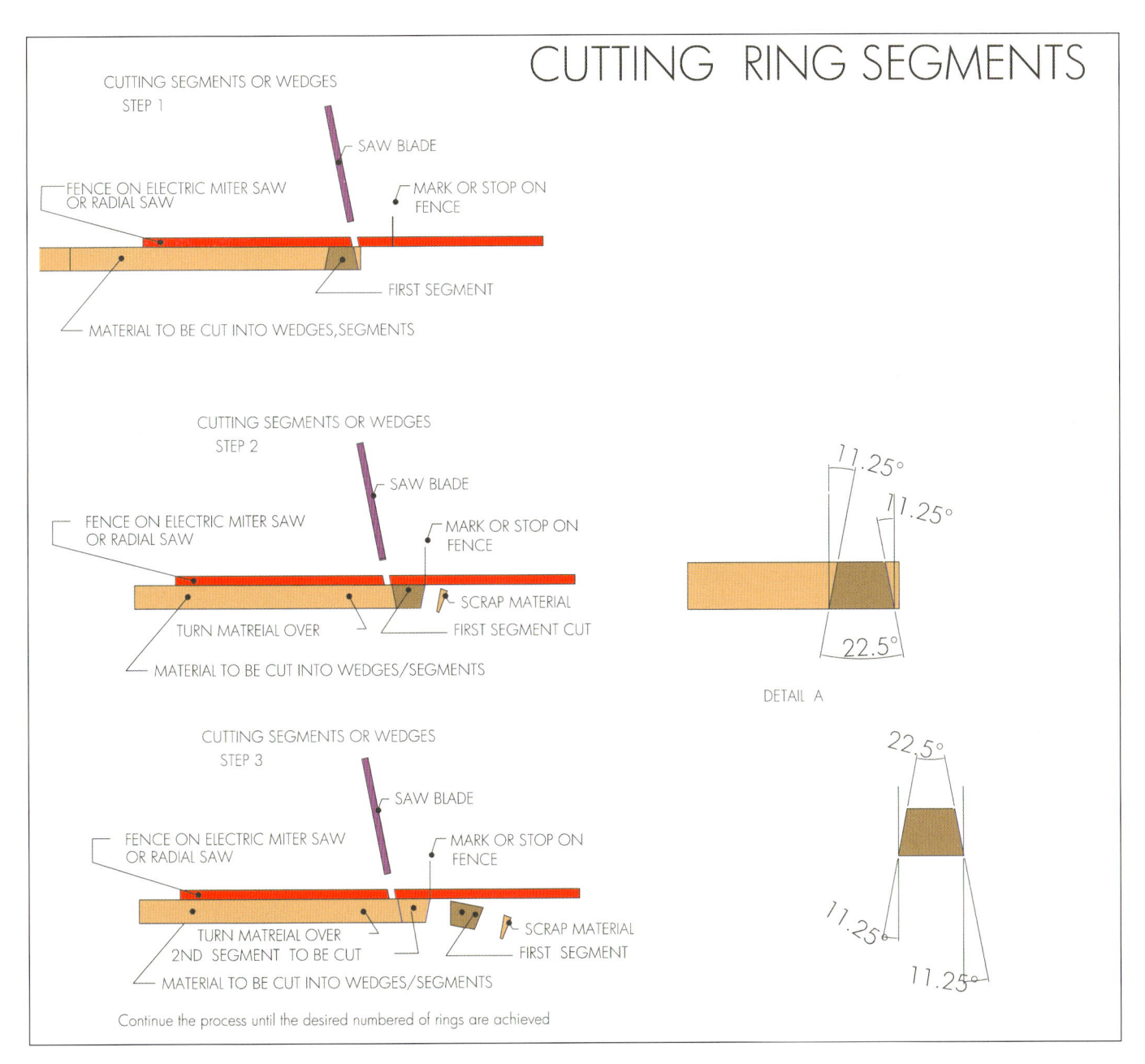

Diag. 1A

Introduction and Basic Segmented Turning **7**

Having cut the segments to the correct angle, the first ring is ready to be assembled and glued together (see Diag. 2). Use a hose or pipe clamp (see Fig. 6) to clamp the ring together tightly enough that no light comes through the joints. When you have the perfect fit (see Fig. 7), it is ready to be glued.

Apply Titebond or a woodworkers glue to both sides of each segment. Lay the segment on a sheet of wax paper large enough for the whole ring. Glue one segment and fit it to the next segment continuing this process around the ring. Clamp the circumference of the ring with a hose clamp. Tighten this firmly. Using a mallet or hammer, lightly tap each segment gently to make sure the segments are flush with the adjoining segment. Then put the ring in a press (see chapter 2) and compress the ring flat until it is completely dry. Be sure you use wax paper under the ring and above the ring to prevent gluing the ring to the press or to your table.

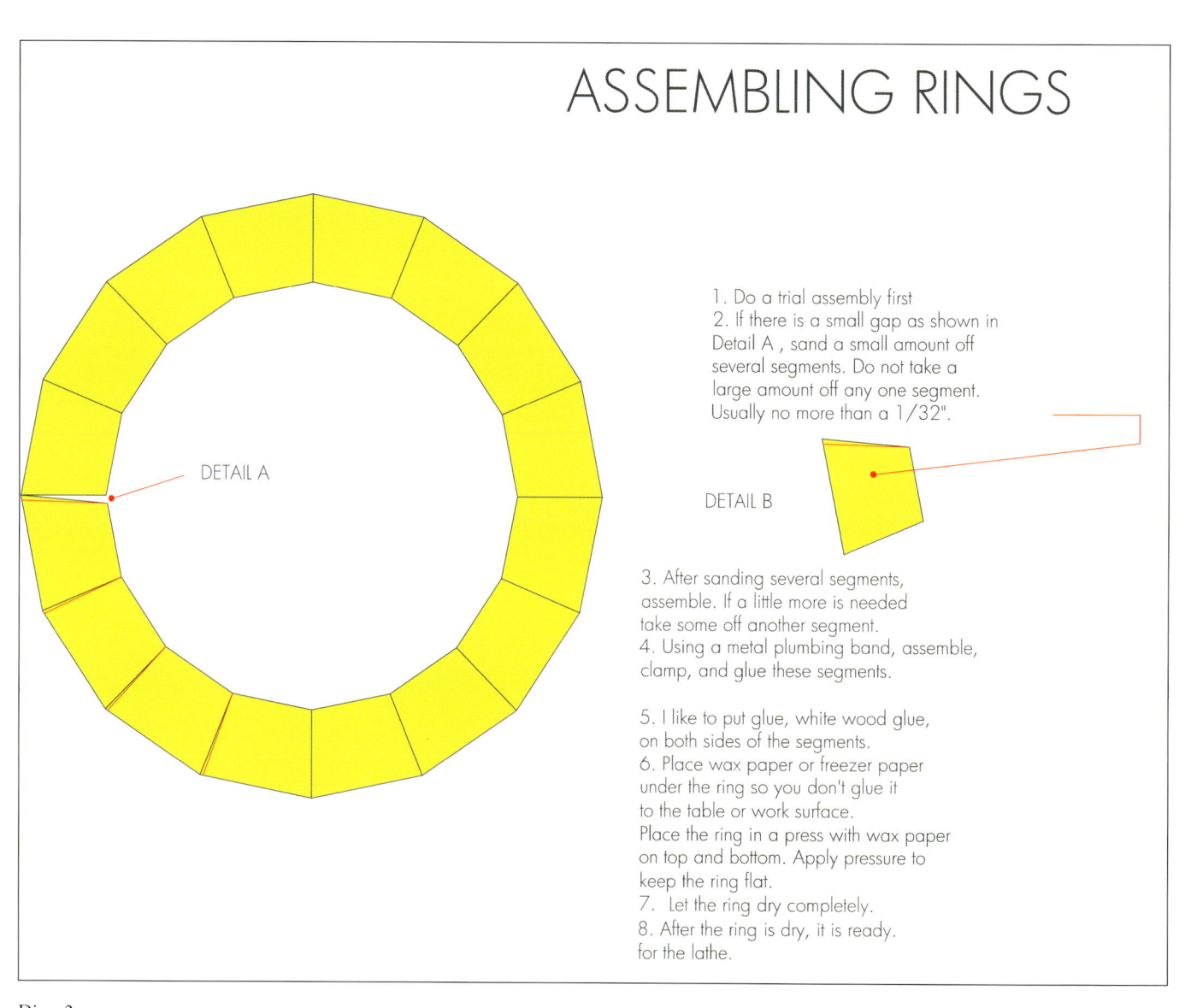

ASSEMBLING RINGS

DETAIL A

1. Do a trial assembly first
2. If there is a small gap as shown in Detail A, sand a small amount off several segments. Do not take a large amount off any one segment. Usually no more than a 1/32".

DETAIL B

3. After sanding several segments, assemble. If a little more is needed take some off another segment.
4. Using a metal plumbing band, assemble, clamp, and glue these segments.

5. I like to put glue, white wood glue, on both sides of the segments.
6. Place wax paper or freezer paper under the ring so you don't glue it to the table or work surface.
Place the ring in a press with wax paper on top and bottom. Apply pressure to keep the ring flat.
7. Let the ring dry completely.
8. After the ring is dry, it is ready for the lathe.

Diag. 2

Introduction and Basic Segmented Turning

Fig. 6: Clamping a ring with a hose or pipe clamp commonly used by plumbers. Notice that I've actually used two clamps.

Fig. 7: Checking for cracks and spaces against a light source.

Make a scrap disk about 11" in diameter—this size should accommodate any lamp in the book. I usually use oak or birch plywood. Attach the disk to your lathe's faceplate (see Fig. 8).

Fig. 8: The 11" disk attached to the lathe faceplate.

Turn the lathe on and use a pencil to mark concentric circles (see Fig. 9) on the wood disk as it turns. Press the pencil lightly to make the circles. Make your first circle a little smaller, by about 1/2", than the ring you are working on. Then make another circle approximately an inch larger than your first circle. Continue making circles until the total surface area marked with circles is larger than your ring. You will use these circles to center your first ring on the faceplate.

Fig. 9: Concentric circles marked on the disk.

Attach this first ring to the disk with Cyanoacrylate (CA) glue, D-3, or using recessed screws (see Figs. 10 and 10A). With the ring attached to the disk, it can be flattened using a diamond nose lathe tool (see Fig. 11). Check for flatness using a straight edge, such as a framing square (see Fig. 12). Once the ring is flattened on one side it can be taken off the disk.

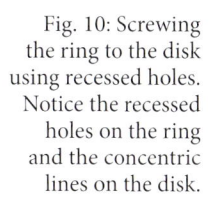

Fig. 10: Screwing the ring to the disk using recessed holes. Notice the recessed holes on the ring and the concentric lines on the disk.

Introduction and Basic Segmented Turning

Lamps can either have a solid piece of wood for the bottom or the bottom can be a segmented ring. If a solid piece of wood is used you will not be able to reach inside of the lamp. Certain lamps (see Rope and Lace Lamp on page 48) must have an open ring on the bottom so you can reach into the lamp and weave the rope in and out.

When using a solid piece of wood on the bottom, you should sand one side flat and smooth with a belt sander. Make sure this is perfectly flat by checking it with a straight edge (see Fig. 12). Once this is perfectly flat it is ready to be attached to a flat round disk and then the faceplate. The 11" disk I use should accommodate any of the rings made in this book.

Fig. 10A: Make sure the holes are deeply recessed. This protects the screws from being hit when you're turning the rings.

Fig. 11: Flattening the ring with a diamond nose lathe tool.

Fig. 12: Check for flatness using a straight edge.

If a segmented ring is used for the first ring instead of a solid board, this ring must be smooth on both sides. One side will become the bottom of the lamp and the other side will accept the second ring. If you are using a segmented ring for the bottom of your lamp and you do not want any holes on the bottom of your lamp refer to diagram D-3 for specific instructions.

Once the solid ring is flat on one side or the segmented ring is flat on both sides, either can be attached to the scrap disk. There are two methods I will describe to attach a solid piece of wood or a segmented ring to the scrap disk.

Method one: Draw concentric circles on the round disk (as above in Fig. 9), which will help you to center the first ring or solid board. This first ring can be attached with screws from the faceplate side. The screws may have to be countersunk slightly (see Fig. 10) so your lathe tool will not cut into the heads of the screws. This method will leave several (usually 4 or 5) screw holes on the bottom of your lamp. I usually cover these with a piece of felt.

Method two: Using your scrap disk, glue a piece of paper between the disk and the first ring. I use a manila folder since it is thick, holds well, and releases easily. This will produce a lamp with no holes on the bottom. Once your lamp is complete you can separate the scrap board from the first ring by placing a chisel between these two rings (see Figs. 13 and 13A).

Fig. 13

Fig. 13A

TURNING RINGS

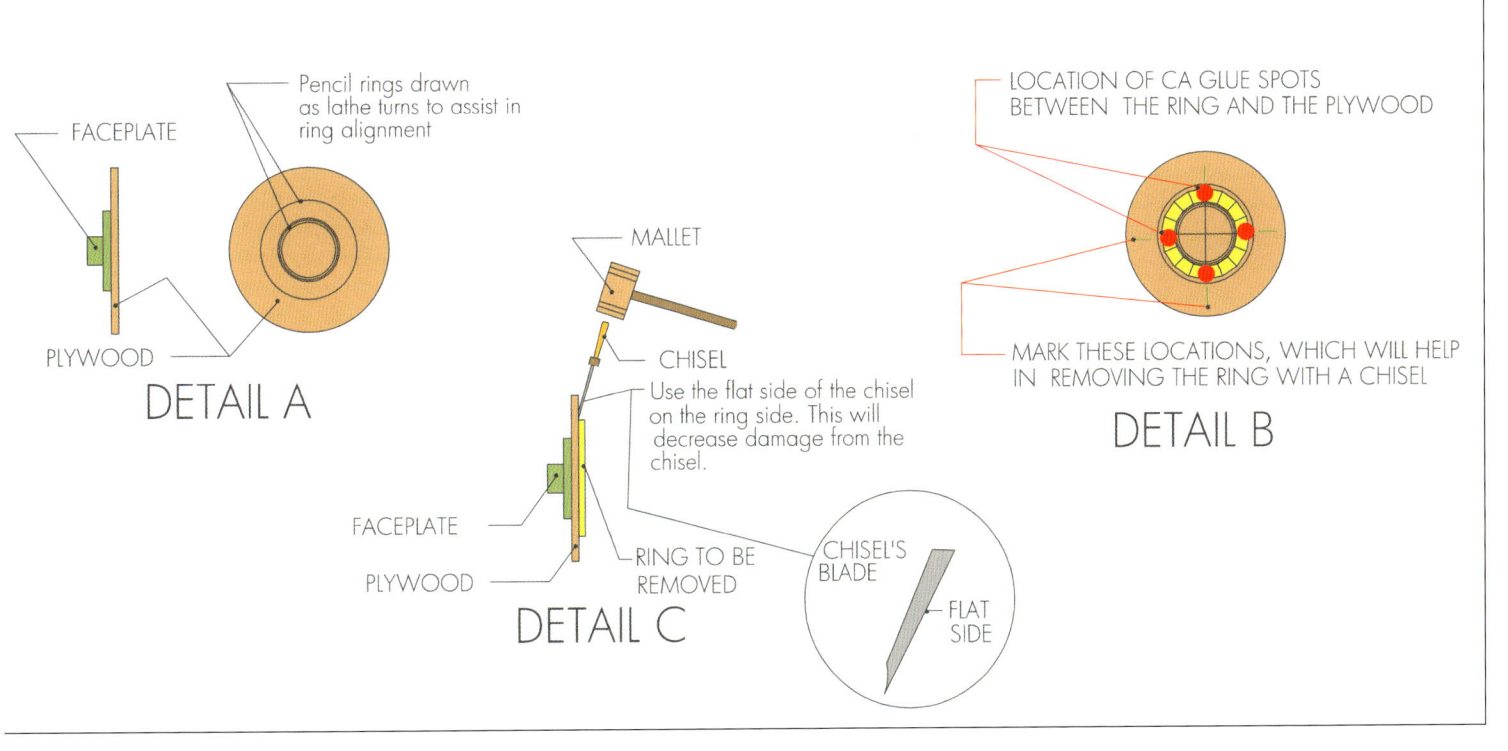

DETAIL A
- FACEPLATE
- PLYWOOD
- Pencil rings drawn as lathe turns to assist in ring alignment

DETAIL C
- MALLET
- CHISEL
- Use the flat side of the chisel on the ring side. This will decrease damage from the chisel.
- FACEPLATE
- PLYWOOD
- RING TO BE REMOVED
- CHISEL'S BLADE
- FLAT SIDE

DETAIL B
- LOCATION OF CA GLUE SPOTS BETWEEN THE RING AND THE PLYWOOD
- MARK THESE LOCATIONS, WHICH WILL HELP IN REMOVING THE RING WITH A CHISEL

Diag. 3

Introduction and Basic Segmented Turning 11

When the first ring is attached and both sides have been flattened, repeat the above process of flattening a new ring and gluing it on for each ring (see Diag. 4).

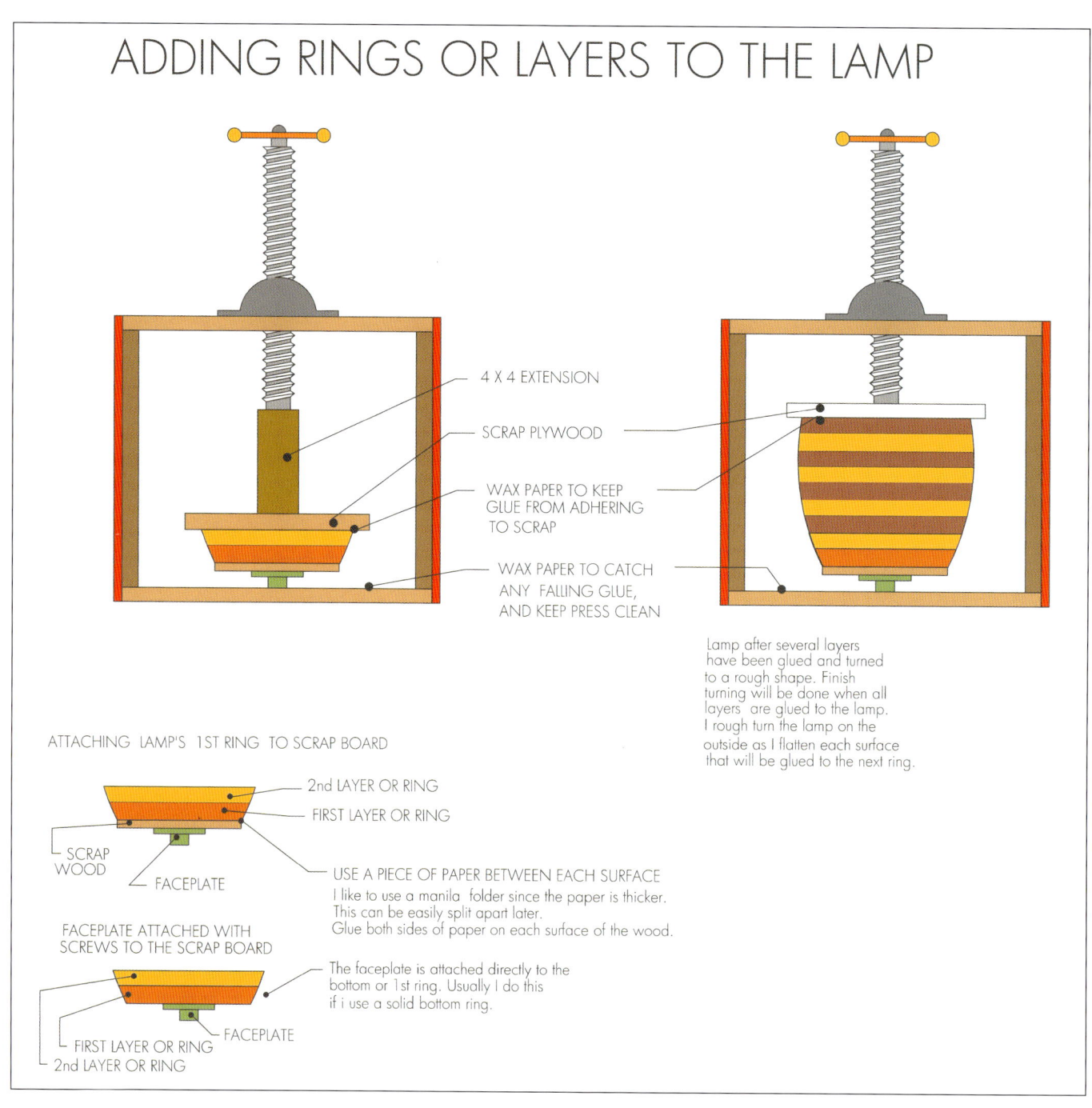

ADDING RINGS OR LAYERS TO THE LAMP

- 4 X 4 EXTENSION
- SCRAP PLYWOOD
- WAX PAPER TO KEEP GLUE FROM ADHERING TO SCRAP
- WAX PAPER TO CATCH ANY FALLING GLUE, AND KEEP PRESS CLEAN

Lamp after several layers have been glued and turned to a rough shape. Finish turning will be done when all layers are glued to the lamp. I rough turn the lamp on the outside as I flatten each surface that will be glued to the next ring.

ATTACHING LAMP'S 1ST RING TO SCRAP BOARD

- 2nd LAYER OR RING
- FIRST LAYER OR RING
- SCRAP WOOD
- FACEPLATE
- USE A PIECE OF PAPER BETWEEN EACH SURFACE
  I like to use a manila folder since the paper is thicker. This can be easily split apart later.
  Glue both sides of paper on each surface of the wood.

FACEPLATE ATTACHED WITH SCREWS TO THE SCRAP BOARD

The faceplate is attached directly to the bottom or 1st ring. Usually I do this if i use a solid bottom ring.

- FIRST LAYER OR RING
- FACEPLATE
- 2nd LAYER OR RING

Diag. 4

Introduction and Basic Segmented Turning

When using more expensive woods, such as black ebony, I try to make the material go as far as possible. An example is the Trunk Lamp (page 64), in which I make the black ebony segments out of two types of wood (see Fig. 14).

Another method to minimize cost and time is to split rings. For example, a ring that is 3/4" thick should first be turned round on the outside, then flatten the face that will accept the next ring. Now use a parting tool and cut straight into the ring from the side. Make this cut deep enough—leave only 1/16" or 1/8" of wood between your parting tool and the opening of the ring. Then use a multi-tool (see Fig. 15), a hand jig saw, or even a backsaw, to cut the ring in half. Be careful not to let the ring you are cutting off fall; they break very easily. If it does break you can fix it with CA glue. Once the ring is split, flatten the new surface of the ring that remains on the lathe. This process works well with lamps with thin rings like the Flower on the Wall Lamp (page 59), which has a lot of 1/8" rings.

Fig. 15: Splitting half a ring off with a multi-tool, leaving the other half on.

Fig. 14: Oak is used on the inside half of this ring to economize on the high cost of black ebony.

The process of cutting, trial testing, gluing, pressing, and adding additional rings is used on all the lamps throughout this book. The designs of each lamp, dimensions, colors, and types of woods, will vary, but the process of joining the rings will be the same.

Designing your own lamp involves determining the correct ring and segment sizes to realize your design. Knowing that a circle has 360 degrees, you can easily determine the angles of a segment by dividing the number of segments you want into 360 degrees. For example, a ring that uses 16 segments, divided into 360 degrees, gives you an angle of 22 1/2° per segment. This means each segment would have a 22 1/2° degree angle from one side to the other or a 11 1/4° angle cut on each side.

In Diag. 5 you will see common ring sizes and the grain direction on the face of the segment. The angle is cut on each side, which is labeled "end grain." Make the segment with the end grain as shown. When you turn this you will only see the face of the wood, no end grain will show.

Use Diags. 5A, 5B and 5C as references for designing your own segmented project. First, determine the size and shape of your project: lamp, bowl, box, or other segmented creation. Once you have determined the shape of your project, you can decide on the number of segments needed for a particular diameter of any ring. An example would be if your first ring is 6" in diameter, you would need to decide how many segments you want. Refer to a chart having the number of segments you want, look down to where it says 6", and it will tell you the exact outside measurement for that particular segment. The chart will also give you the exact angle you will need to cut the segment.

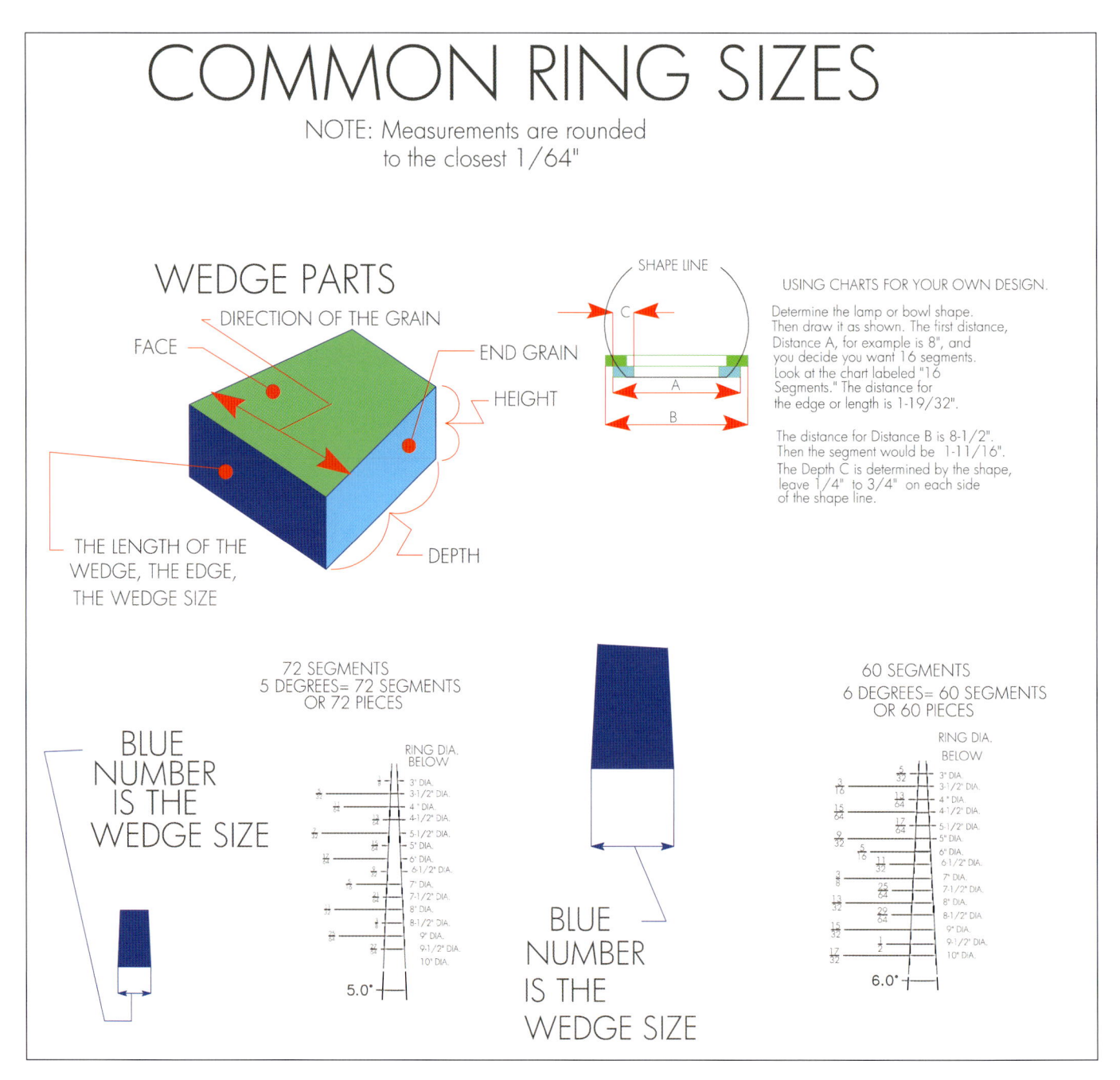

COMMON RING SIZES

NOTE: Measurements are rounded to the closest 1/64"

WEDGE PARTS

- DIRECTION OF THE GRAIN
- FACE
- END GRAIN
- HEIGHT
- DEPTH
- THE LENGTH OF THE WEDGE, THE EDGE, THE WEDGE SIZE

SHAPE LINE

USING CHARTS FOR YOUR OWN DESIGN.

Determine the lamp or bowl shape. Then draw it as shown. The first distance, Distance A, for example is 8", and you decide you want 16 segments. Look at the chart labeled "16 Segments." The distance for the edge or length is 1-19/32".

The distance for Distance B is 8-1/2". Then the segment would be 1-11/16". The Depth C is determined by the shape, leave 1/4" to 3/4" on each side of the shape line.

72 SEGMENTS
5 DEGREES= 72 SEGMENTS OR 72 PIECES

BLUE NUMBER IS THE WEDGE SIZE

5.0°

60 SEGMENTS
6 DEGREES= 60 SEGMENTS OR 60 PIECES

BLUE NUMBER IS THE WEDGE SIZE

6.0°

Diag. 5

14 *Introduction and Basic Segmented Turning*

COMMON RING SIZES

NOTE: Measurements are rounded to the closest 1/64"

45 SEGMENTS
8 DEGREES= 45 SEGMENTS OR 45 PIECES

BLUE NUMBER IS THE WEDGE SIZE

Wedge Size	Ring Dia. Below
13/64	3" DIA.
9/32	3-1/2" DIA.
5/16	4" DIA.
23/64	4-1/2" DIA.
11/32	—
25/64	5" DIA.
27/64	6" DIA.
29/64	6-1/2" DIA.
15/32	7" DIA.
17/32	7-1/2" DIA.
9/16	8" DIA.
19/32	8-1/2" DIA.
5/8	9" DIA.
43/64	9-1/2" DIA.
45/64	10" DIA.

8.0°

40 SEGMENTS
9 DEGREES= 40 SEGMENTS OR 40 PIECES

BLUE NUMBER IS THE WEDGE SIZE

Wedge Size	Ring Dia. Below
15/64	3" DIA.
9/32	3-1/2" DIA.
5/16	4" DIA.
23/64	4-1/2" DIA.
7/16	5" DIA.
15/32	6" DIA.
25/64	6-1/2" DIA.
33/64	7" DIA.
9/16	7-1/2" DIA.
5/8	8" DIA.
43/64	8-1/2" DIA.
3/4	9" DIA.
25/32	9-1/2" DIA.
—	10" DIA.

9.0°

36 SEGMENTS
10 DEGREES= 36 SEGMENTS OR 36 PIECES

BLUE NUMBER IS THE WEDGE SIZE

Wedge Size	Ring Dia. Below
17/32	3" DIA.
—	3-1/2" DIA.
29/64, 16	4" DIA.
21/32	4-1/2" DIA.
45/64	5-1/2" DIA.
25/32	5" DIA.
53/64	6" DIA.
—	6-1/2" DIA.
7/8	7" DIA.
59/64	7-1/2" DIA.
31/32	8" DIA.
1	8-1/2" DIA.
1 9/32	9" DIA.
1 5/32	9-1/2" DIA.
	10" DIA.

10.0°

32 SEGMENTS
11.25 DEGREES= 32 SEGMENTS OR 32 PIECES

BLUE NUMBER IS THE WEDGE SIZE

Wedge Size	Ring Dia. Below
19/64	3" DIA.
11/32	3 1/2" DIA.
25/64	4" DIA.
7/16	4-1/2" DIA.
35/64	5-1/2" DIA.
—	5" DIA.
19/32	6" DIA.
41/64	6-1/2" DIA.
47/64	7" DIA.
—	7-1/2" DIA.
25/32	8" DIA.
27/64	8-1/2" DIA.
57/64	9" DIA.
15/16	9-1/2" DIA.
63/64	10" DIA.

11.3°

Diag. 5A

Introduction and Basic Segmented Turning

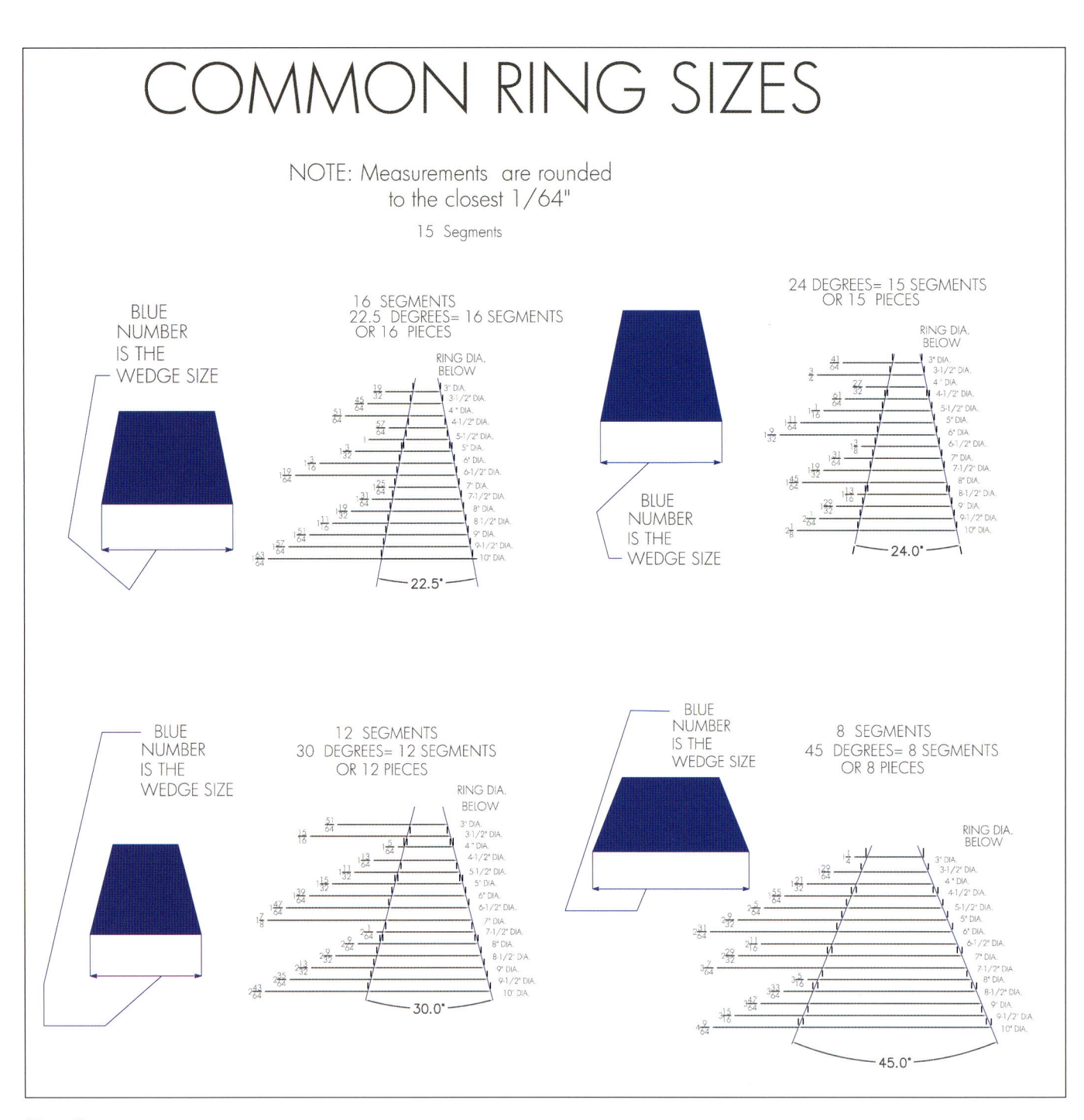

Diag. 5B

Introduction and Basic Segmented Turning

COMMON RING SIZES

NOTE: Measurements are rounded to the closest 1/64"

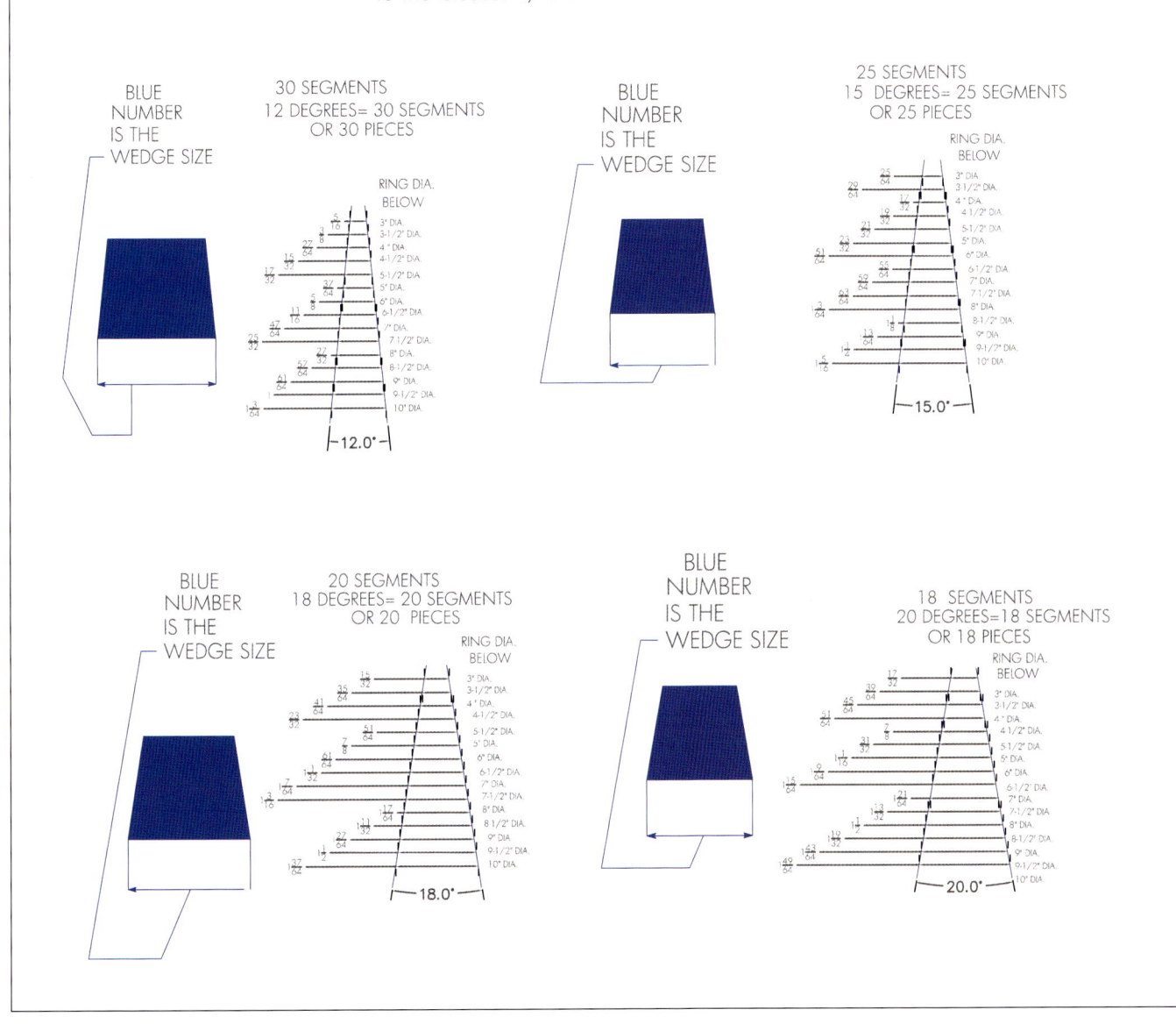

Diag. 5C

II. Topic Section: Processes and Techniques

This chapter describes the processes and techniques you will use to make many of the lamps throughout the book.

I. Building Figures: When building figures, such as the deer (page 55) or schoolhouses (page 115), construct these row by row. As an example, we will look at the deer in the Navajo Deer Lamp, (see Diag. 6 and Fig. 16). The legs are glued up in a long section, making sure that when you cut the individual legs you will see the grain from the side or the face, not the end grain. Next, cut the body and let it overhang on each end. It is cut a little bit longer than the dimensions given in the book. Glue these two together. I use CA glue on a lot of these parts but not all. Then sand the blocks square and flat on a disk sander. The side of the legs and the side of the body are now flush.

This process is used throughout the book to make various figures.

Fig. 16: Detail of deer in Navajo Deer Lamp (page 19).

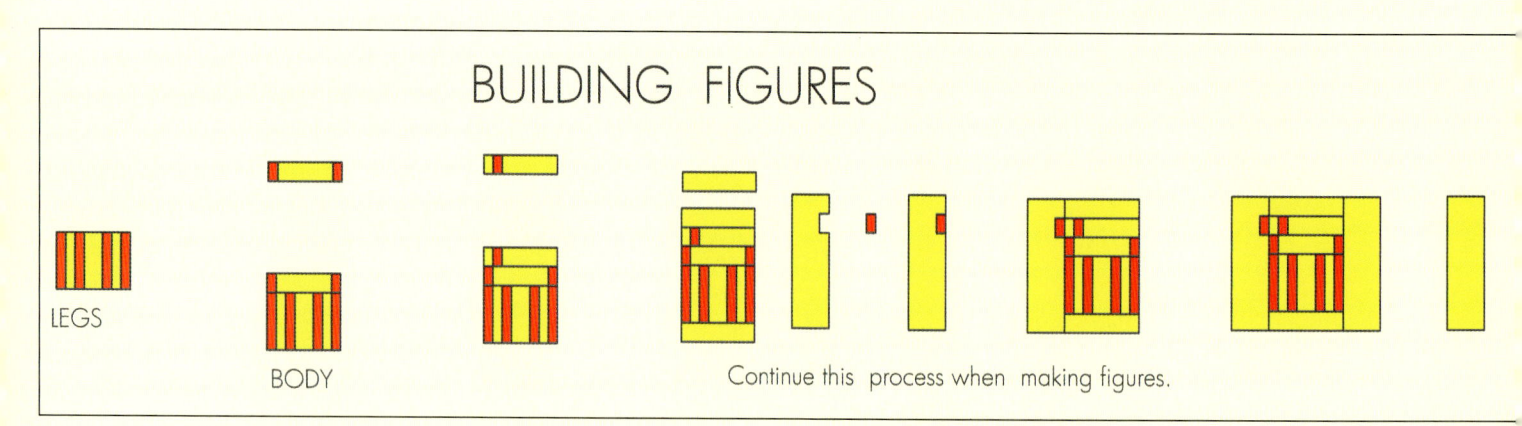

BUILDING FIGURES

LEGS

BODY

Continue this process when making figures.

Diag. 6

Topic Section: Processes and Techniques **19**

II. Dado Jig For Disk: The holding device that is made out of plywood should be made so the disk slides in tightly and touches the table saw's surface. The disk can be held in with a small plumber type band clamp. Then you can slide the straight edge of the jig against the table saw's fence to cut dados in the disk. See Diagram 6A.

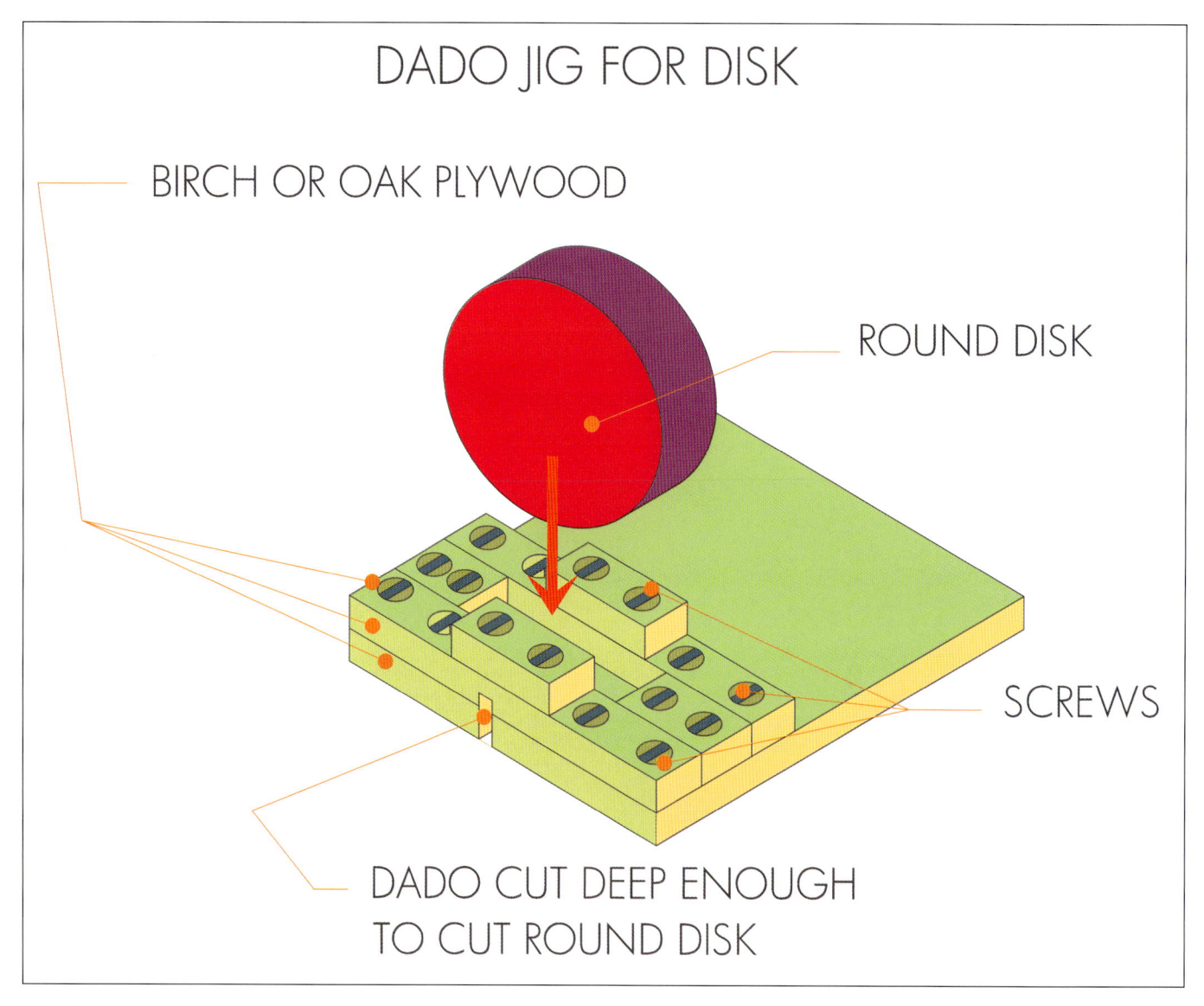

DADO JIG FOR DISK

BIRCH OR OAK PLYWOOD

ROUND DISK

SCREWS

DADO CUT DEEP ENOUGH TO CUT ROUND DISK

Diag. 6A

20 *Topic Section: Processes and Techniques*

III. Equal Parts of a Circle: To determine the spacing of five equally marked locations on a lamp, use the following chart, which may need to be enlarged according to your lamp base size. Place the bottom of your lamp on the concentric circle on the drawing that is closest in diameter to the bottom of your lamp. Using the red line in the drawing, you can transfer the location anywhere on the lamp using a framing square held perpendicular to the red line. Given a variety of equally spaced locations, you can pick out the number of equal parts that you want. An example for using this chart would be the Trunk Lamp (page 64). Five or six equal locations would be ideal for this lamp.

To lay out equal parts see the list below:
Three equal parts: Diag. 7
Four equal parts, Diag. 8
Five equal parts, Diag. 9
Six equal parts, Diag. 10
Seven equal parts, Diag. 11
Eight equal parts, Diag. 12
Nine equal parts, Diag. 13
Ten equal parts, Diag. 14
Eleven equal parts, Diag. 15

NOTE: Permission is granted to enlarge the equal parts of a circle patterns for personal use.

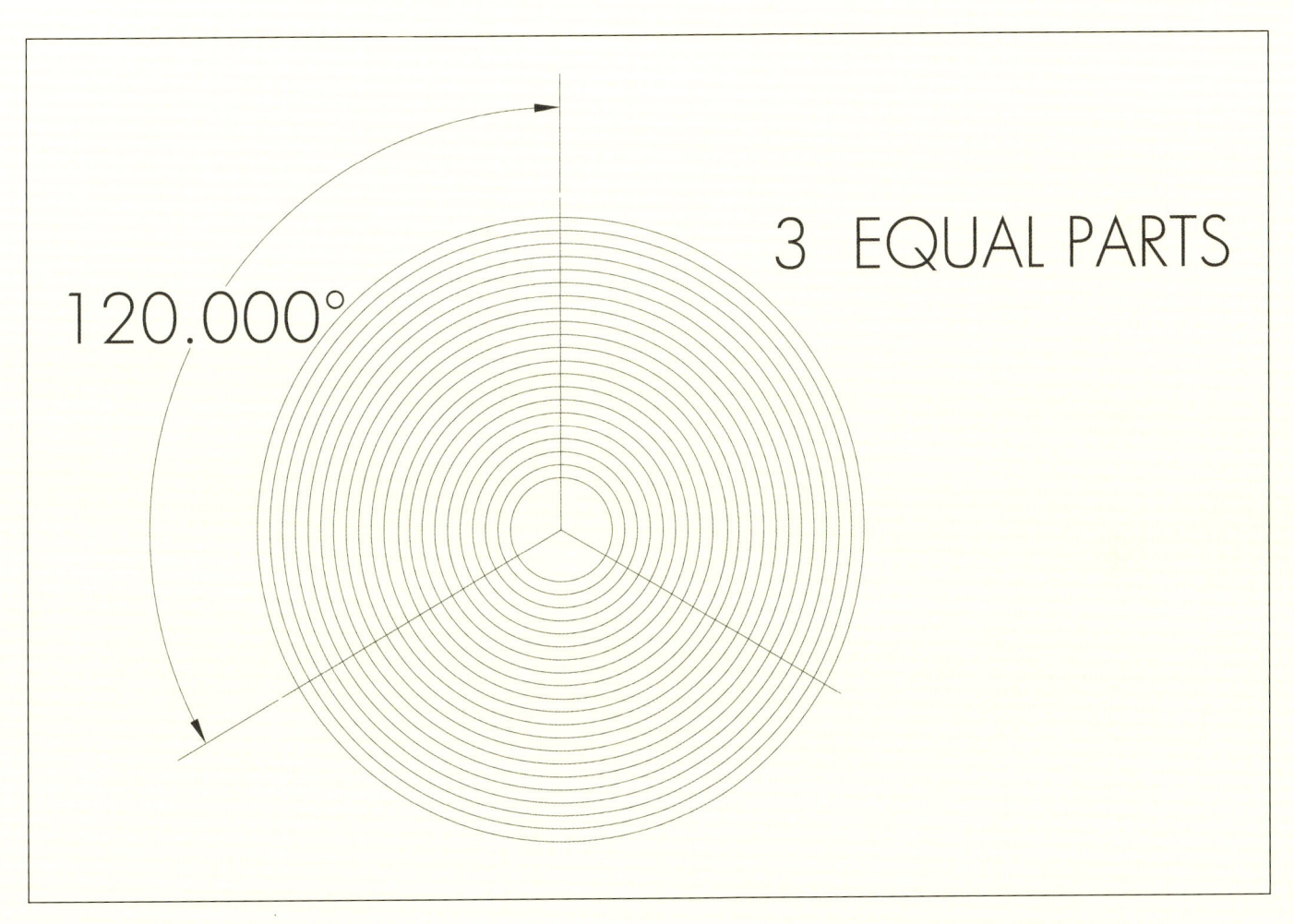

Diag. 7

Topic Section: Processes and Techniques

4 EQUAL PARTS

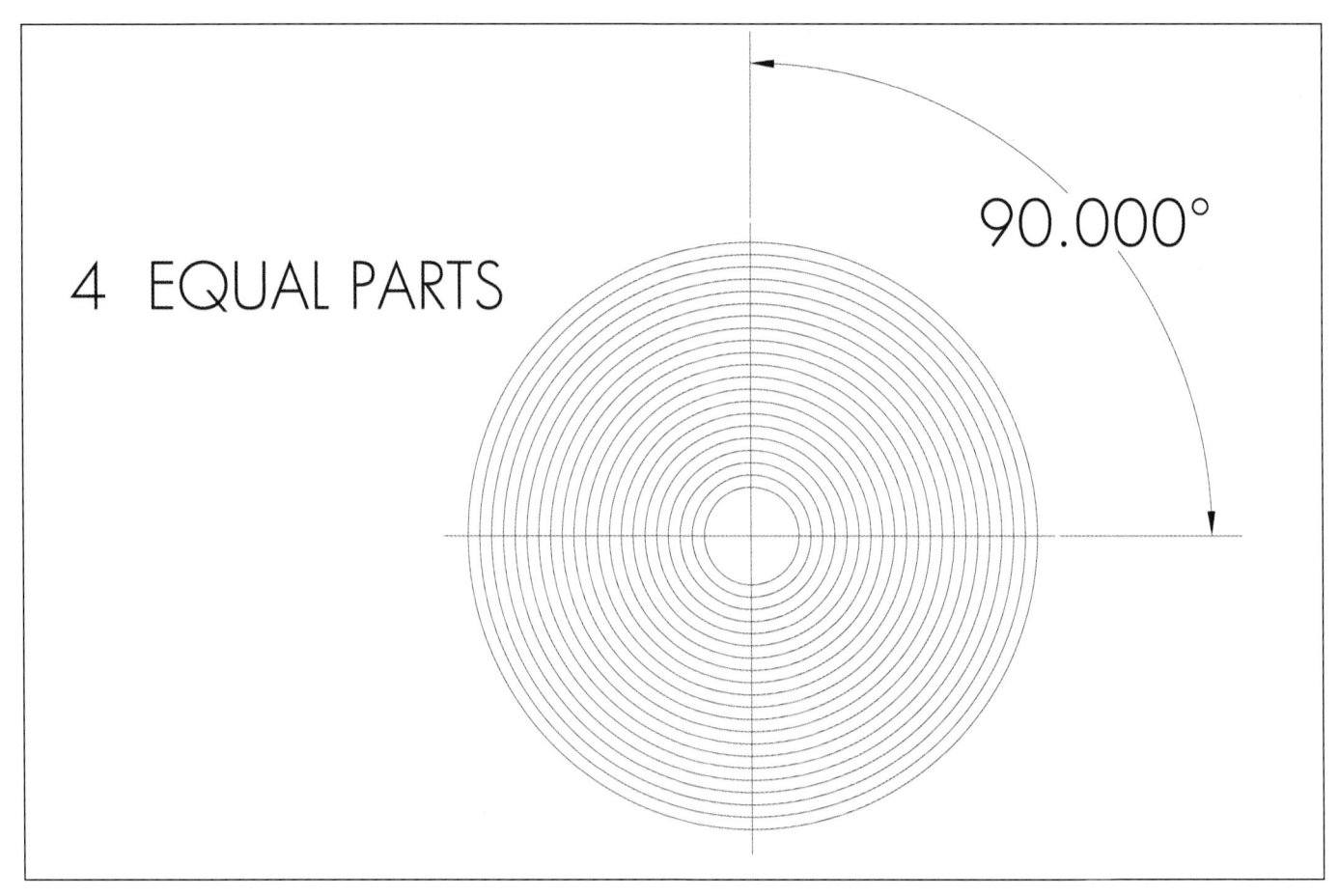

90.000°

Diag. 8

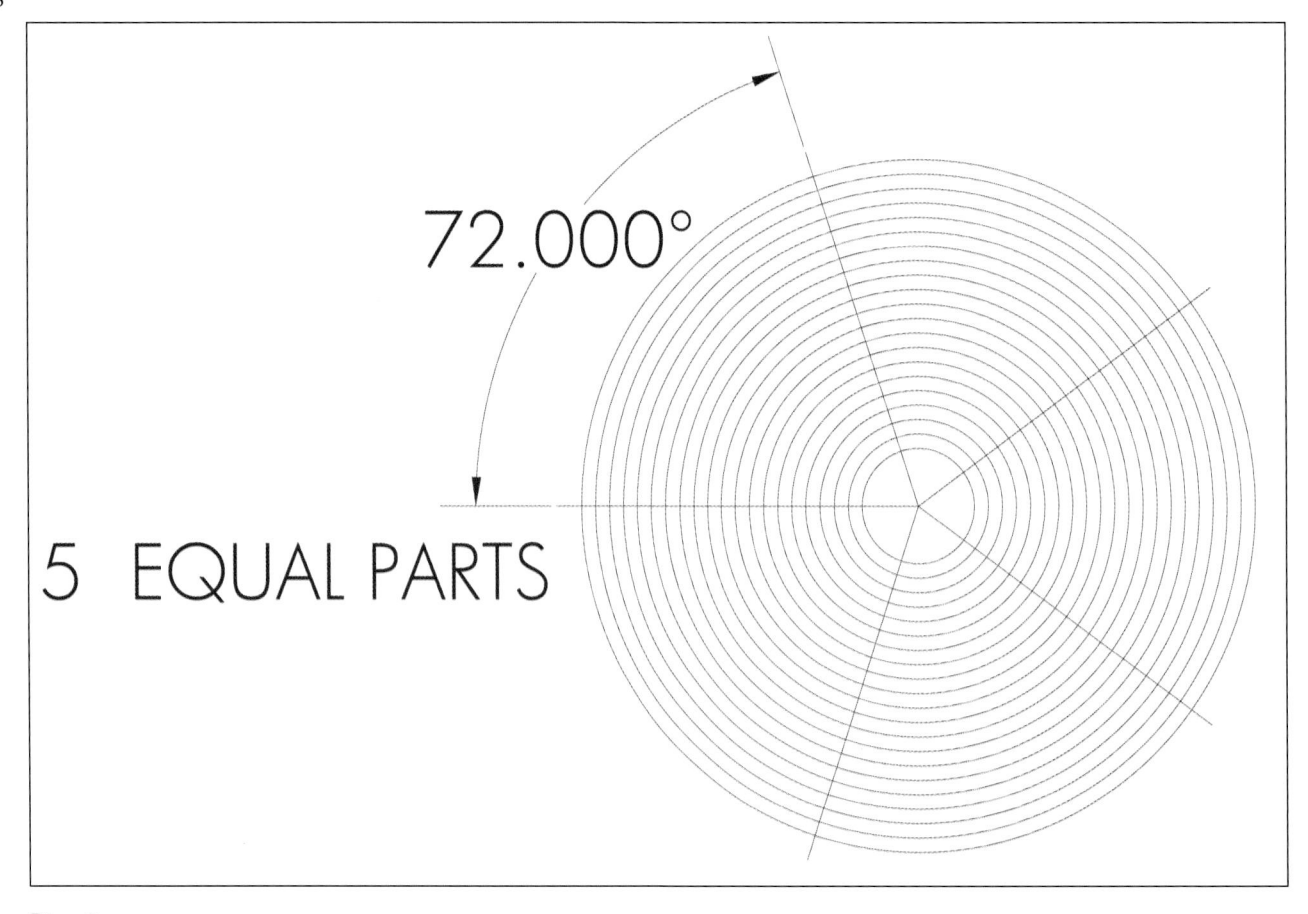

72.000°

5 EQUAL PARTS

Diag. 9

Topic Section: *Processes and Techniques*

60.000°

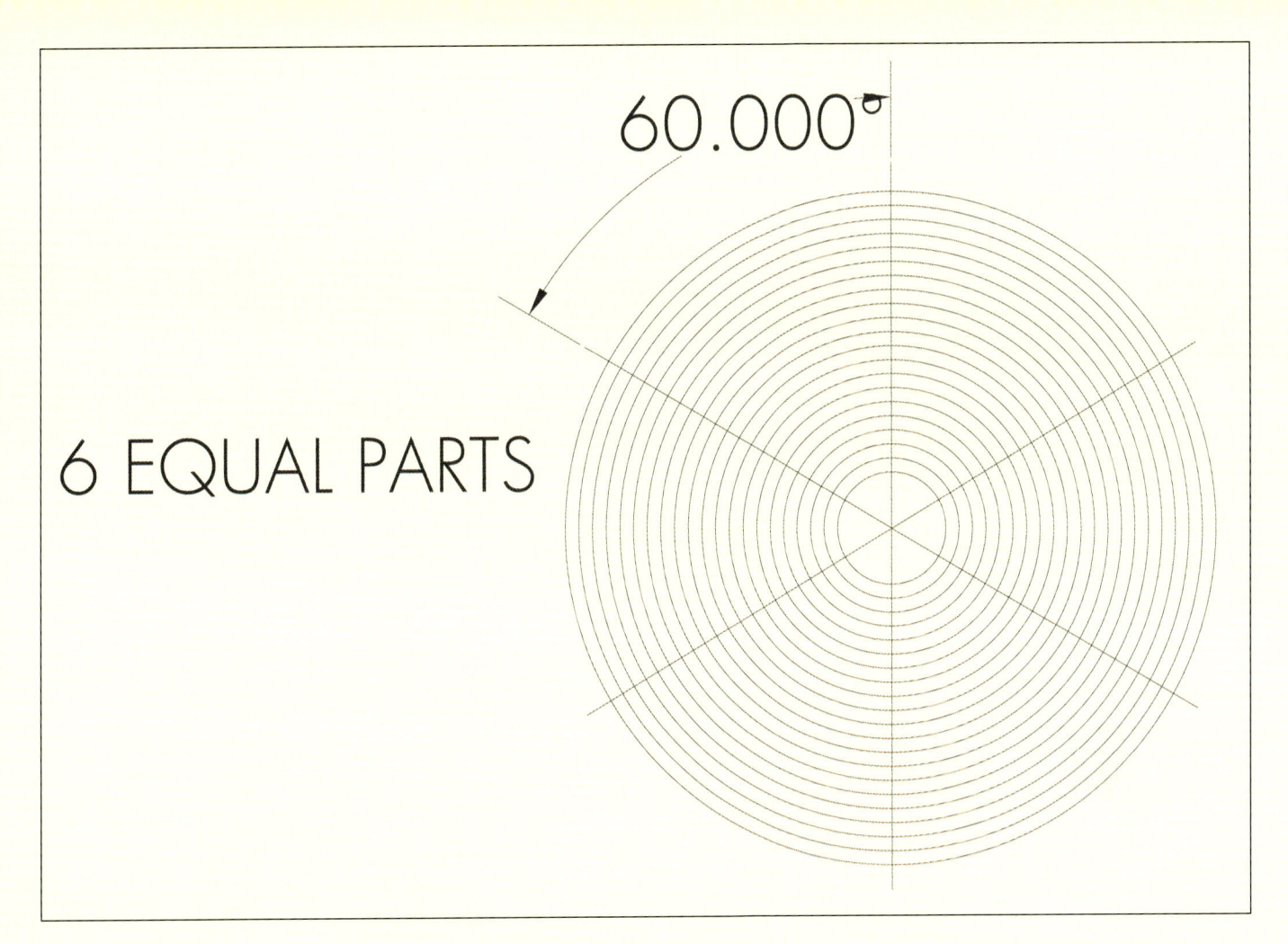

6 EQUAL PARTS

Diag. 10

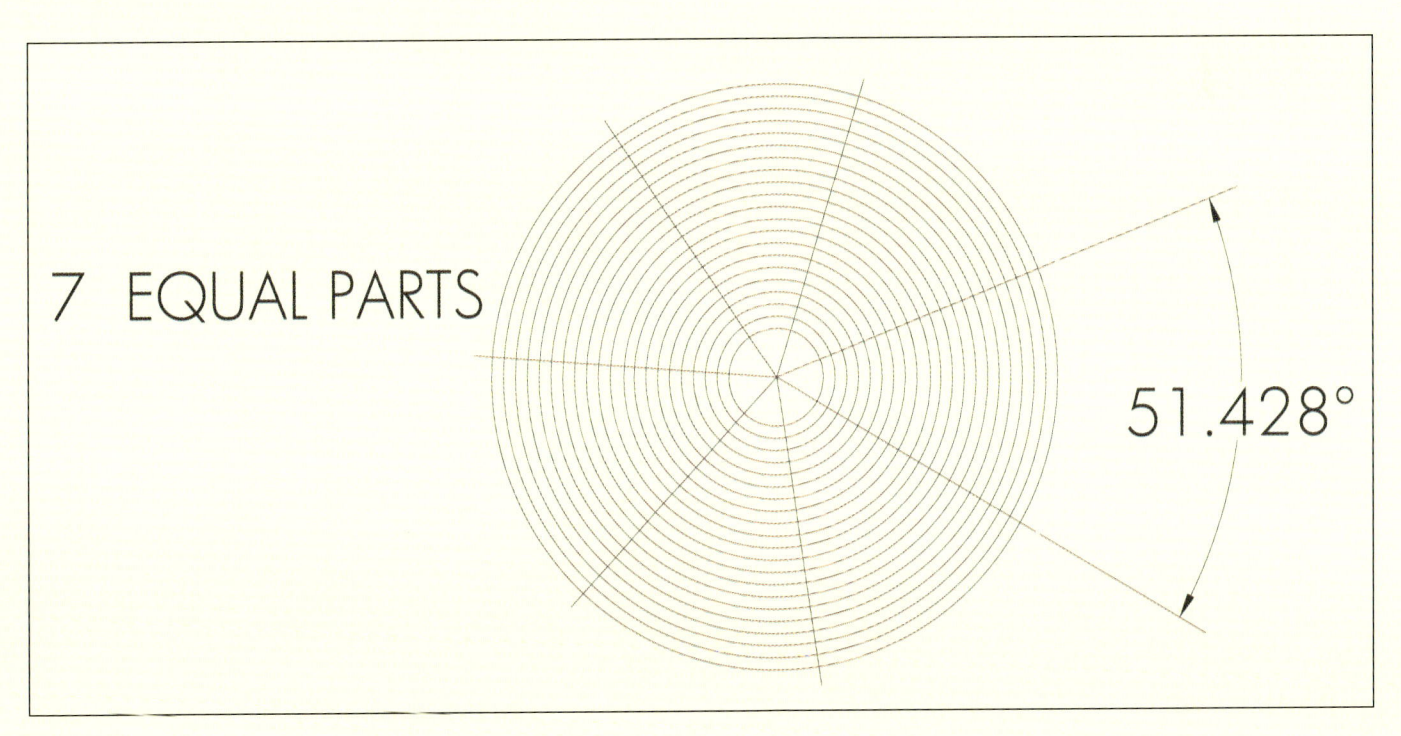

7 EQUAL PARTS

51.428°

Diag. 11

Topic Section: Processes and Techniques

45.000°

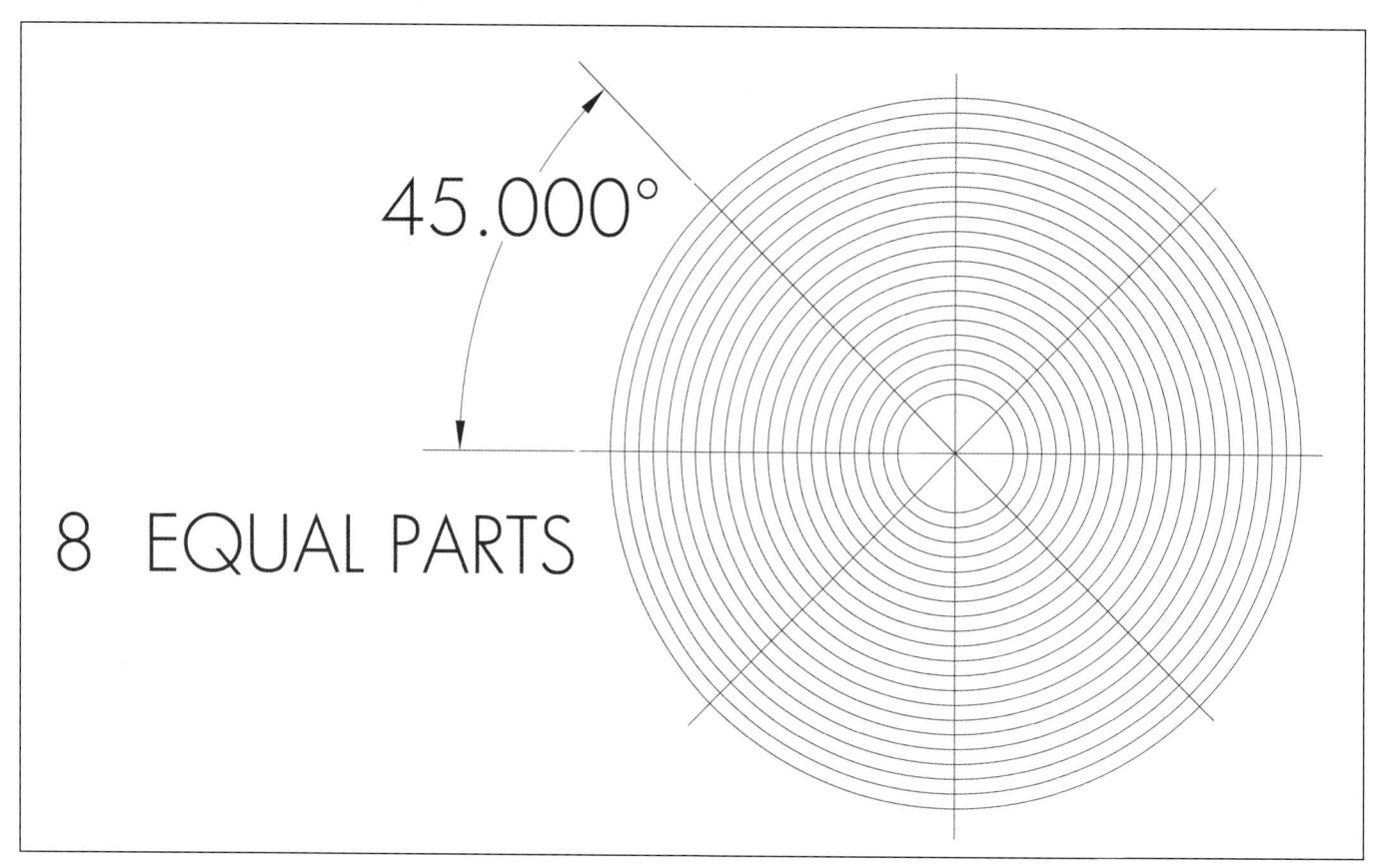

8 EQUAL PARTS

Diag. 12

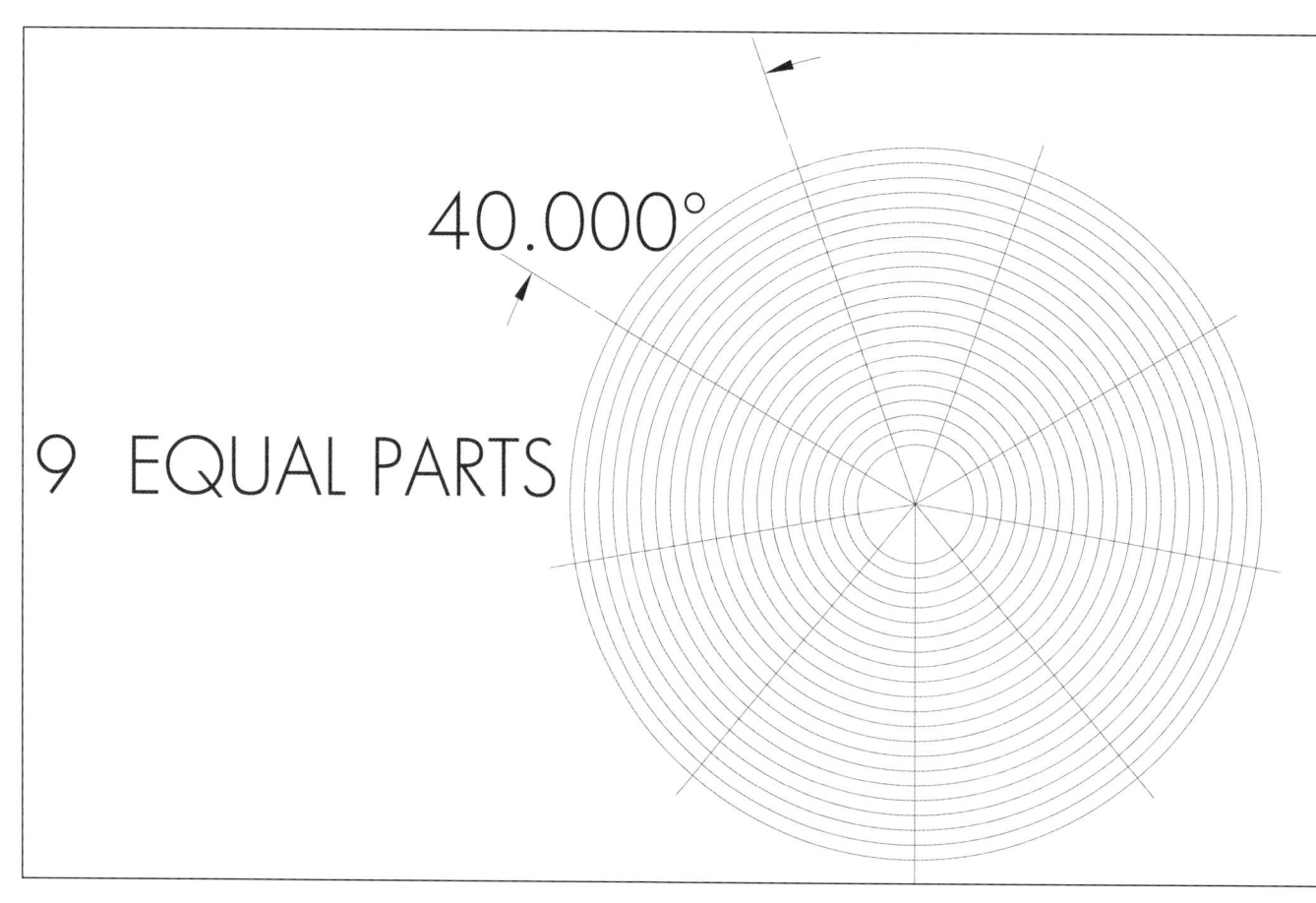

40.000°

9 EQUAL PARTS

Diag. 13

10 EQUAL PARTS

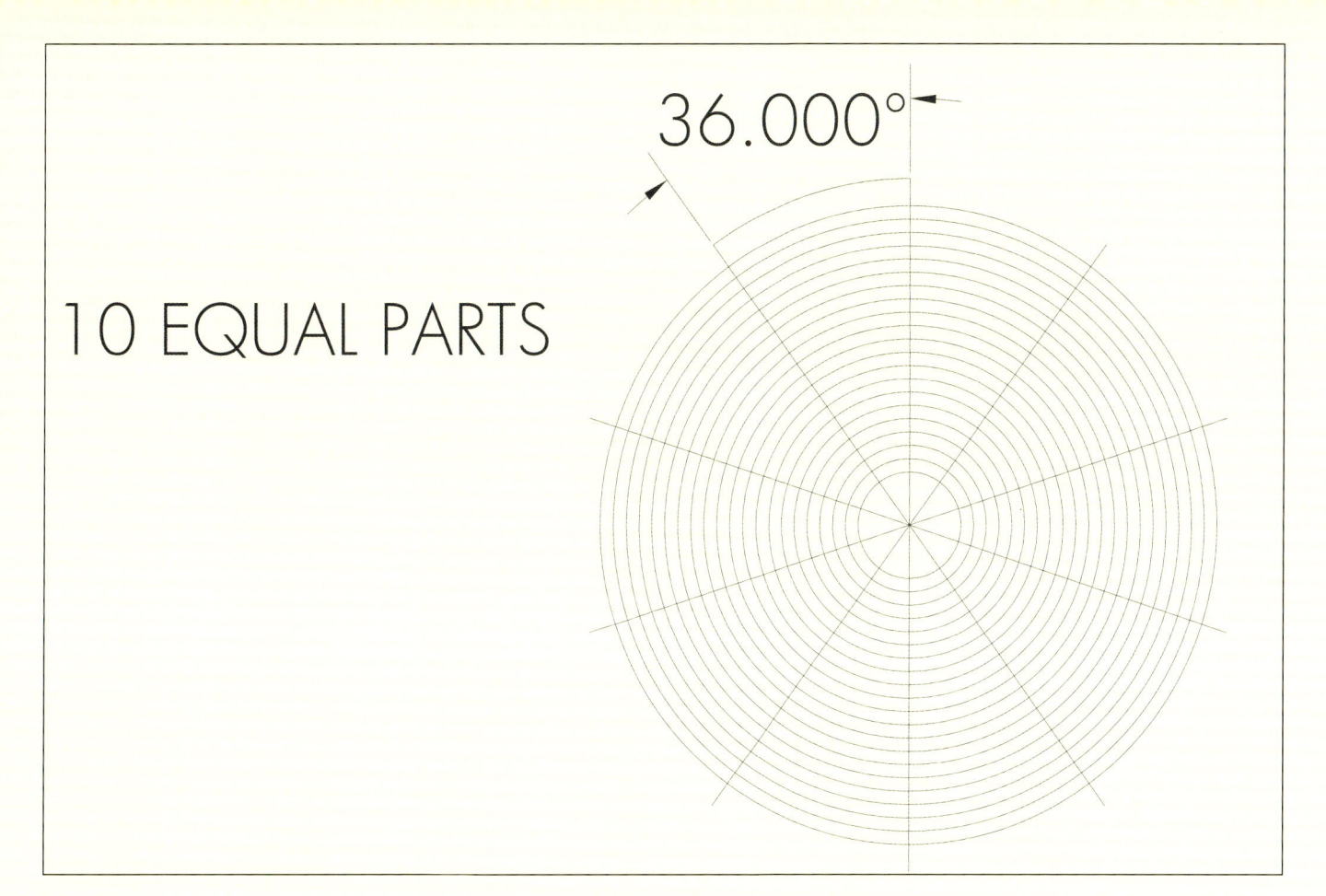

36.000°

Diag. 14

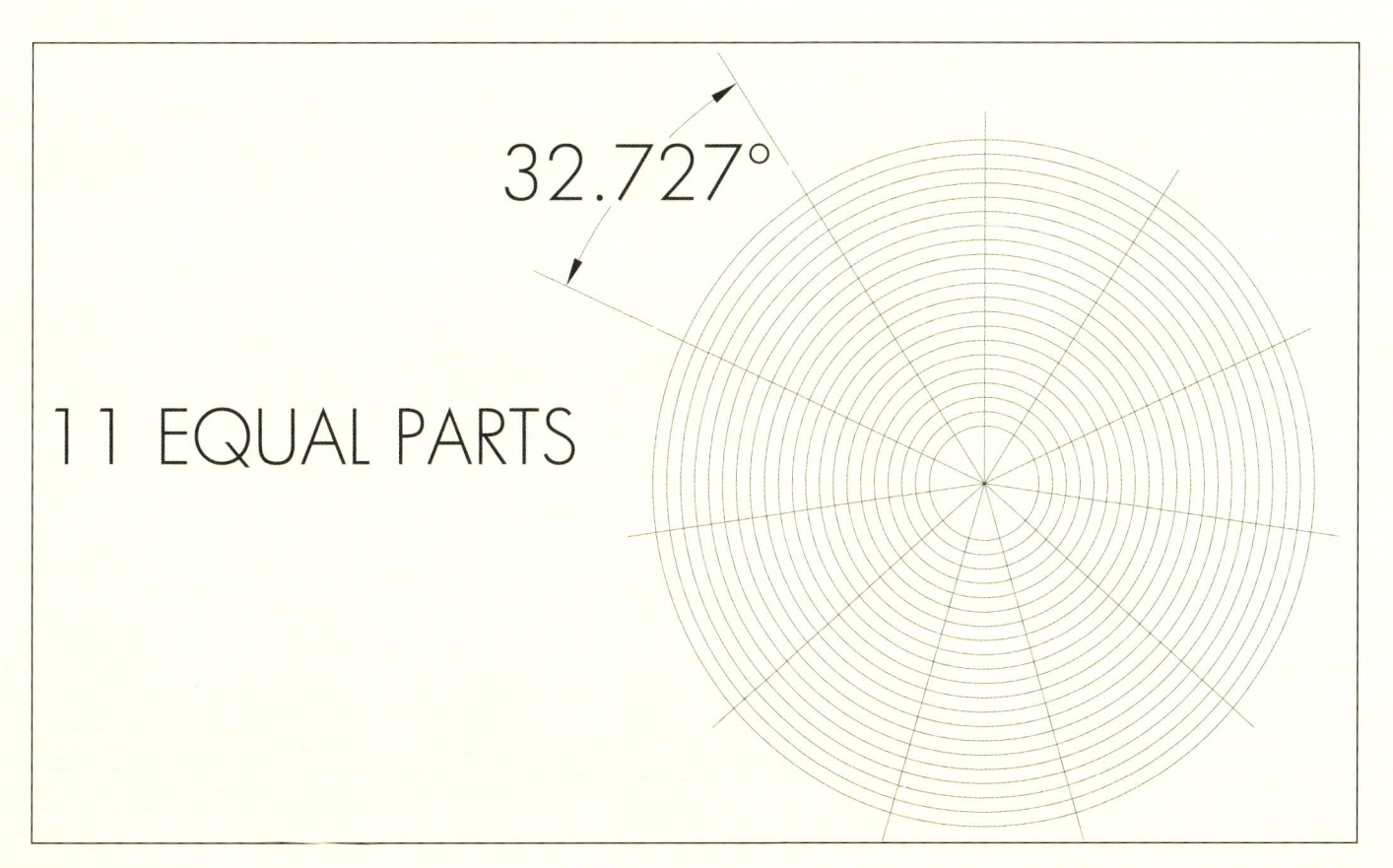

11 EQUAL PARTS

32.727°

Diag. 15

Topic Section: Processes and Techniques **25**

IV. Glues

Titebond Original Wood Glue: This glue is an aliphatic resin glue that sets up fairly fast. When turning rings be sure it is completely dry.

Titebond Dark Wood Glue: This glue leaves a darker glue line than white glue, which is ideal when using dark wood.

Glue Gun: I use an inexpensive hot glue gun for attaching rope on the Barrel Lamp (page 46).

CA Glue (Cyanoacrylate): This "instant glue" is a quick set glue that can set even faster with an accelerator. It is available at most woodworking sites, such as Woodwerks Store.

I use this to attach rings to the scrap board disk that is attached to the lathe faceplate. Attaching with CA glue leaves no holes. I also used it to attach the ladybugs for the Ladybugs Stump Lamp (page 82). It dries clear.

Stick Fast or Clear Epoxy: This can also be used with a variety of other materials. See glues in websites.

V. Hole Patterns:
When turning a cylinder to tightly fit in a drilled hole, make a template as seen in Fig. 17. Drill the hole in the pattern with the same bit that will be used in your project. Cut away about 2/3 of the pattern leaving you an arced template. This template can be used to match the diameter of the cylinder to get a very exact fit.

VI. Inlaying Walnuts:
Start the walnut inlaying process by sanding the sides of the walnut to make it somewhat smooth (see Fig. 18). Cut the walnut in half with a coping saw, holding the nut in a vice or clamp (see Fig. 19). Remove the meat of the nut with a pick. I like making this project because I can eat the scrap for a snack. Place the walnut half against the project and trace around the nut, (see Fig. 20). Use a Forstner bit and drill about 1/2" to 3/4" deep. Make sure the size bit you use is a little bit smaller than the nut you traced (see Fig. 21). Carve out the rest of the space for the walnut with a power carving tool, a Dremel tool works well (see Fig. 22). Insert the walnut half (see Fig. 23). Apply glue to the edge of the nut and tap it in gently. Then sand over the nut with an orbital sander (see Fig. 24). Space the walnut halves randomly around your project.

Fig. 17: Wooden template being used to check diameter.

Fig. 18: Sanding a walnut on a belt sander.

Fig. 19: Cutting a walnut in half.

Topic Section: Processes and Techniques

Fig. 20: Tracing the shape of the nut on the lamp.

Fig. 21: Drilling a hole for the nut, using a Forstner bit.

Fig. 22: Hollowing out the space to inlay the walnut shell.

Fig. 23: Gluing the walnut shell in and tapping gently. It should protrude out of the hole about 1/64 of an inch.

Fig. 24: Sanding the walnut shell flush with an orbital sander.

Topic Section: Processes and Techniques **27**

VII. Janka Hardness Scale: The Janka Scale rates a wood's hardness, its density. This measurement is made by pushing a steel ball half way into the wood. The surface of the wood is used for this test not the end grain. The scale indicates the amount of pressure that it takes to force the ball into the wood.

The hardest wood on the Janka Scale and the hardest wood in the world is lignum vita, which requires 4,500 pounds of force. The following chart shows common wood species—some are used in this book but not all. The Janka Scale is a tool used commonly in the hardwood flooring manufacturing business.

Lignum Vita	4500
Brazilian Ebony	3692
Brazilian Walnut	3684
Ebony	3220
Bloodwood	2900
Brazilian Cherry	2350
Purple Heart	1860
Tigerwood	1850
Hickory	1820
Rosewood	1780
African Paduak	1725
Locust	1700
Wenge	1630
Zebrawood	1575
Sweet Birch	1470
Hard Sugar Maple	1450
Kentucky Coffee Tree	1390
White Oak	1366
White Ash	1320
Beech	1300
Northern Red Oak	1290
Yellowheart Pine	1225
Coco Bolo	1136
American Walnut	1010
Teak	1000
American Cherry	950
Soft or Ambrosia Maple	950
Cedar	900
Southern Yellow Pine	870
American Red Elm	860
Lacewood	840
Sycamore	770
Douglas Fir	660
Sassafras	630
Chestnut	540
Poplar	540
Hemlock	500
White Pine	420
Basswood	410
Balsa	100

VIII. Lady Bugs

• Black ebony and paduak were used in the Lady Bug Stump Lamp (page 82). Glue a piece of black ebony about 3/8" wide or more and 3/4" thick between two strips of paduak. The paduak needs only to be about 3/4" wide and 3/4" thick. Make about 40 ladybugs. The lamp only needs about 30 but a few extra is a good idea. Sand or plane all sides smooth. The plug cutter works best on a very smooth surface (see Diag. 16).

• On a drill press, cut the plugs about 1/2" deep.

Lady bugs on Lady Bug Stump lamp.

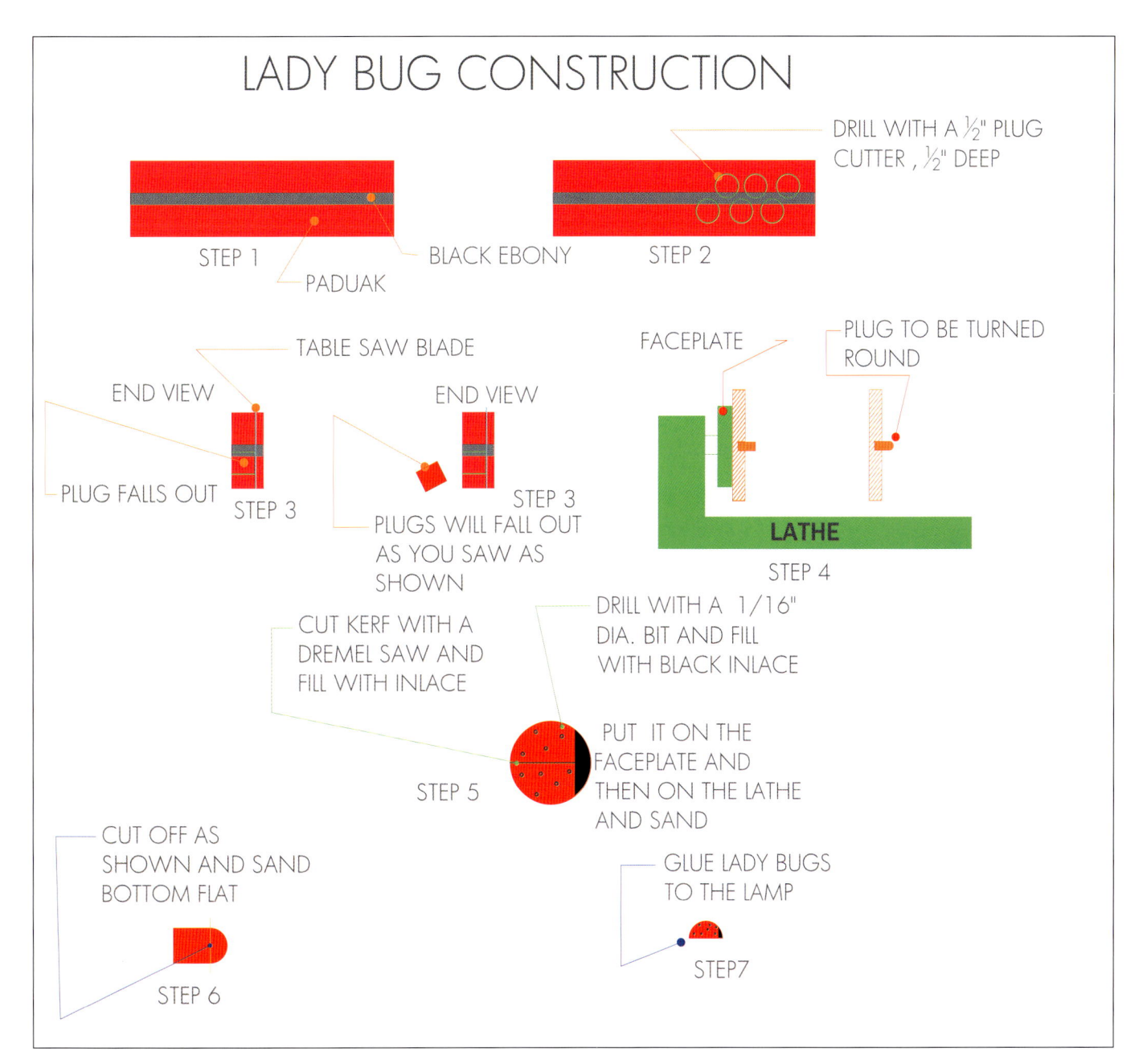

LADY BUG CONSTRUCTION

STEP 1 — PADUAK, BLACK EBONY

STEP 2 — DRILL WITH A ½" PLUG CUTTER, ½" DEEP

STEP 3 — END VIEW, TABLE SAW BLADE, PLUG FALLS OUT

STEP 3 — END VIEW, PLUGS WILL FALL OUT AS YOU SAW AS SHOWN

STEP 4 — FACEPLATE, PLUG TO BE TURNED ROUND, LATHE

STEP 5 — CUT KERF WITH A DREMEL SAW AND FILL WITH INLACE. DRILL WITH A 1/16" DIA. BIT AND FILL WITH BLACK INLACE. PUT IT ON THE FACEPLATE AND THEN ON THE LATHE AND SAND

STEP 6 — CUT OFF AS SHOWN AND SAND BOTTOM FLAT

STEP 7 — GLUE LADY BUGS TO THE LAMP

Diag. 16

Topic Section: Processes and Techniques

• Use a push stick on the table saw and make a saw cut so the kerf releases the plug (see Fig. 25). Do this on both sides. The plugs should fall out and be smooth on the bottom.

Fig. 25: Plugs falling out as they are being cut on table saw.

• Mount a board on the faceplate of your lathe. I cut the board round just to have a smooth rotating object. Using a chuck mounted in your tailstock, drill a 1/2" hole in the board about 1/4" deep. Drilling this on the lathe will precisely center the plug in relation to the lathe. Then press a plug from step 3 in the hole and turn it round on top.

• Hold the plugs in a scrap board for these next steps (see Fig. 27). Use a saw blade in a Dremel tool and cut the straight line in the back of the ladybug. This line represents the division between the wings. I used a 1/6" bit and drilled three holes on each side about 3/32" deep. Fill this with Inlace (see topic XX, "Websites," on page 40 for Inlace suppliers). Once dried, put the plug back on the lathe and using a scraping tool cut the excess Inlace off. This requires a very thin cut. Sand and finish, I use a spray lacquer in a can.

• Hold the ladybug with a pair of vice grips and sand the bottom on a disk or belt sander, leaving the final height of the ladybug at 1/4" or less.

• Once the lamp is finished with a surface finish, such as lacquer, it is ready to have the ladybugs glued on. Glue the ladybugs to the lamp randomly using a thick CA glue. I used about 30 ladybugs. Be sure not to wax the project because the glue will not adhere well.

Fig. 27: This board is used to hold the ladybugs while the straight line is cut with a dremel tool and small holes drilled.

IX. Lamp Top Inserts: Lamp inserts are simply pieces of scrap solid wood or plywood (see Fig. 28). I use these to strengthen the top of the lamp. These are glued inside the lamp (see Fig. 29) to give the threaded pipe more bearing surface on the sides of the pipe. Usually the top ring on most lamps is 3/4" thick; by using a 3/4" insert you gain 1 1/2" of wood for the threaded pipe to adhere too. Since the threaded pipe holds the harp, the socket, and the shade this will strengthen and keep the threaded pipe in a vertical position (see Diag. 17).

Fig. 28: I use Titebond to glue the inserts.

Topic Section: Processes and Techniques

Fig. 29: Glue the insert in the top of the lamp.

LAMP TOP INSERTS

INSERT IS 3/4" THICK

DRILL 3/8 HOLE FOR THREADED PIPE

TOP OF LAMP

DRILL A 3/8 HOLE FOR THREADED PIPE

INSERT MADE OF SOLID WOOD

SCRAP WOOD

INSIDE OF LAMP

Diag. 17

Topic Section: Processes and Techniques   31

X. Lathe Tools: Shown in Diag. 18 are the six basic lathe tools used in turning. They can be divided into two categories: cutting tools and scraping tools. Cutting tools include the gouge, skew, and the parting tool. Scraping tools are the flat nose, round nose, and diamond nose. The cutting tools can also be used for scraping.

Gouges: These tools are used mainly in spindle turning for turning square material between centers. I never use them for faceplate turning. Gouges come standard in most sets of basic lathe tools and in many sizes.

Skew: The skew can be used for flat surfaces, smoothing, cutting "V"-shaped grooves, square shoulders, and similar shapes.

Diamond Nose and Flat Nose: both of these are scraping tools. I use the diamond nose or flat nose on outside curved surfaces as well as on flat surfaces.

Round Nose: The round nose is another scraping tool used for cutting curves, especially inside the curves such as a cove.

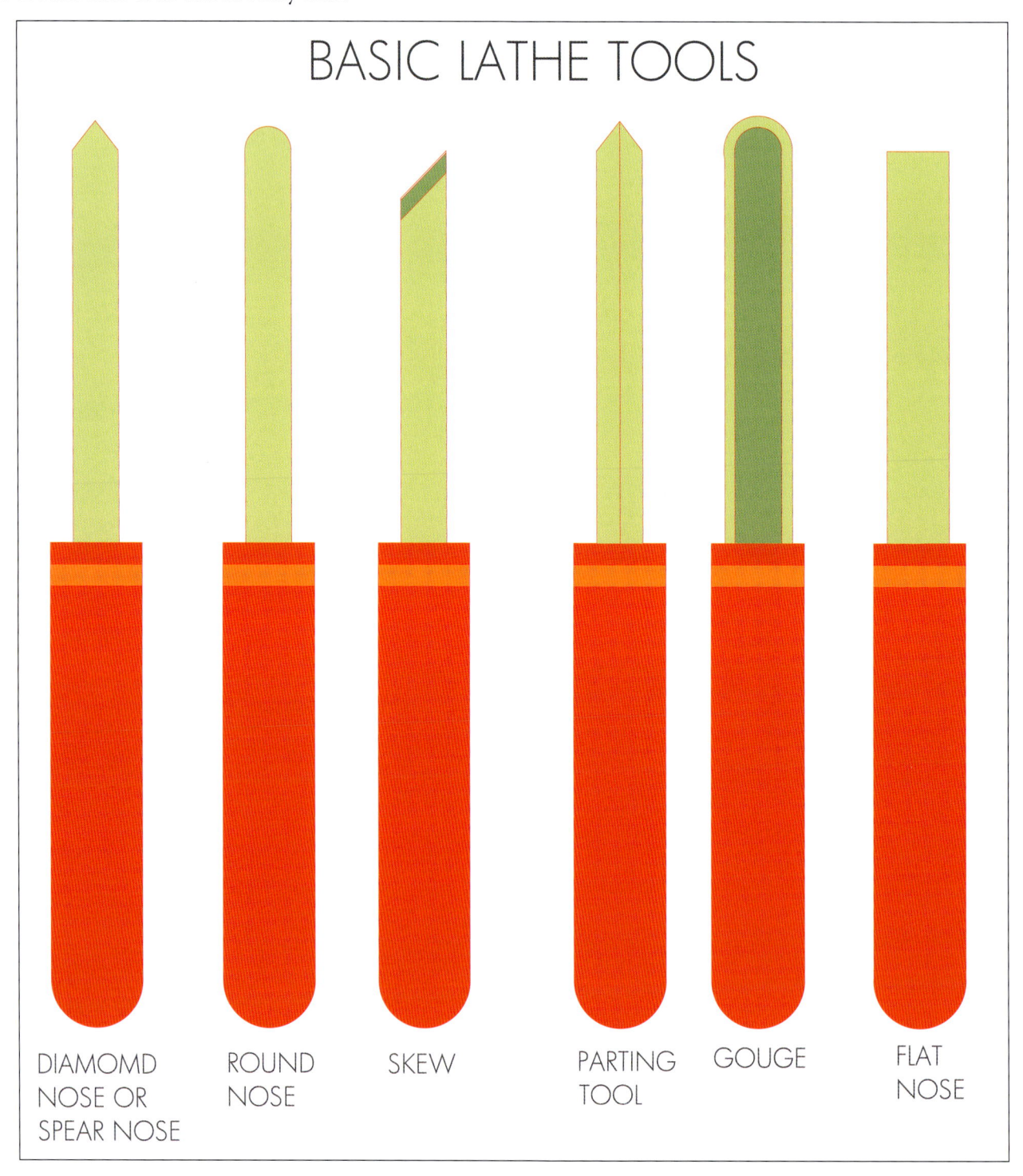

BASIC LATHE TOOLS

DIAMOMD NOSE OR SPEAR NOSE | ROUND NOSE | SKEW | PARTING TOOL | GOUGE | FLAT NOSE

Diag. 18

Topic Section: Processes and Techniques

Parting Tool: The parting tool is used to cut straight in; an example is shown in Fig. 30. Notice the square cut on each end of the cylinder, which is done with the parting tool.

Fig. 30: This straight-in cut is made with a parting tool

XI. Pulling Wire Through A Lamp: Some lamps are solid on the bottom and require "fishing" a line through the lamp; an example is the Navajo Lamp (see page 53). Tie a small nail on a thin fishing line or string to act as a weight. Let this dangle from the top of the lamp through the threaded pipe and into the lamp. Get a coat hanger and make a little hook on the end, use this hook to catch the fishing line. Gently pull the fishing line through the hole on the side of the lamp near the bottom.

Cut the electrical wire in a "V" shape on the end of the wire, tie a string to the wire or use CA glue and pull the electrical wire gently through the lamp.

I usually leave 8 to 10 feet of wire coming from the lamp (see Diag. 19).

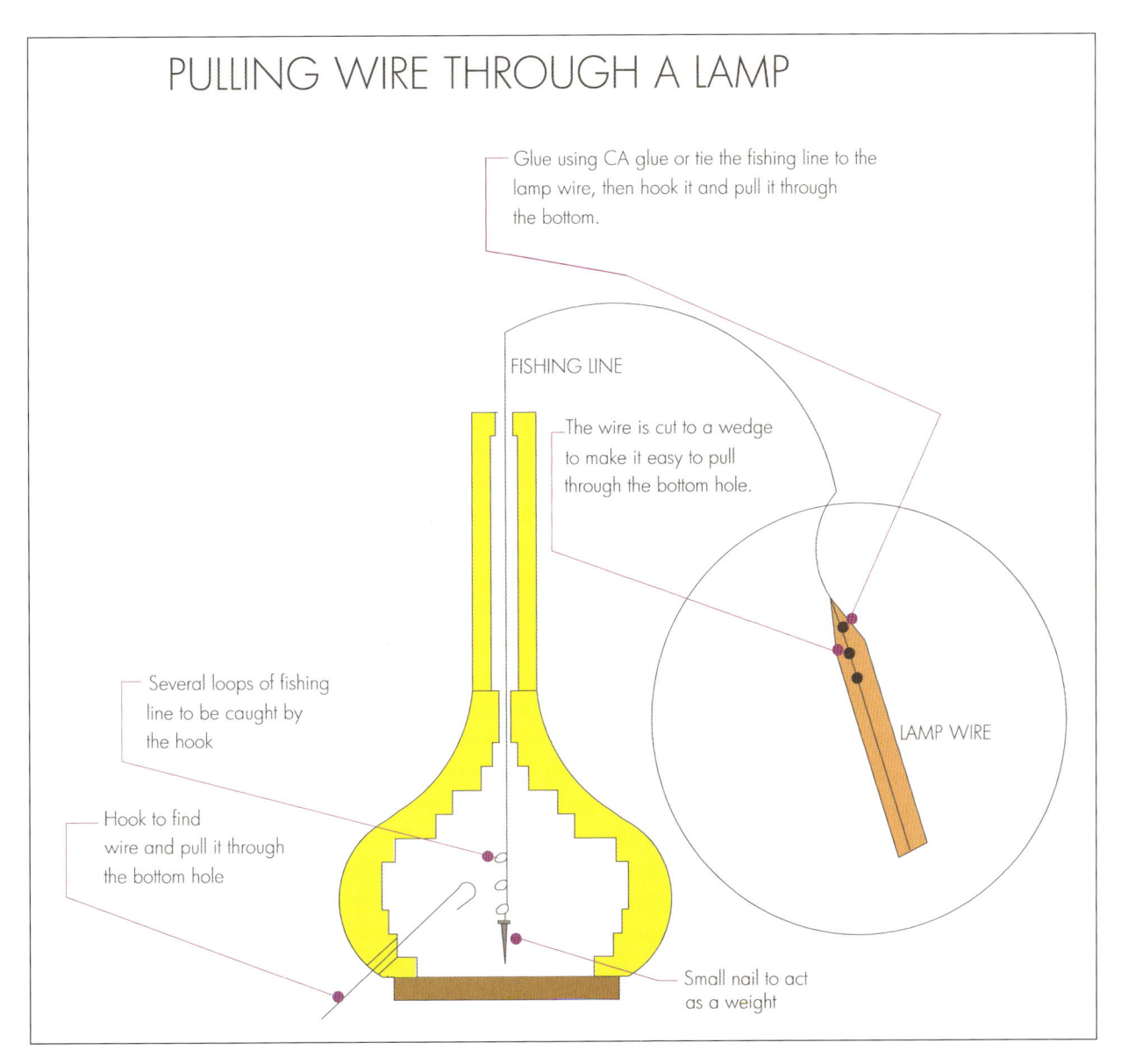

PULLING WIRE THROUGH A LAMP

- Glue using CA glue or tie the fishing line to the lamp wire, then hook it and pull it through the bottom.

FISHING LINE

- The wire is cut to a wedge to make it easy to pull through the bottom hole.

- Several loops of fishing line to be caught by the hook

- Hook to find wire and pull it through the bottom hole

LAMP WIRE

- Small nail to act as a weight

Diag. 19

Topic Section: Processes and Techniques

XII. Rope and Lace Weaving: I suggest using a practice board for the Rope and Lace Lamp (see page 48). It's quicker and much easier than working inside the lamps. See practice weaving board in Fig. 32.

• The rope starts inside, where you should tie a knot. Pull ample rope through leaving a "U" shape as shown in Fig. 31.

• The rope again comes out and loops over the "U" leaving another "U" shape. Get the first "U" nice and tight.

• This process continues around the lamp. Be sure to keep the rope tight with a consistent appearance. At the end, tuck the rope inside the lamp and apply CA glue to the rope and the inside of the last hole.

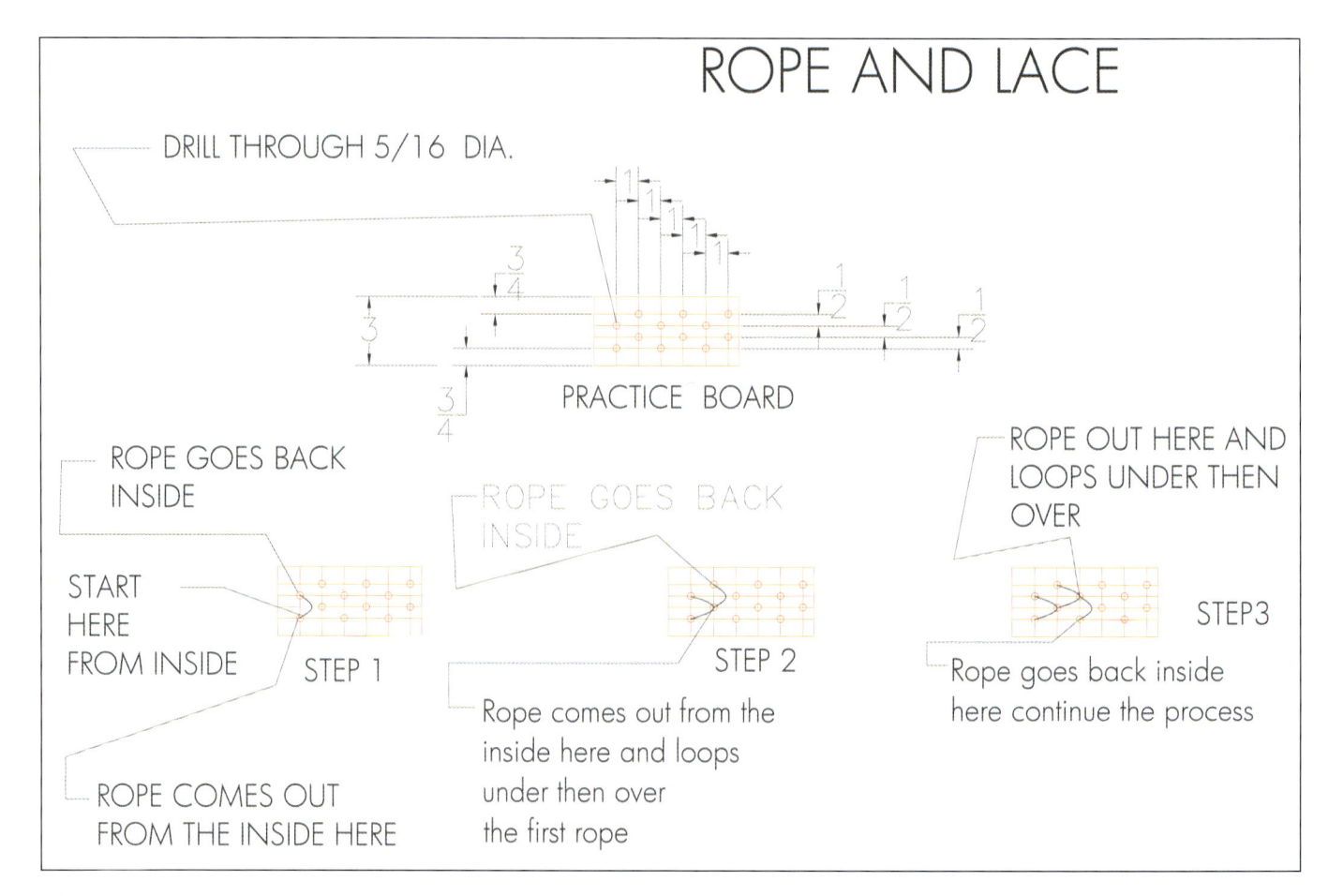

Diag. 20

Fig. 31: Weaving the manila rope.

34 Topic Section: Processes and Techniques

Topic Section: Processes and Techniques

XIII. Rope Weave Lamp: When making the Rope Weave Lamp (see page 51), it is best to lay out the holes on a piece of scrap wood as shown in Fig. 32. Practicing it first on a flat board is much easier than reaching inside the lamp to practice. Lay out the holes using a framing square (see Fig. 33). The finish should be applied to the lamp *before* weaving the rope.

Fig. 32: A practice weaving board.

XIV. Specifications on Lamp:

Lamp Name	Harp Size	Shade Bottom Dia.	Shade Top Dia.	Height	Shade
Bad Day in the Shop	10	16	7	10 ½	Bell
Barrel Lamp	12	18	8	13	Coolie
Dot Lamp	10	17	7	14	Coolie Straight
Flower on the Wall Lamp	14	18	8	12 ½	Hexagon Bell
Kokopelli	13	21	7	14	Coolie Straight
Lady Bug Stump Lamp	10 ½	14 ½	8 ½	11 ½	Coolie Straight
Navajo Deer Lamp	10	18	9 ½	11 ½	Red Coolie
Pagoda	12	18	9	13 ½	Hexagon Bell
Pink Ivory Lamp	10	16	7	10 ½	Bell
Quilted Milk Can Lamp	14	21	10	17	Coolie Straight
Rope and Lace Lamp	15	18	10	17	Coolie Straight
Rope Weave Lamp	13	18	10	13	Coolie Straight
There's A Spider on That Post, Grandpa!	10	21	7	12	Coolie Straight
Sunbonnet Sue Lamp	10	18	9 ½	11 ½	Bell
Trunk Lamp	13	18	10	13	Black Coolie
Walnut Nut Lamp	14	21	10	17	Coolie-Straight

XV. Templates and Patterns: When matching a cylinder's diameter to the diameter of a hole, first make a template, as shown in Fig. 34. Drill the hole the size required and at the same time drill a hole to make a pattern the same size. Then you can use a pattern when you turn your cylinder as used in the Quilted Milk Can Lamp (see page 112) or There's a Spider on That Post, Grandpa! (see page 73).

Fig. 33: Laying out the holes for weaving.

Fig. 34: Using a template to insure a snug fit.

Topic Section: Processes and Techniques

Topic Section: Processes and Techniques 37

XVI. Turning Tall Lamps: This is the process used on the Navajo Deer Lamp (see page 53). Place a new ring on the lamp with no center hole. Using the tailstock, crank the dead center into the lamp. Then flatten the ring, by cutting with a scraping tool, with the exception of where the dead center hits. Next, drill a 1/2" hole in the exact center, using the lathe, or a drill press. If you are using the lathe you will need a chuck that has a Morse taper that fits your lathe. Repeat this process for each of the rings until you reach the desired height of the lamp. On the last one or two rings, drill a 3/8" hole for your threaded pipe to fit tightly.

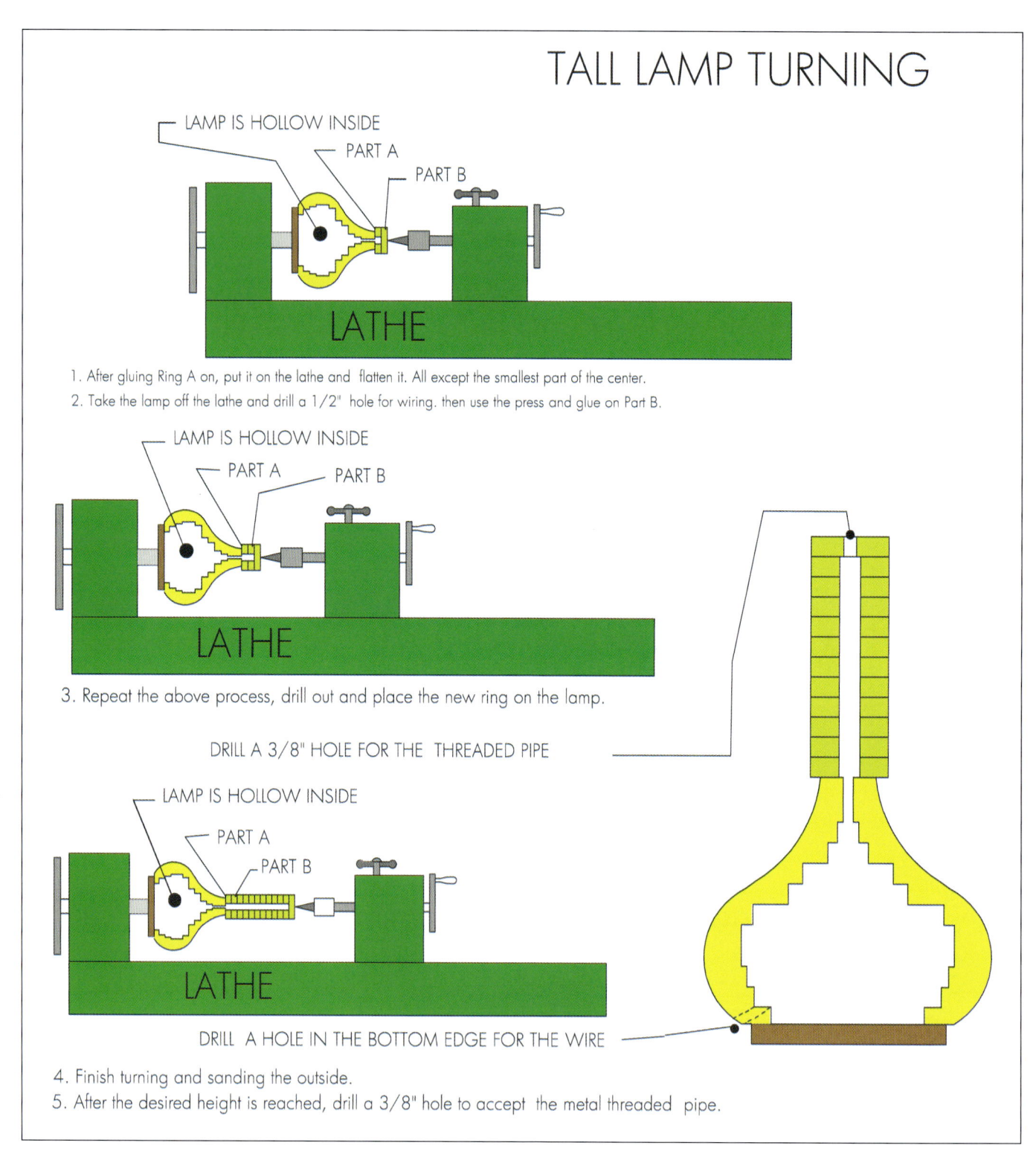

TALL LAMP TURNING

LAMP IS HOLLOW INSIDE
PART A
PART B
LATHE

1. After gluing Ring A on, put it on the lathe and flatten it. All except the smallest part of the center.
2. Take the lamp off the lathe and drill a 1/2" hole for wiring. then use the press and glue on Part B.

LAMP IS HOLLOW INSIDE
PART A   PART B
LATHE

3. Repeat the above process, drill out and place the new ring on the lamp.

DRILL A 3/8" HOLE FOR THE THREADED PIPE

LAMP IS HOLLOW INSIDE
PART A
PART B
LATHE

DRILL A HOLE IN THE BOTTOM EDGE FOR THE WIRE

4. Finish turning and sanding the outside.
5. After the desired height is reached, drill a 3/8" hole to accept the metal threaded pipe.

Diag. 20A

38 *Topic Section: Processes and Techniques*

XVII. Turning Flat Surfaces: When flattening the surface, like on the Walnut Nut Lamp (see page 69) or There's a Spider on That Post, Grandpa! (see page 73), use the following method:

First, turn both ends to the required diameter using outside calipers to check the diameter. Next, check for high and low spots by using a straight edge. For a straight edge, you can use a square, a level, or anything that is straight. Mark the high spots and gradually turn the piece, checking it regularly with your straight edge. Be sure not to go too deep. Continue this process until you have a completely flat surface (see Fig. 35).

XVIII. Using a Pattern: On certain lamps, such as the Dot Lamp (see page 43), I use a pattern made from a manila folder or sometimes 1/4" lauan plywood. When turning the sphere of the Dot Lamp, use the pattern as a guide. Gradually refine the turning to match the pattern (see Fig. 36). Notice that only about 1/3 of the circle is used when making the pattern.

Fig. 35: Checking for low and high spots when turning straight, flat surfaces.

Fig. 36: Checking for roundness using a paper pattern.

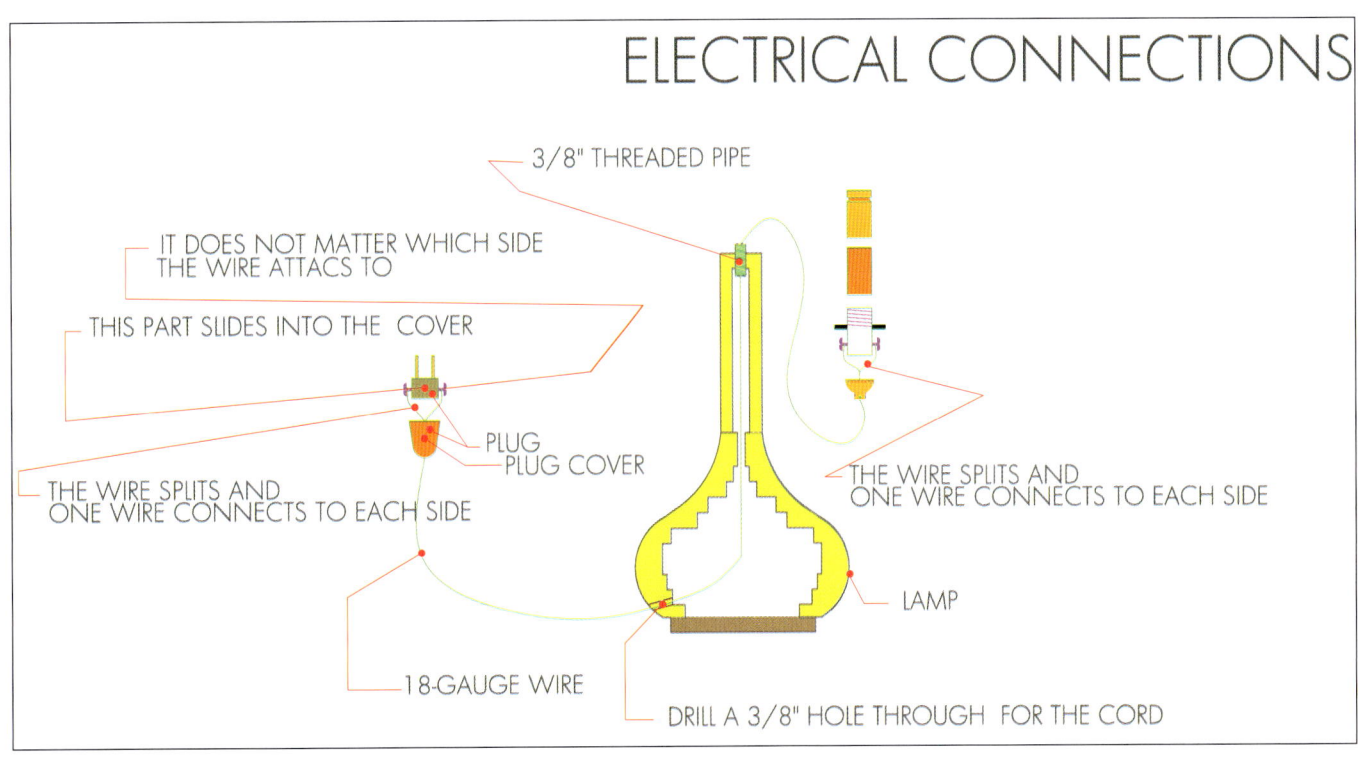

ELECTRICAL CONNECTIONS

- 3/8" THREADED PIPE
- IT DOES NOT MATTER WHICH SIDE THE WIRE ATTACS TO
- THIS PART SLIDES INTO THE COVER
- PLUG
- PLUG COVER
- THE WIRE SPLITS AND ONE WIRE CONNECTS TO EACH SIDE
- THE WIRE SPLITS AND ONE WIRE CONNECTS TO EACH SIDE
- LAMP
- 18-GAUGE WIRE
- DRILL A 3/8" HOLE THROUGH FOR THE CORD

Diag. 21

Topic Section: Processes and Techniques

XIX. Wiring A Lamp: I use an 18-gauge wire and try to leave about 8 or 10 feet of cord. The drawing shows how to wire the plug and the socket.

Polarity does not matter. In other words, it doesn't matter which screw the wire goes on—either the plug or the socket. If you have a grounding wire it does matter, but most lamp wires have just two wires and not a ground.

XX. Websites

The following vendors offer supplies and materials that you will need for making segmented lamps:

Leather (www.tandyleatherfactory.com): You can find belts, straps, buckles, leather glue, leather finish, and almost anything else associated with leather.

Lamp sockets (www.lampsockets.com): This site has high quality lamp sockets and all sorts of unusual and hard-to-find lamp parts.

Tacks (www.kennedyhardware.com): They have an assortment of tacks, which I used on the trunk lamp, as well as buckles and other trunk hardware.

Inlace inlay and other items for lathe work are available through the following:

www.woodturnerscatalog.com
www.woodwerks.com
www.woodcraft.com
www.rockler.com

Confetti Oil Lamp Vase
(www.woodturnerscatalog.com)

III. Segmented Lamp Projects

Now that you are familiar with the basic skills required to make a segmented lamp, you are ready to start a project. I have organized the lamp projects by complexity, starting with confetti lamps, which are an excellent beginner project. As you work through the projects in this book, the level of difficulty increases: the number of pieces involved goes up and the size of the lamp increases. Enjoy.

Confetti Lamp

These little oil lamps make a great weekend project, and are ideal for the novice woodturner.

Basically, these lamps are vessels for holding a small jar containing lamp oil and a wick. The company selling these small lamp oil jars promotes them as having three good uses. First, they say, they are good for power outages. So, a few weeks back, our power went out and sure enough these little lamps worked like a charm.

Second, these lamps are supposedly great for parties. I tried these little lamps out when a few friends were over recently and again, to my surprise, they were the hit of the party.

The third use, the company says, is for romance. By this time, I was pretty convinced that these little lamps really work. So, late one night I got all spruced up, put on some Old Spice, and got ready to hit the sack. I lit up a confetti lamp and shortly thereafter my wife walked in. "Cute", she said with a smile. So at this point, I'm thinking, *WOW! These things really do work*. I hustled downstairs to get another confetti lamp. At this point, I'm thinking ,these baby's burn for about 45 minutes, two lamps, this is all going to work out fine.

Without going into more detail, I have to say, my wife fell asleep. So they don't work for romance. I guess two out of three isn't bad.

Bloodwood and Birdseye Maple Confetti Lamp

Fig. 37: Bloodwood and birdseye maple confetti lamp

- Glue ring one up using eight segments.
- Then glue this ring with CA glue to a flat disk attached to a faceplate. Flatten it on one side.
- Turn ring one over and glue the flattened side to the faceplate and flatten the other side of ring one.
- With both sides flattened, it should be turned to the required thickness.
- Glue up ring two using sixteen segments. Put it on the lathe in a similar manner and flatten one side.
- Use a press and glue it to ring one.
- Glue a scrap board inside as shown in Diag. 22. This is for your confetti jar to sit on.
- Glue up the remaining rings three, four, and five. Turn to the shape shown and be sure the jar fits in the top hole correctly.
- For confetti lamp vases, see websites on page 40.

CONFETTI LAMP OIL LAMP

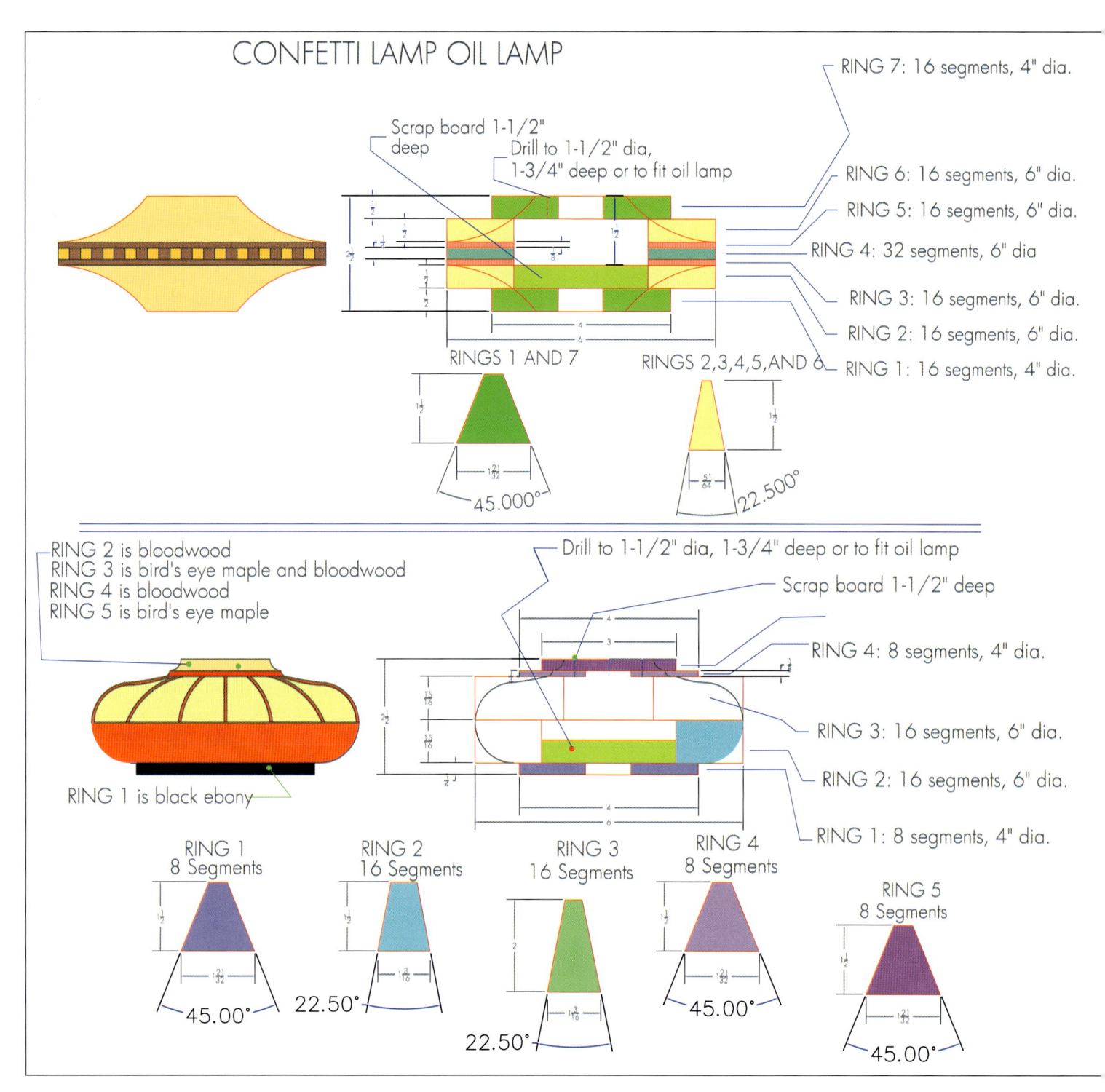

RING 7: 16 segments, 4" dia.
RING 6: 16 segments, 6" dia.
RING 5: 16 segments, 6" dia.
RING 4: 32 segments, 6" dia
RING 3: 16 segments, 6" dia.
RING 2: 16 segments, 6" dia.
RING 1: 16 segments, 4" dia.

Scrap board 1-1/2" deep
Drill to 1-1/2" dia, 1-3/4" deep or to fit oil lamp

RINGS 1 AND 7 — 45.000°
RINGS 2, 3, 4, 5, AND 6 — 22.500°

RING 2 is bloodwood
RING 3 is bird's eye maple and bloodwood
RING 4 is bloodwood
RING 5 is bird's eye maple
RING 1 is black ebony

Drill to 1-1/2" dia, 1-3/4" deep or to fit oil lamp
Scrap board 1-1/2" deep

RING 4: 8 segments, 4" dia.
RING 3: 16 segments, 6" dia.
RING 2: 16 segments, 6" dia.
RING 1: 8 segments, 4" dia.

RING 1 — 8 Segments — 45.00°
RING 2 — 16 Segments — 22.50°
RING 3 — 16 Segments — 22.50°
RING 4 — 8 Segments — 45.00°
RING 5 — 8 Segments — 45.00°

Diag. 22

Tulip Wood and Purpleheart Confetti Lamp

Fig. 38: Tulip wood and purpleheart confetti lamp

The process for gluing up this Confetti Lamp is exactly the same as above. The ring sizes may be different and the final shape is different but the whole process is the same.

42 *Segmented Lamp Projects*

Dot Lamp

Materials: Use wenge, a very dark wood, and cotton wood, which is very light in color, for this lamp.

Refer to Diags. 23–25 when making this lamp:

• The base (Part A), the lower ball, (Part B), and the upper ball (Part D) are made as separate parts.

• Part A is attached to Part B with three screws placed in the bottom of Part A.

• Part B and Part D are attached to each other using Part C, a cylinder (see Diag. 25).

• Parts B, C, and D are glued together. But before gluing them, be sure to drill a 3/4" hole through Part C for the wire.

• For the top cylinder, Part E, I used a piece of maple which is much harder and stronger than the cotton wood.

• Drill a 3/8" hole in Part E for the 3/8" threaded pipe to fit in.

• When turning Part B, see topic XVIII, "Using A Pattern," on page 39.

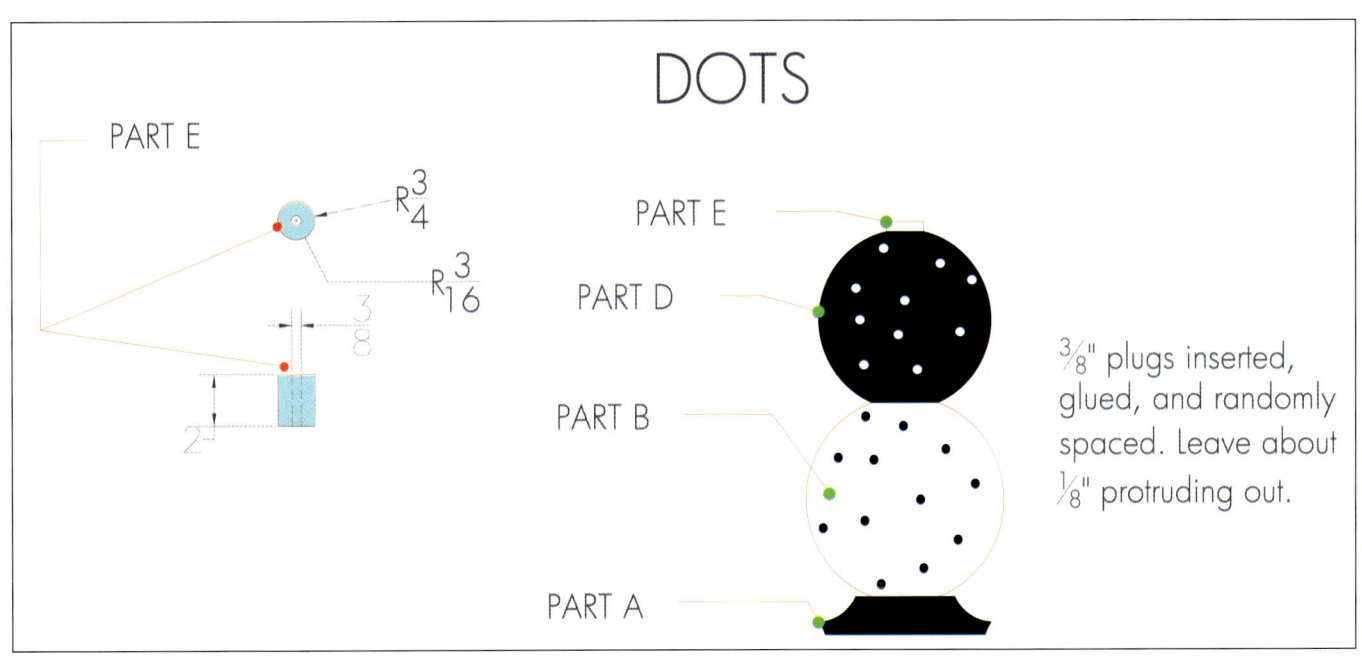

DOTS

3/8" plugs inserted, glued, and randomly spaced. Leave about 1/8" protruding out.

Diag. 23

Dot Lamp

DOTS

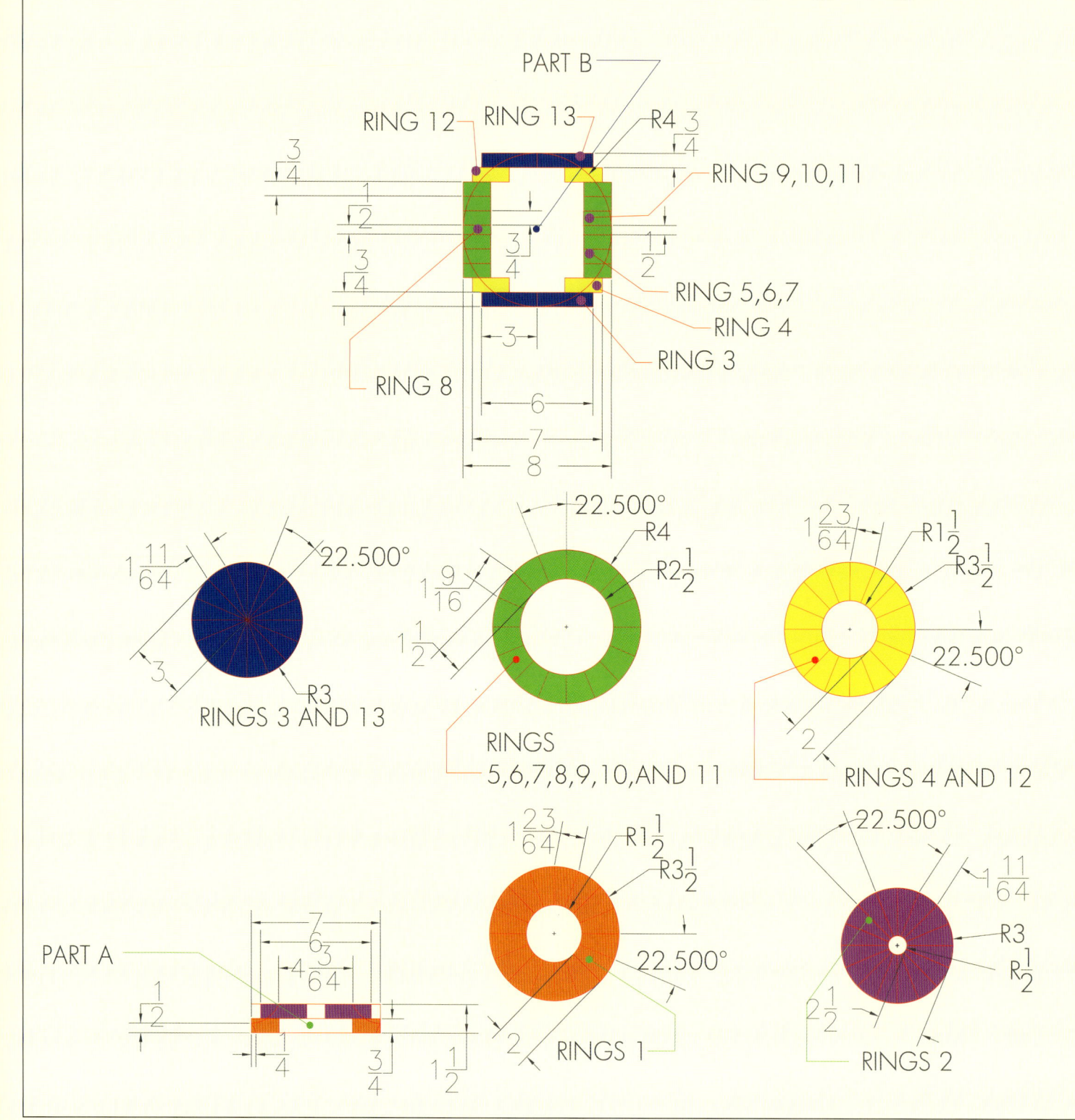

Diag. 24

44 Segmented Lamp Projects

DOTS

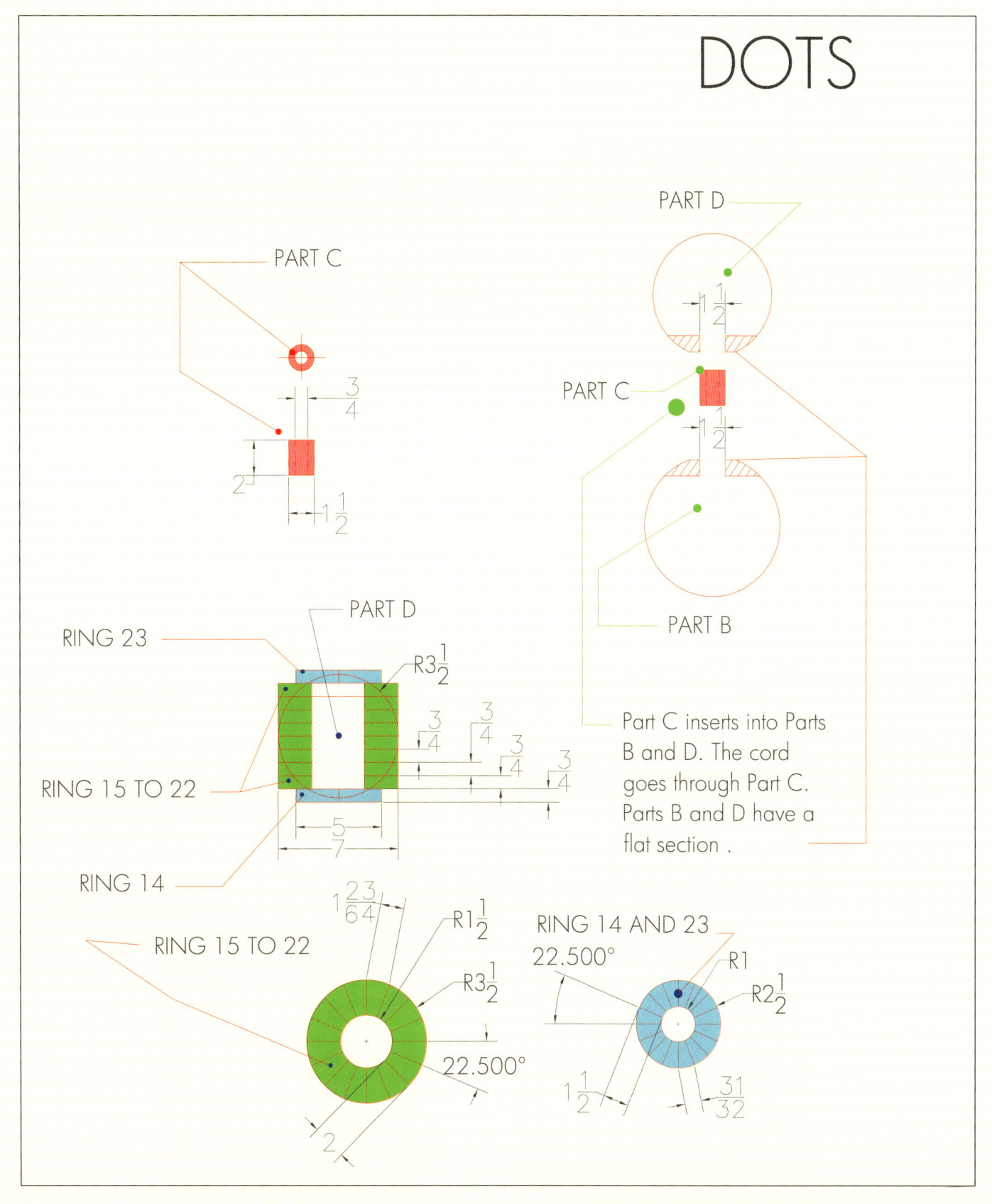

PART D

PART C

PART C

PART B

Part C inserts into Parts B and D. The cord goes through Part C. Parts B and D have a flat section.

RING 23

PART D

R$3\frac{1}{2}$

RING 15 TO 22

RING 14

RING 15 TO 22

$1\frac{23}{64}$

R$1\frac{1}{2}$

R$3\frac{1}{2}$

22.500°

RING 14 AND 23

22.500°

R1

R$2\frac{1}{2}$

$1\frac{1}{2}$

$\frac{31}{32}$

Diag. 25

Dot Lamp 45

Barrel Lamp

Materials: The Barrel Lamp is made of red oak (the light color wood) and walnut (the dark wood). I use a 1/4" hemp rope.

Refer to Diag. 26 when making this lamp:
• Turn this lamp in two parts, joining them at the center, at ring 15. Keep in mind that the bottom section is an exact mirror image of the top section and both have 15 rings.
• For this lamp use a solid piece of wood, not segmented, for the top ring (Ring 1) as well as the corresponding bottom piece (see Fig. 39).
• To start the lamp glue Ring 1 to a piece of plywood with paper between them (see Diag. 4 on page 12). Note that the top and the bottom rings are exactly the same. In fact, the top section, Rings 1–14, is a mirror image to rings in the bottom section, Rings 15–28.
• As you work your way from ring to ring, rough turn the project to within an 1/8" of the finished diameter. Doing this keeps the project round and eliminates vibration.
• After both sections are turned, make sure both center rings have the exact same diameter.
• Glue the top section of rings to the bottom section, keeping the center part as exactly on center with each other as possible.
• Before taking the faceplate off of one end, be sure you know where the exact center is since this end will attach to the tailstock using the dead center. A ball bearing center works best.
• To align these two parts you need to drill a 1/8" diameter hole in the bottom of one of these parts. This must be done on the lathe to ensure the hole is in the exact center of the bottom. Use a chuck with a Morse taper bit that will fit into your tailstock.

This hole should be drilled through Ring 1 and the scrap board before any other rings are added. If Ring 1 is an open ring then you will be drilling through the scrap board only. Slide your tailstock with the chuck and drill bit in it to within about 1/4" of where you will start the hole. Tighten the tailstock down to the bed of the lathe and slowly crank the chuck into Ring 1 and through the scrap board.

In this operation your drill bit will not turn but the project will turn and it will drill a hole exactly in the center. This section of the lamp will become the section placed against the tailstock when gluing it to the other section, which is held in place by a faceplate attached to the headstock. The bottom section and the top section can be glued while on the lathe using your tailstock as a clamp that can be tightened to hold the two sections together firmly. Be sure to put some wax paper on the bed of your lathe so you don't have glue dripping on it.
• Once the lamp is completely dry it can be turned to its finished diameter. Remove the scrap wood and sand the top and bottom.
• See topic XI, "Pulling Wire Through A Lamp," on page 33.

Fig. 39: The barrel lamp after gluing the two sections together and turning.

46 *Segmented Lamp Projects*

BARREL LAMP

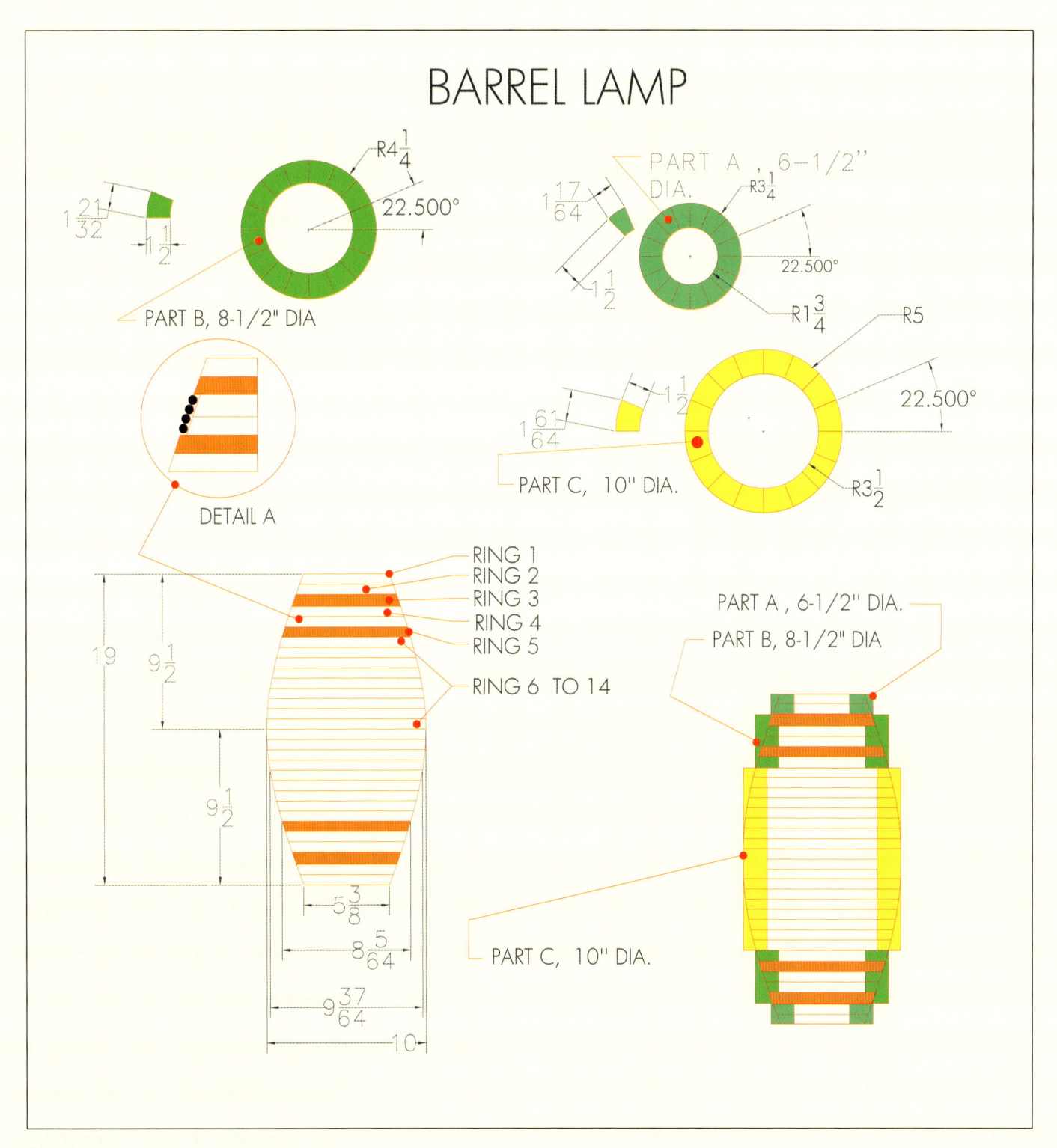

Diag. 26

Barrel Lamp 47

• Finish the lamp using a hot glue gun to apply the rope (see Figs. 40 and 41).

Fig. 40: Using a hot glue gun to attach the hemp rope.

Fig. 41: Pressing on the rope as the hot glue sets.

Rope and Lace Lamp

Materials: The Rope and Lace Lamp is made from yellowheart and lacewood.

Refer to Diag. 27 when making this lamp:
• Parts B and C are identical to Parts E and F. The below instructions are for Parts E and F—Parts B and C are made in the same manner.
• Make Part E first. Start by turning Ring 3 on one side so it is flat and smooth.
• Take Ring 3 off the lathe, turn it over, and put it back on the lathe using concentric circles to align it to the exact center. Turn the second side smooth and flat.
• Make and attach Rings 4 and 5 and turn Part E to its finished dimensions.
• Follow the same process to make Part C.
• Turn Part D (Rings 7–10) using a similar method for the first ring.

Segmented Lamp Projects

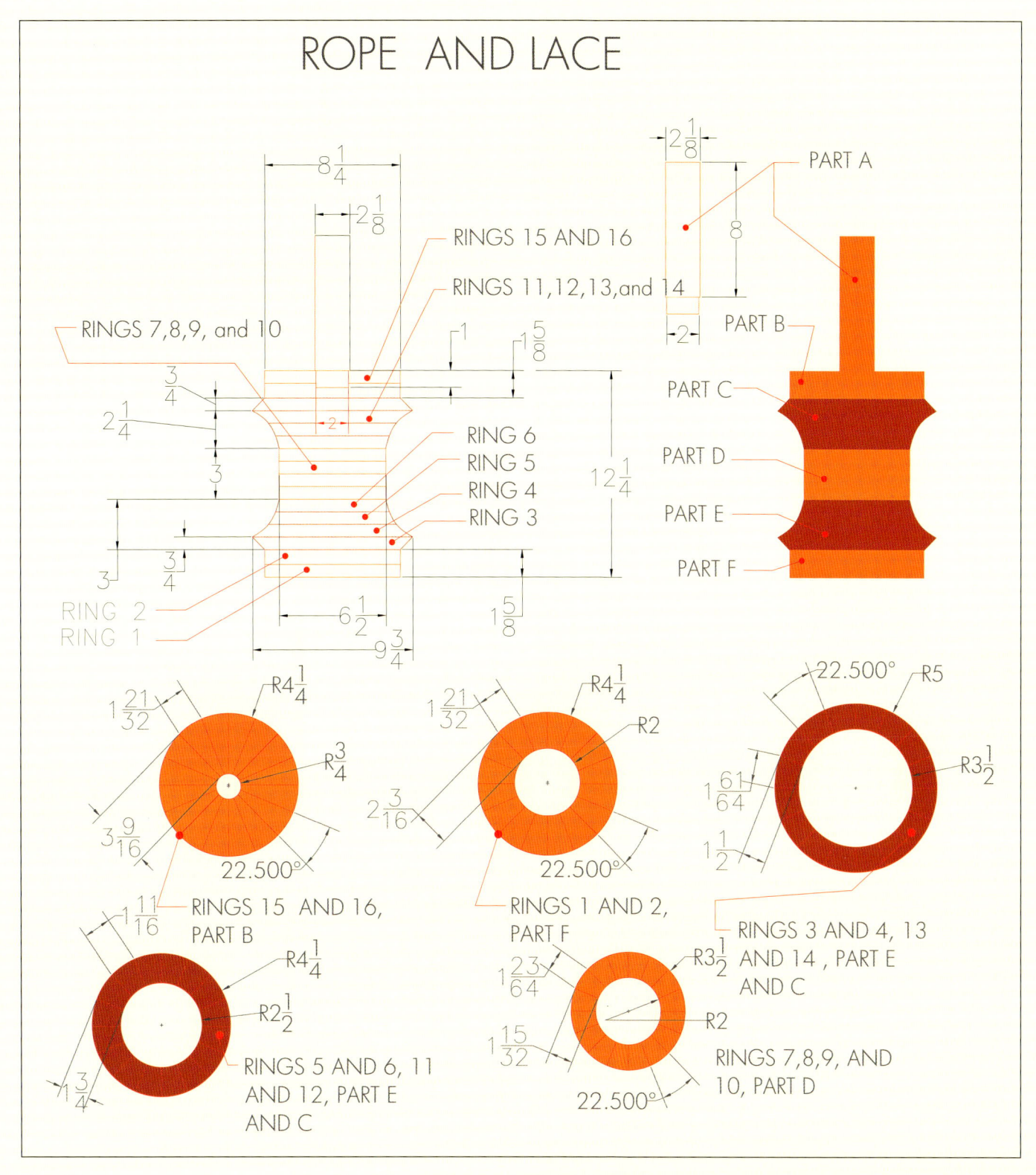

ROPE AND LACE

Rope and Lace Lamp — Diag. 27 — 49

- Glue Part D to Part E, then draw concentric circles on part D (see Fig. 42).

Fig. 42: Diag. concentric lines used for aligning the next ring.

- With part C turned to its finished dimensions, glue Part C to Part D (see Fig. 43).

Fig. 43: Gluing Part C and D using the lathe's tailstock as a press or a clamp

- With Parts E, D, and C glued together (see Fig. 44), Part D is ready to be turned to match up with Parts E and C.

Fig. 44: This shows Parts C, D, and E after they have been glued

- Next, lay out and drill the holes for the lacing (see Fig. 45).
- Turn Part F and Part B.
- Drill a 2" hole through Part B and glue it to Part C. Make sure you there isn't any squeeze out.
- Attach Part F to part E with countersunk screws from the bottom.
- Turn Part A and drill a 3/8" hole through the center for the cord.

Fig. 45: Lay out the holes using a measuring tape used for sewing.

- Glue Part A into Part B and see topic XII, "Rope and Lace Weaving," on page 34 (see Fig. 46).

Fig. 46: Lacing the lamp.

Segmented Lamp Projects

Rope Weave Lamp

Materials: The black wood is wenge and the red wood is bloodwood. The light wood is birch. For the rope, use a 1/8" decorative rope, found in most fabric stores.

Refer to Diag. 28 when making this lamp:
• The top and bottom halves of this lamp are mirror images of each other.
• Prepare Ring 1: screw it to a scrap disk on a faceplate, countersinking the holes, and flatten on both sides (see Chapter 1).
• Glue up Ring 2, flatten it on one side, and glue it to Ring 1 in a press.
• Repeat this process through Ring 13, then start making duplicates of Rings 1-12 for the top half.
• Glue the two halves together, making sure they line up concentrically. Once these are glued, place them on the lathe and turn.
• Lay out the holes for the rope, see the detailed drawings in Diag. 28 and Fig. 33 on page 52. You may need to make a slight adjustment if your lamp varies in diameter.
• Use a scrap board to practice weaving the rope (see Fig. 32 on page 36). Then drill the holes in the lamp on the drill press. On this step you will need an extra hand. My wife usually helps to hold the lamp horizontally on the drill press table. We place the lamp on a towel to prevent it from scratching.
• After you drill the holes, you may want to put the lamp on the lathe for a final sanding.
• Drill the 3/8" hole for the threaded pipe and a 3/8" hole at the bottom for the wire to exit.
• Apply a finish to the lamp *before* weaving the rope and then wire the lamp.

ROPE WEAVE LAMP

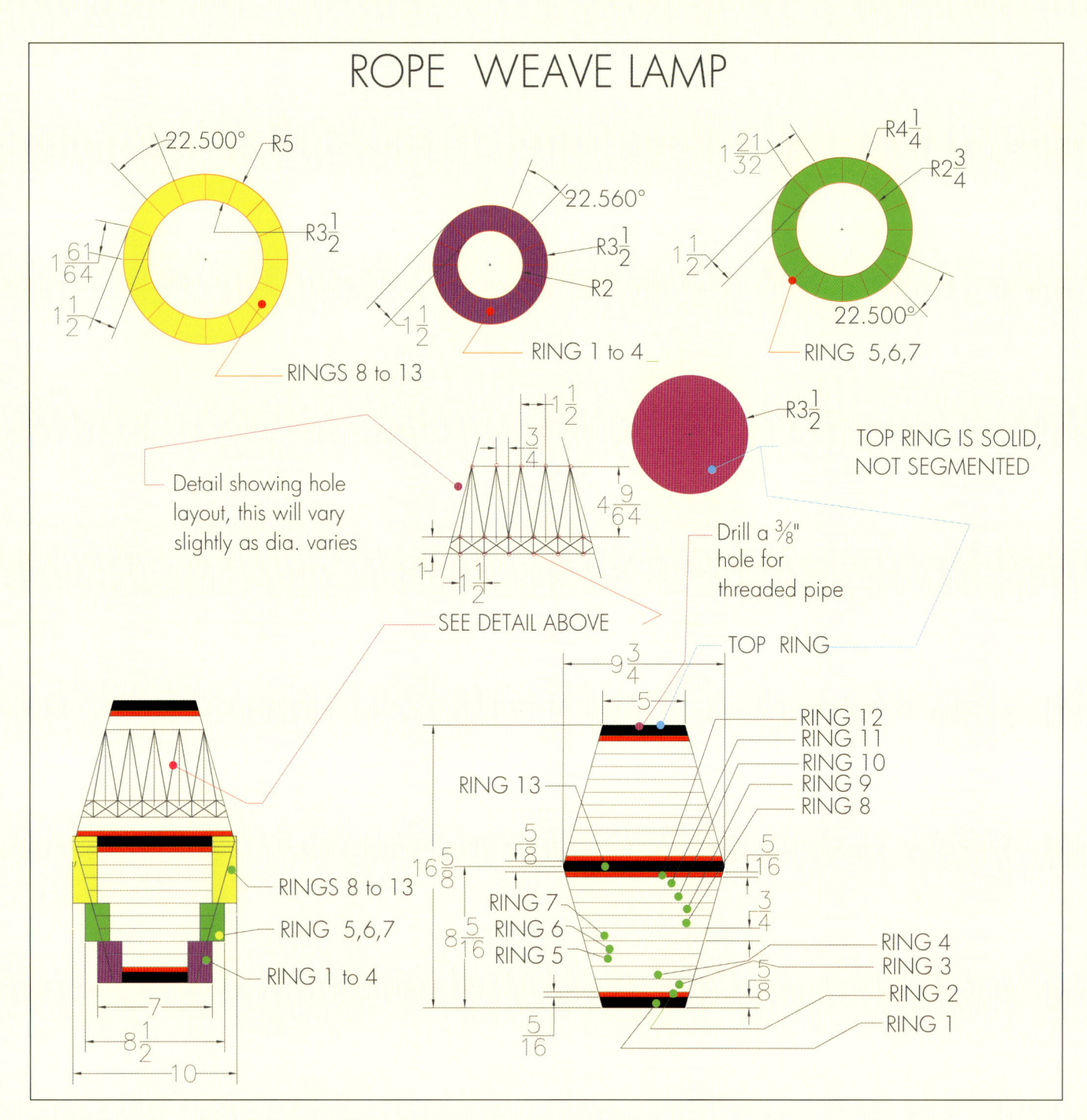

Diag. 28

52 *Segmented Lamp Projects*

Navajo Deer Lamp

Materials: The bottom ring (Ring 1) is a solid piece of walnut. Ring 4 and 6 are walnut segmented rings. Ring 26 and 28 are bloodwood segmented rings. Bloodwood is also used for the checkered part in the neck of the lamp.

Refer to Diags. 29–33 when making this lamp:

- Glue Ring 1 to a scrap board with a piece of paper between the two, see Chapter 1. Attach this to a faceplate and turn the walnut piece flat and to the correct thickness.
- Make Rings 2–4: These rings are glued up, flattened on one side, and glued to the previous ring.
- Once these four rings are glued together, turn them to within 1/4" of their final shape. By taking the corners off the rings, you keep the lamp round and eliminate vibration.
- Glue the deer up as shown in Diag. 30. After each step be sure to touch up the squareness using a disk sander. An example would be in step 2, making the body of the deer, the diagram shows it being one inch long but it should be made 1/8" longer so it hangs over the leg section which was made in step one. Then it can be sanded flat on the outside. There are eight deer required for the lamp, I usually make an extra one and make all nine deer at the same time.
- Once the deer are made, use a similar procedure to make the diamond sections.
- The deer and the diamond make up Ring 5 and can be cut at 11 1/4° on each side. This should give you a block that is 22 1/2° from side to side. NOTE: I usually design a holding jig to hold these as I cut them on the miter box.
- Cut the walnut spacers that go between the segments and glue up Ring 5.
- At this point, you would follow the same process of making the ring, putting it on the lathe, flattening it, and gluing it to the previous ring. Do this for the remaining rings to complete the lamp. See topic XVI, "Turning Tall Lamps," on page 38.
- Notice that Rings 15 through 30 have only eight segments, unlike Rings 1 through 14 that have sixteen segments. I use eight segments for Rings 15 through 30 because the diameter is smaller. If I were to use sixteen segments on this part of the lamp, the segments would be real small and chip easily. Also, larger segments are safer to cut. Using eight segments will make each segment considerably larger, about twice the size.

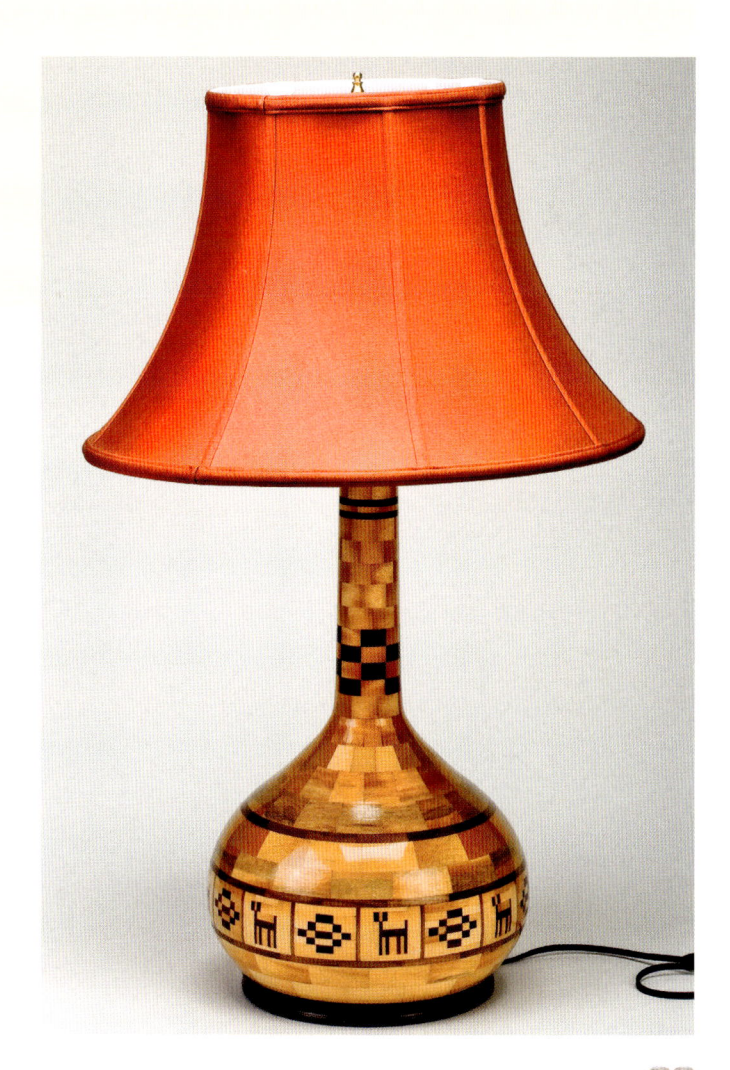

Navajo Deer Lamp

NAVAJO LAMP

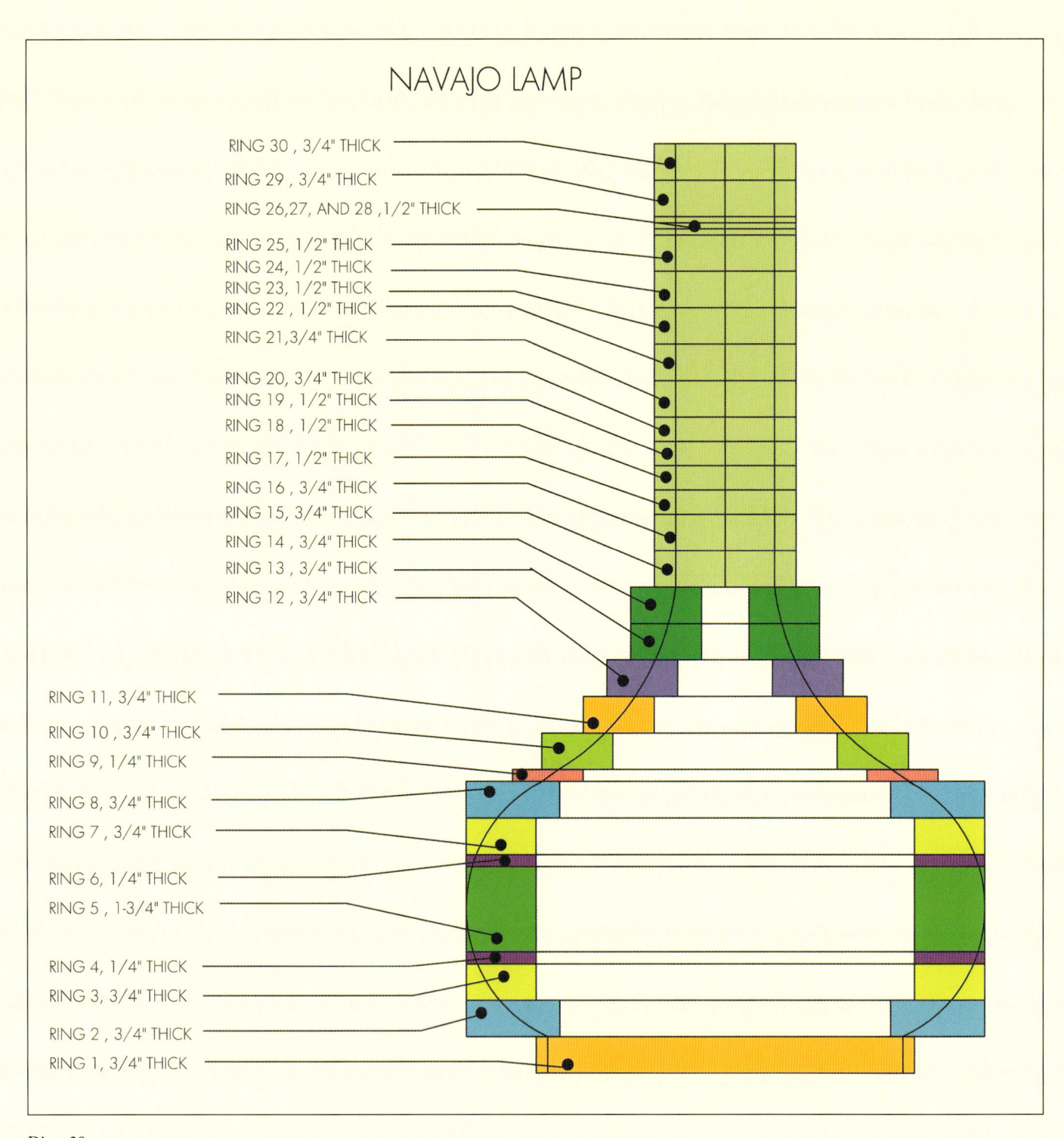

RING 30, 3/4" THICK
RING 29, 3/4" THICK
RING 26, 27, AND 28, 1/2" THICK
RING 25, 1/2" THICK
RING 24, 1/2" THICK
RING 23, 1/2" THICK
RING 22, 1/2" THICK
RING 21, 3/4" THICK
RING 20, 3/4" THICK
RING 19, 1/2" THICK
RING 18, 1/2" THICK
RING 17, 1/2" THICK
RING 16, 3/4" THICK
RING 15, 3/4" THICK
RING 14, 3/4" THICK
RING 13, 3/4" THICK
RING 12, 3/4" THICK
RING 11, 3/4" THICK
RING 10, 3/4" THICK
RING 9, 1/4" THICK
RING 8, 3/4" THICK
RING 7, 3/4" THICK
RING 6, 1/4" THICK
RING 5, 1-3/4" THICK
RING 4, 1/4" THICK
RING 3, 3/4" THICK
RING 2, 3/4" THICK
RING 1, 3/4" THICK

Diag. 29

54 *Segmented Lamp Projects*

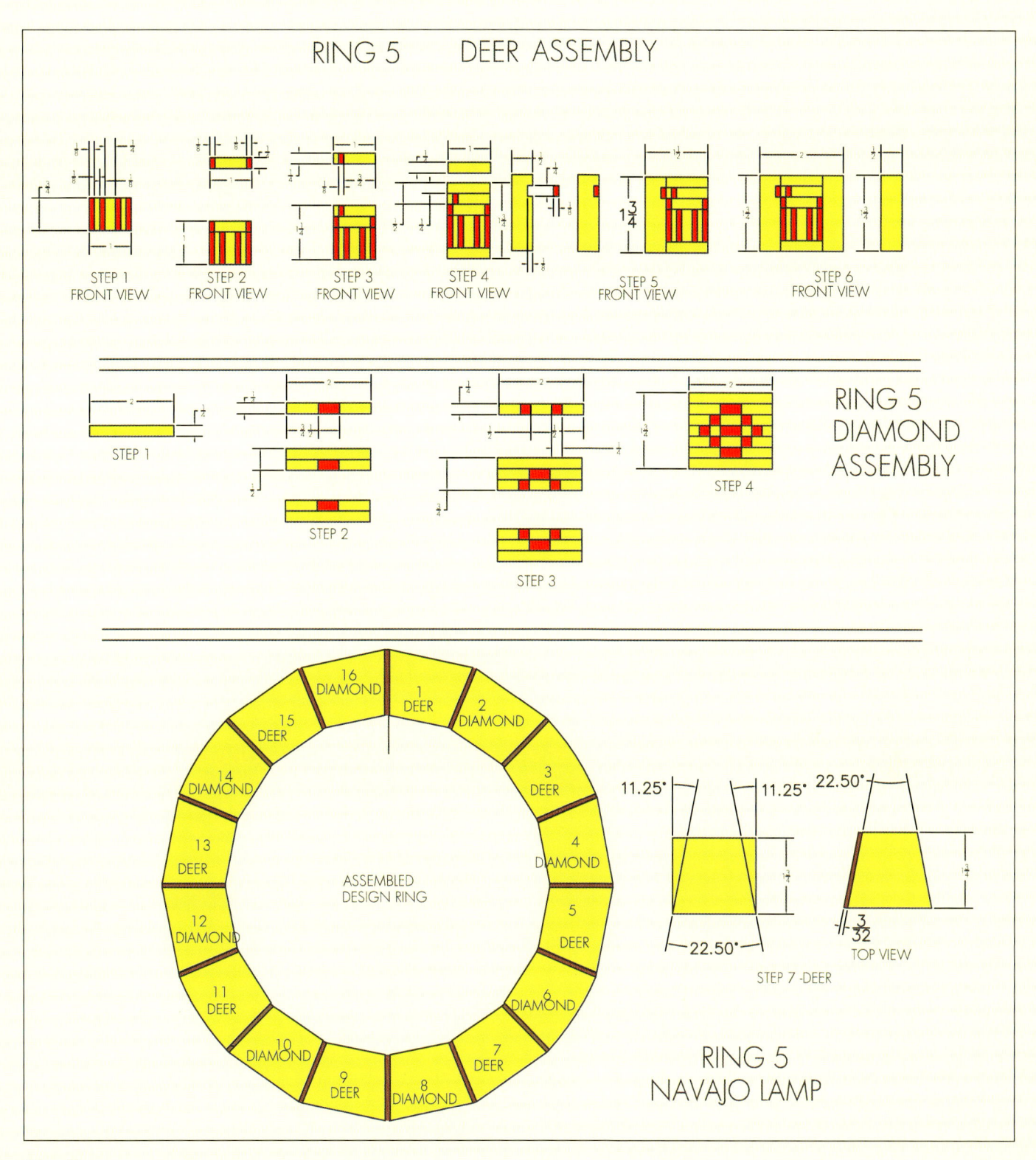

Diag. 30

Navajo Deer Lamp

NAVAJO LAMP WEDGE SIZES

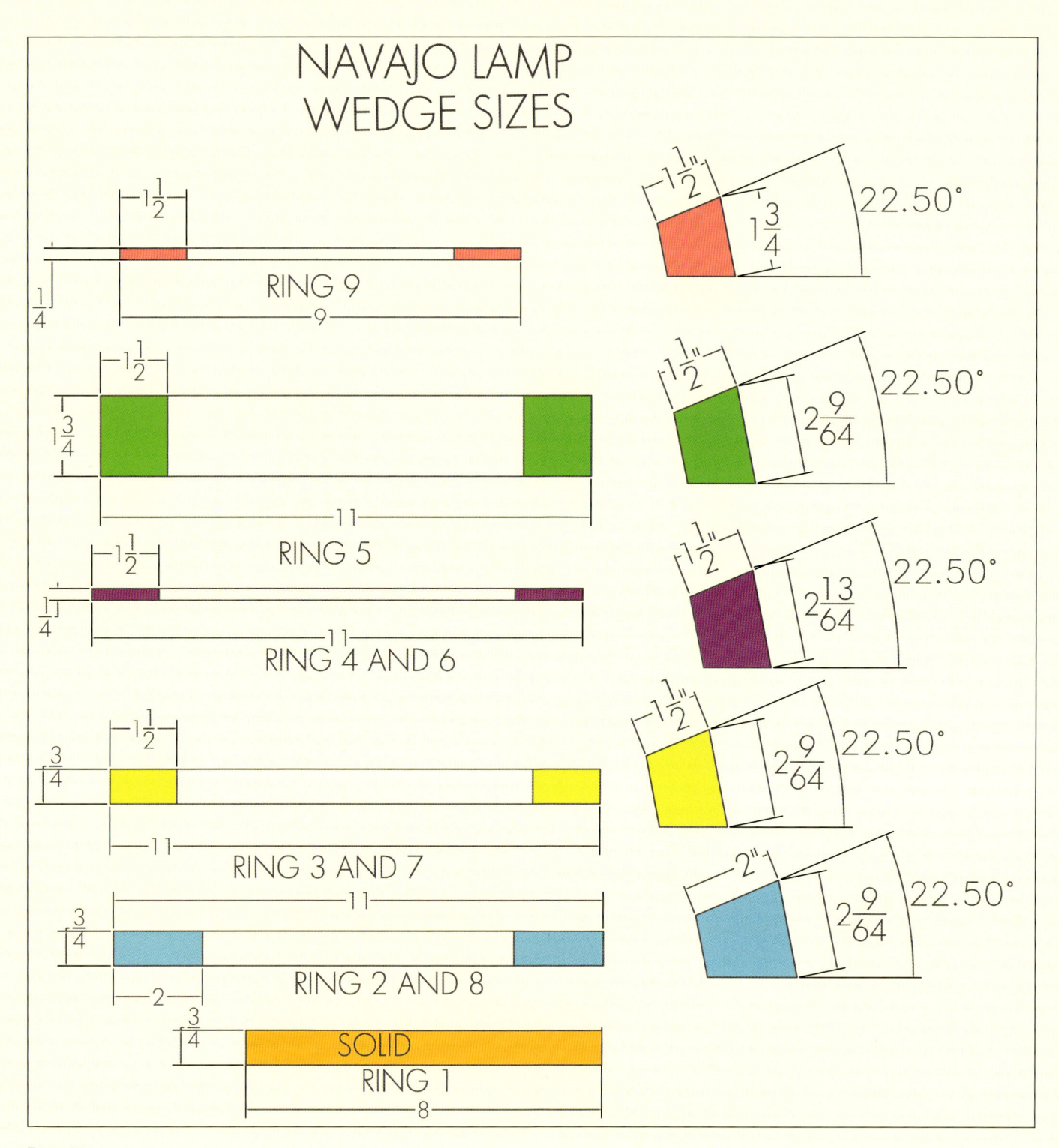

Diag. 31

NAVAJO LAMP WEDGE SIZES

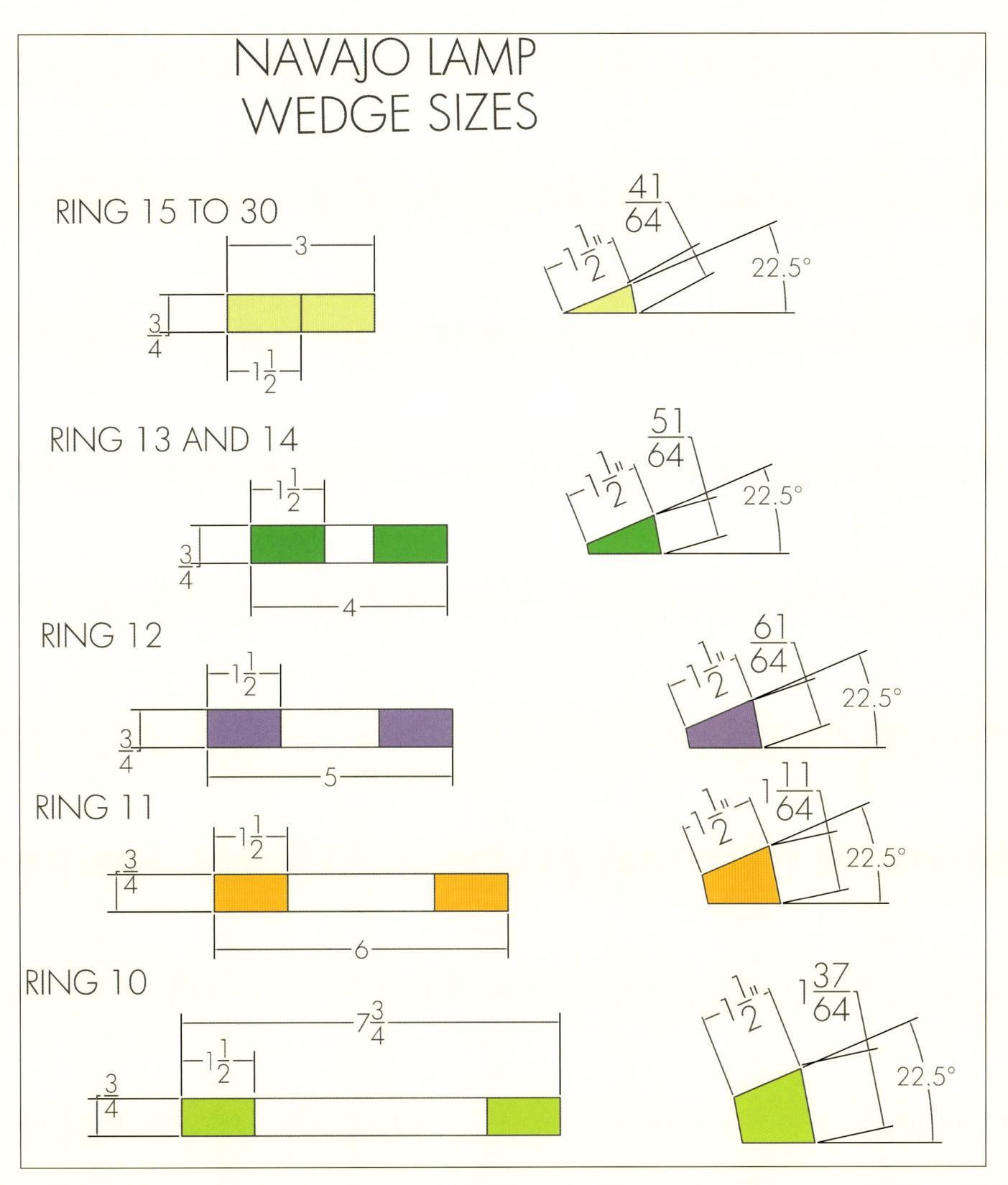

RING 15 TO 30

- 3
- 3/4
- 1 1/2
- 41/64
- 1 1/2"
- 22.5°

RING 13 AND 14

- 1 1/2
- 3/4
- 4
- 51/64
- 1 1/2"
- 22.5°

RING 12

- 1 1/2
- 3/4
- 5
- 61/64
- 1 1/2"
- 22.5°

RING 11

- 1 1/2
- 3/4
- 6
- 1 11/64
- 1 1/2"
- 22.5°

RING 10

- 7 3/4
- 1 1/2
- 3/4
- 1 37/64
- 1 1/2"
- 22.5°

Diag. 32

Navajo Deer Lamp

NAVAJO LAMP

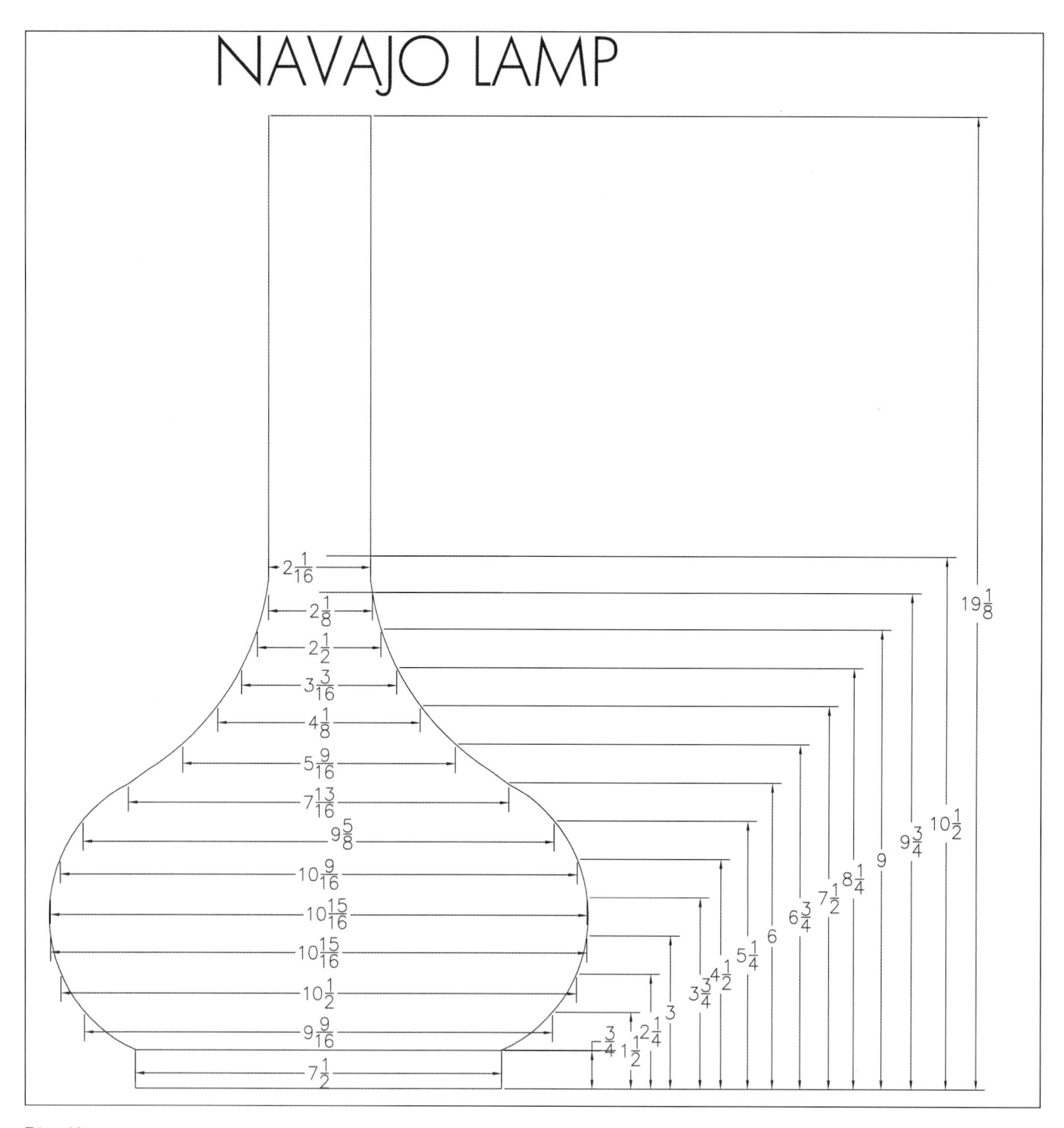

Diag. 33

58 *Segmented Lamp Projects*

Flower on the Wall Lamp

Materials: Wenge is used for the first ring, the brick pattern is purpleheart and birch, and the flower is beech and coco bolo.

Refer to Diags. 34–36 when making this lamp:

Flower on the Wall Lamp

FLOWER ON THE WALL
RING DESCRIPTION

BEECH WITH COCO BOLO

DETAIL B

BEECH

RING 32 and 33 are 6" dia.

RING 29, 30 and 31 are 7" dia.

RING 30 is 1/8" thick

RING 28 is 1/8" thick

RING 27 and 28 are 7-7/8" dia.

RING 17, 18, 19, 20, 21, 22, 23, 24, 25, and 26 are 8-1/8" dia.

RING 18, 20, 22, 24, and 26 are 1/8" thick

RING 13, 14, 15 and 16 are 7 1/8" dia.

RING 14 and 16 are 1/8" thick

RING 9, 10, 11, and 12 are 7-1/8" dia.

RING 5, 6, 7, and 8 are 7" dia.

RING 6 and 8 are 1/4" thick

RING 1, 2, 3, and 4 are 6 1/2" dia.

RING 2 and 4 are 1/8" thick

WENGE

PURPLEHEART AND BEECH

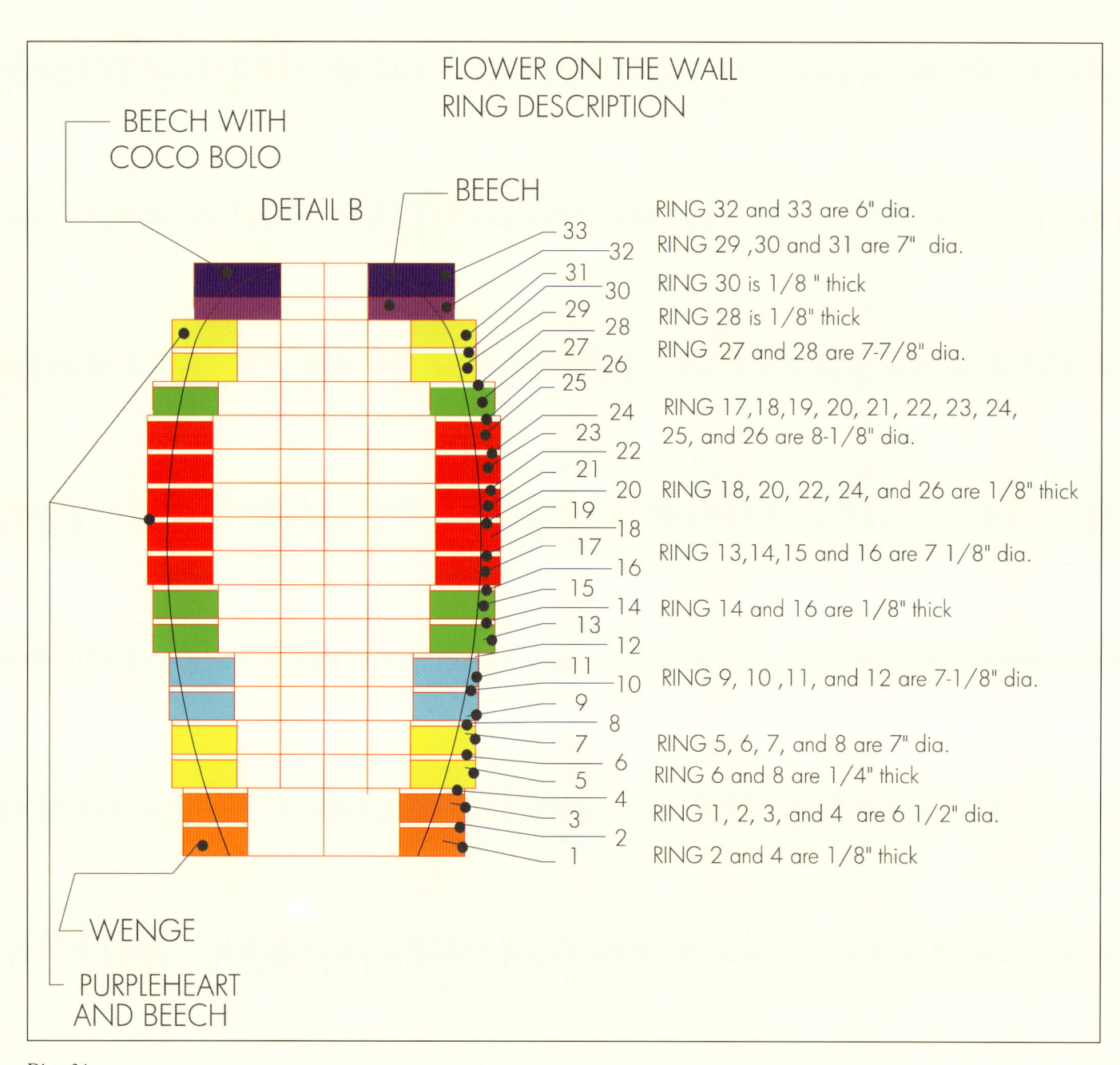

Diag. 34

60 Segmented Lamp Projects

- $1\frac{1}{2}$
- $1\frac{17}{64}$
- 22.5°
- 7" dia ring
- $1\frac{23}{64}$
- 22.5°
- 6" dia ring
- $1\frac{11}{64}$
- 22.5°
- 6 1/2" dia ring
- RING 1, 2, 3, AND 4
- $1\frac{1}{2}$
- RING 5, 6, 7, 8, AND 29, 30, AND 31
- 2
- 6" dia ring
- RING 33

- 8-1/8" ring
- $1\frac{37}{64}$
- 22.5°
- $1\frac{1}{2}$
- RING 17, 18, 19, 20, 21, 22, 23, 24, 25, AND 26
- 7 7/8" dia ring
- $1\frac{17}{32}$
- 22.5°
- $1\frac{1}{2}$
- RING 13, 14, 15, 16, 27, AND 28
- RING 9, 10, 11, AND 12
- 7 1/8" dia ring
- $1\frac{3}{8}$
- 22.5°
- $1\frac{1}{2}$

- 6" dia ring
- RING 32

PURPLE HEART

BEECH

LAYOUT OF RINGS
3, 5, 7, 9, 11, 13, 15
17, 19, 21, 23, 25
27, 29, AND 31
TYPICAL RING

DETAIL A

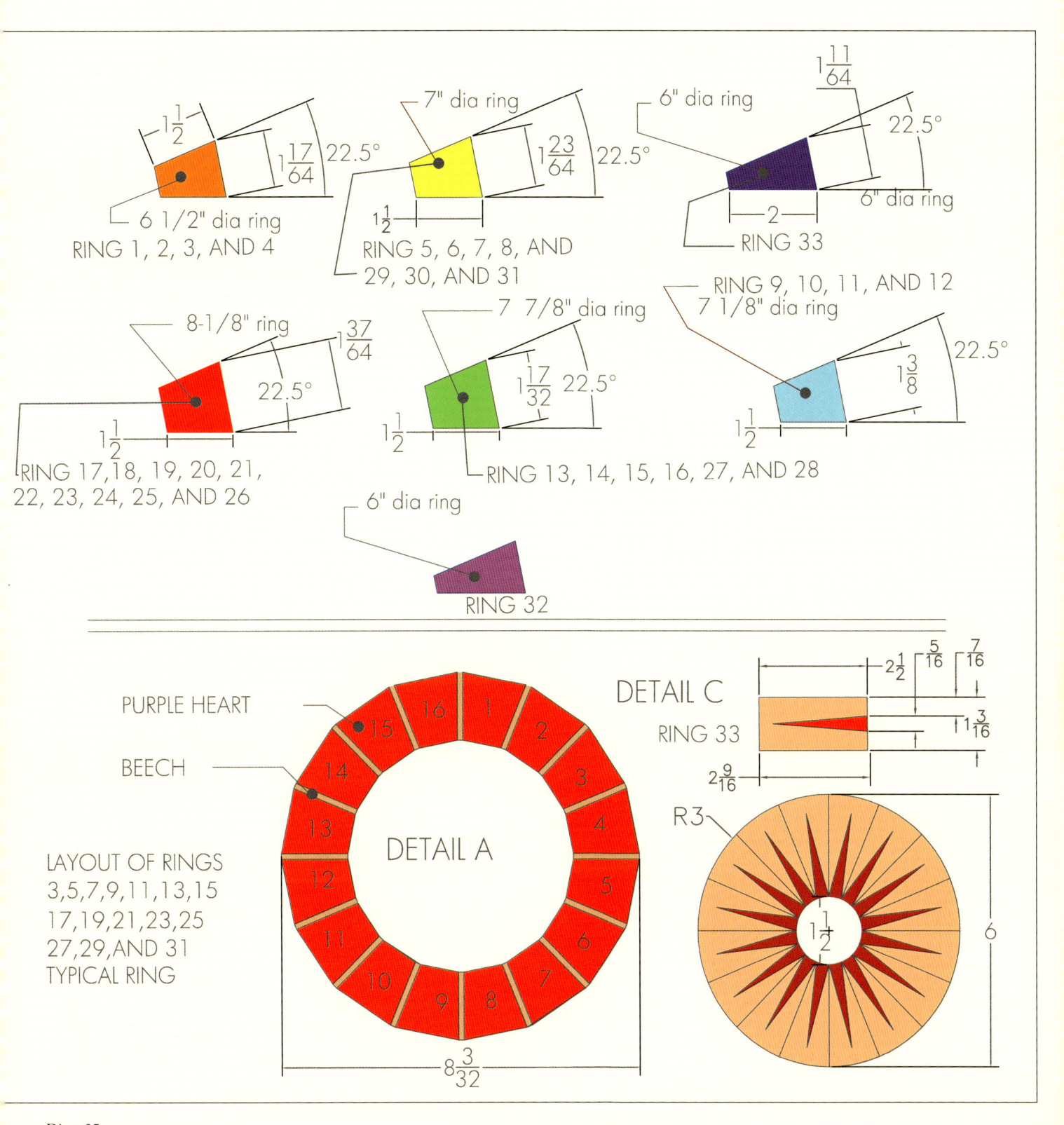

$8\frac{3}{32}$

DETAIL C
RING 33
- $2\frac{1}{2}$
- $\frac{5}{16}$
- $\frac{7}{16}$
- $1\frac{3}{16}$
- $2\frac{9}{16}$

- R3
- $1\frac{1}{2}$
- 6

Diag. 35

Flower on the Wall Lamp **61**

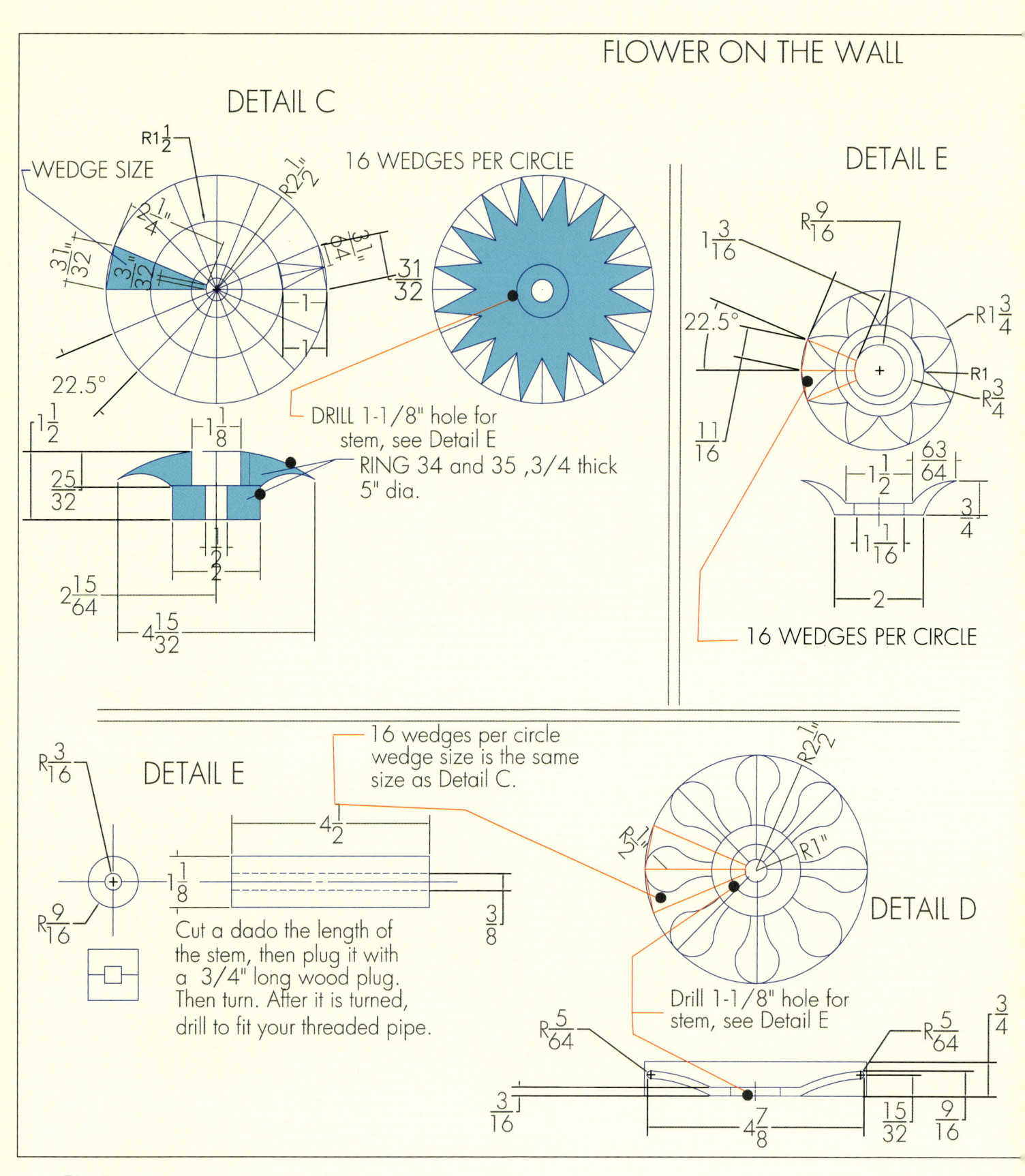

FLOWER ON THE WALL

DETAIL C

WEDGE SIZE
R$1\frac{1}{2}$
R$2\frac{1}{2}$
$2\frac{1}{4}$"
$\frac{3}{4}$"
$\frac{31}{32}$"
$\frac{3}{32}$"
$\frac{31}{32}$
1
1
22.5°

16 WEDGES PER CIRCLE

DRILL 1-1/8" hole for stem, see Detail E
RING 34 and 35, 3/4 thick 5" dia.

$1\frac{1}{2}$
$1\frac{1}{8}$
$\frac{25}{32}$
$\frac{1}{2}$
$2\frac{15}{64}$
$4\frac{15}{32}$

DETAIL E

$1\frac{3}{16}$
R$\frac{9}{16}$
22.5°
R$1\frac{3}{4}$
R1
R$\frac{3}{4}$
$\frac{11}{16}$

$1\frac{1}{2}$
$\frac{63}{64}$
$\frac{3}{4}$
$1\frac{1}{16}$
2

16 WEDGES PER CIRCLE

DETAIL E

R$\frac{3}{16}$
R$\frac{9}{16}$
$1\frac{1}{8}$
$4\frac{1}{2}$
$\frac{3}{8}$

16 wedges per circle wedge size is the same size as Detail C.

Cut a dado the length of the stem, then plug it with a 3/4" long wood plug. Then turn. After it is turned, drill to fit your threaded pipe.

DETAIL D

R$2\frac{1}{2}$
R$1\frac{1}{2}$
R1"

Drill 1-1/8" hole for stem, see Detail E

R$\frac{5}{64}$
R$\frac{5}{64}$
$\frac{3}{4}$
$\frac{3}{16}$
$4\frac{7}{8}$
$\frac{15}{32}$
$\frac{9}{16}$

Diag. 36

Segmented Lamp Projects

- Glue up Ring 1 out of wenge (see Fig. 47). Turn on both sides to a thickness of 5/8".
- Turn Ring 2 on one side and glue it to Ring 1. Turn this to a thickness of 1/8". Continue this process through Ring 32 (Detail A in Diag. 35). If you have problems with the lamp vibrating, you may want to use a stabilizer, at some point, to decrease the chance of Ring 1 breaking off the paper.

Fig. 47: Wenge is used for the first ring. The brick pattern is purpleheart and birch.

Fig. 49: Gluing flower into the lamp with CA glue.

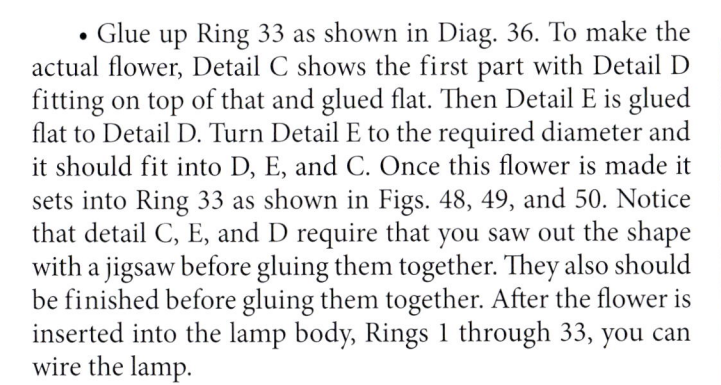

- Glue up Ring 33 as shown in Diag. 36. To make the actual flower, Detail C shows the first part with Detail D fitting on top of that and glued flat. Then Detail E is glued flat to Detail D. Turn Detail E to the required diameter and it should fit into D, E, and C. Once this flower is made it sets into Ring 33 as shown in Figs. 48, 49, and 50. Notice that detail C, E, and D require that you saw out the shape with a jigsaw before gluing them together. They also should be finished before gluing them together. After the flower is inserted into the lamp body, Rings 1 through 33, you can wire the lamp.

Fig. 48: The flower is ready to be inserted into the lamp.

Fig. 50: Detail of the finished flower.

Flower on the Wall Lamp

Trunk Lamp

Materials: Use wormy chestnut for the Trunk Lamp. The black rings are black ebony and the leather is a piece of strap leather (see topic XX, "Websites," on page 40 for leather suppliers).

Refer to Diag. 37 when making this lamp:

Segmented Lamp Projects

TRUNK LAMP

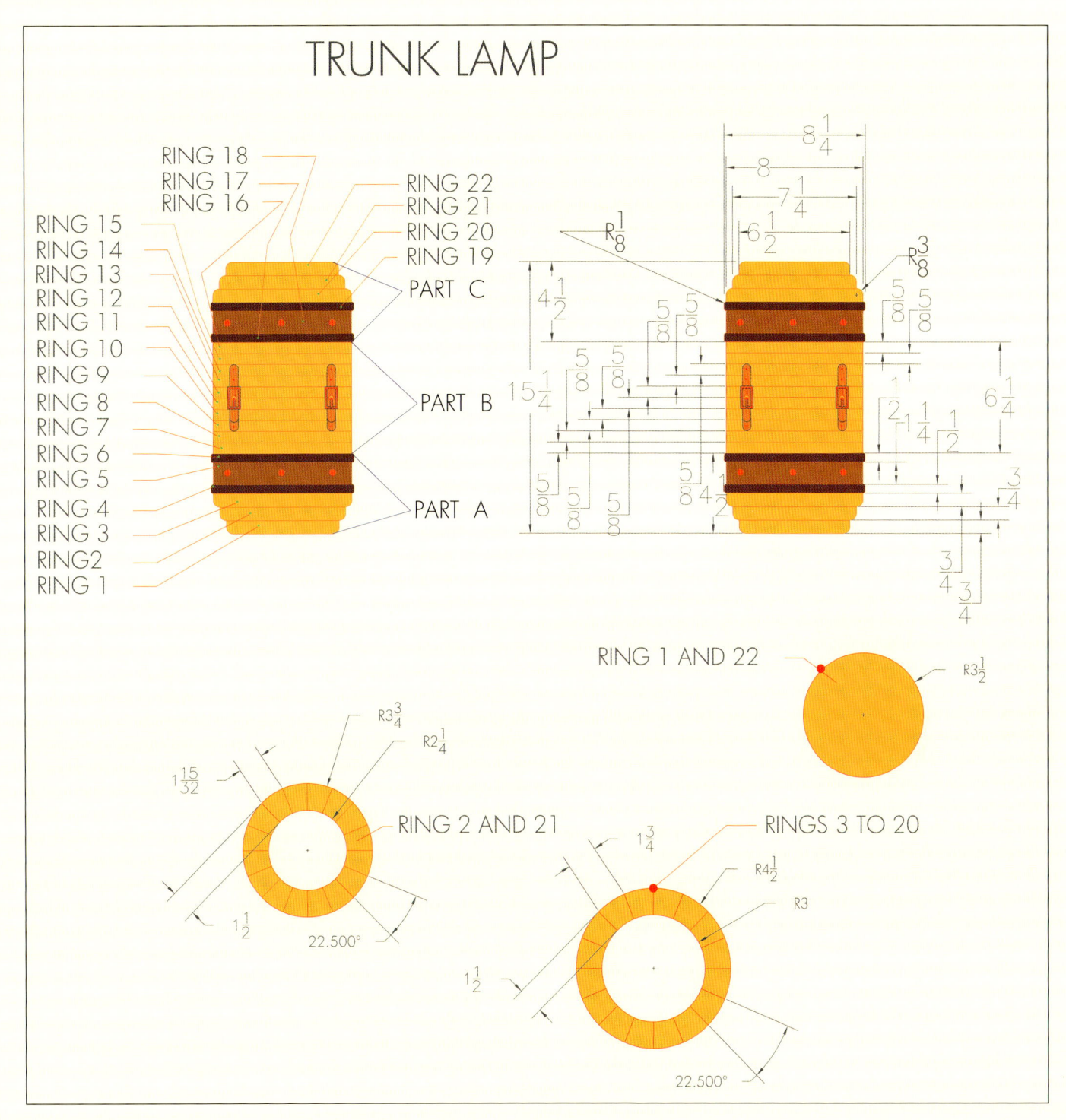

Diag. 37

Trunk Lamp

- Make the midsection, Part B, first. Drill the first ring (Ring 6) to be put on the lathe (see Fig. 51).
- Put Ring 6 on the lathe as shown in Fig. 52—flatten and smooth one side. Turn the ring over and attach it onto the plywood disk from the backside. Then flatten and smooth. Leave Ring 6 on the faceplate.

Fig. 51: Drilling recessed holes to hold ring on the scrap disk.

Fig. 52: The ring is ready to be flattened.

- Turn Ring 7, flatten it, glue it to Ring 6, and put it in the press without taking the faceplate off of Ring 6. After Ring 6 and 7 are dry, put them back on the lathe and flatten ring seven. Repeat this process thru ring sixteen, which will complete Part B. After Part B is assembled, turn it to about 1/4" of its final size.
- Start the black ebony rings, Ring 4, 6, 17, and 19. Remember to add a layer of oak to the black ebony wedges to save on cost (see Fig. 14 on page 13). Black ebony is usually very expensive.
- Make Ring 1 next. Glue it to a plywood disk with thick paper—I like manila folders—between the disk and Ring 1. Use the same process as described above to make Part A and Part C. For Rings 5 and 18 I use an inexpensive wood or even scrap wood, since they are covered with leather and do not show on the finished lamp.
- Add another piece of scrap wood to Part C as shown in Figs. 53 and 54. This supports the threaded pipe at the top of the lamp. See topic IX, "Lamp Inserts," on page 30.

Fig. 53: Gluing in the top insert, which will add thickness for the 3/8" hole that will be drilled for the threaded pipe

Fig. 54: A tight fit on the edges is not necessary here.

- After Parts A, B, and C are made (see Fig. 55), put them in the press and glue them. Be sure to use the concentric lines to align and center these parts as closely as possible.

66 *Segmented Lamp Projects*

With the lamp glued up in one piece, place it on the lathe (see Fig. 56).

Notice there is still plywood on each end. In some cases, you may want to glue the parts together on the lathe using the lathe as a press. In particular, this method is effective when gluing the part closest to the tailstock.

- Turn the lamp to its finished dimensions.

- Make sure the leather strap fits exactly (see Fig. 57). The leather strap should be flush on top with the black ebony.

- Sand the lamp and apply finish to the outside of the lamp.

Fig. 55: These two sections are ready to be glued together.

Fig. 57: Fitting the leather in between the black ebony rings.

- Cut the leather strap to length (see Fig. 58) using a razor blade knife. Then cut the 1/2" strips for the buckle.

Fig. 56: Preparing the lamp for final turning.

Fig. 58: Cut the leather with an exacto knife.

Trunk Lamp 67

• You may have to decrease the thickness of the leather strips (see Fig. 59) and cut the end of the 1/2" strips of leather (see Fig. 60).

• Decide how many buckles you want on your lamp and lay them out using the "Equal Parts of a Circle" chart in topic III on page 21. You will need to copy and enlarge these charts so the lamp can sit on the chart. Line up the bottom of your lamp with the closest concentric circle and the lines on the chart will show you where to place the buckle. Once this is done, cut a small groove using a Dremel tool so the buckle will lay flat (see Fig. 62). Drill the holes for the tacks.

• Next, the leather needs to be distressed. I do this by making stress marks or dents using various tools. As an example, I might put a screwdriver, a nail head, or other metal objects on the leather and tap it with a hammer so it will make an indentation in the leather. Sometimes I use a chain. These distress marks will add a rustic flavor and an aged look to the project, blending in well with the wormy chestnut. The leather should be dyed to your liking.

• Glue the 1/2" leather strips (see Fig. 61), and attach them as shown in Fig. 62.

• Next, attach the strap leather between the black ebony (see Fig. 63). The tacks are spaced equally (see Fig. 64).

• Take the scrap wood of the ends of the lamp off using a chisel placed on the paper layer. Work your way gently tapping at the paper seam and the plywood should split right off.

• Sign your name on the bottom, then finish the top and bottom of the lamp. Wire the lamp.

Fig. 59: Sanding the leather to decrease its thickness.

Fig. 60: Trimming the end of the 1/2" leather strip with an exacto knife.

Fig. 61: Use a thick CA glue to glue the 1/2" strips to the lamp.

Fig. 62: Putting the buckle and the leather strip into the recessed holes.

Segmented Lamp Projects

Fig. 63: Using tacks to help hold the strip.

Fig. 64: The finished lamp with scrap wood still attached to the ends.

Walnut Nut Lamp

Materials: On this lamp, the staves are made of hickory. The walnuts are walnuts and the top, Ring A, is walnut wood. Ring B is bloodwood and Ring C, the solid insert, is hickory.

Refer to Diag. 38 when making this lamp:
• Start this lamp by making staves on a table saw. Set the correct angle and make one practice piece. Then cut this practice piece into 16 wedges.

Walnut Nut Lamp **69**

• Put these wedges together as if this were a normal ring. If you are lucky enough to get this to come out right the first time, you don't need to make adjustments. But in my case I needed to make adjustments a couple of times to get the ring to come out without any gaps. When you have the correct angle cut your final 16 staves. It may be a good idea to cut a 17th stave for a spare.

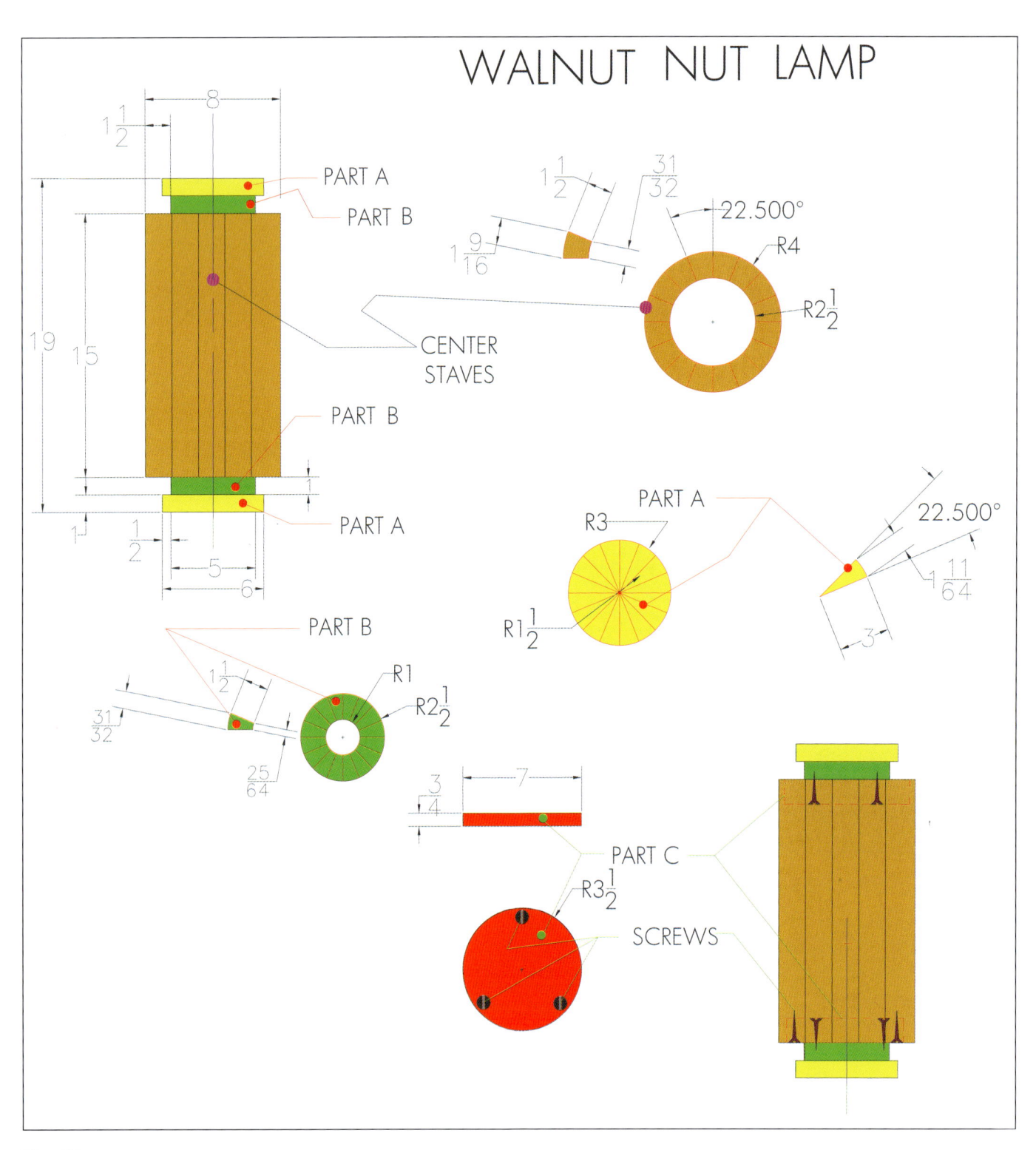

Diag. 38

Segmented Lamp Projects

- Glue these staves together (see Figs. 65 and 66), keeping the bottom as flat as possible. Once glued, attach to a round piece of plywood, which is then attached to the faceplate (see Fig. 67).

Fig. 65: Preparing to glue staves.

Fig. 66: I put the staves together with a clamp as a trial run before gluing them.

Fig. 67: The faceplate and scrap disk after being attached to the flattest end of the staves.

- Turn the center staves to the specified diameter as in Fig. 68.

Fig. 68: Using a straight edge to turn the stave flat. Notice the pencil marks indicating a low section.

- Use a parting tool to cut a groove around both ends of the piece (see Fig. 069). Leave about 1/8" of the wood in the groove. It is best to cut the groove on the tailstock end first. After cutting the grooves sand each end.

Fig. 69: Using a multi-tool to cut the groove on each end of lamp.

Walnut Nut Lamp 71

- Make a pattern with lauan plywood on the lathe (see Fig 70). Attach the pattern to the top of the stave section with a couple of very small brads to hold it in place. Then cut out the top of the stave section with a router, as in Fig. 71. Rout deep enough so Part C will fit snuggly and be flush. Repeat this process for the bottom of the staves.
- Turn two each of Part A and B, then glue Part A to Part B. These parts can be turned to their finished diameter and sanded. Then attach Parts A and B to Part C. Glue these parts to the top and bottom of the stave section.
- Drill the holes for the threaded pipe at the top and a hole at the bottom for the wire to come out.
- See topic VI, "Inlaying Walnut, " on page 26. This explains in some detail how to inlay the walnuts in a random pattern. I used about 25 walnuts.

Fig. 70: Making a pattern out of lauan plywood.

Fig. 71: Routing out the top and bottom section of the staves for part C.

Segmented Lamp Projects

There's a Spider on That Post, Grandpa!

Materials: I used wormy chestnut for the post. The web at the top is made of coco bolo rosewood and birch. The spider is black ebony.

Refer to Diags. 39 and 40 when making this lamp:

• Start this lamp by making Part B, the post. This part is made similar to barrel construction, that is, it uses staves or long segments. On these the grain runs up and down. The wormy chestnut gives it a natural weathered and aged look. However, wormy chestnut is not the easiest wood to find. The staves in this lamp were glued up from tongue and groove chestnut flooring which had been salvaged from an old home.

There's a Spider on That Post, Grandpa!

THERE'S A SPIDER ON THAT POST, GRANDPA!

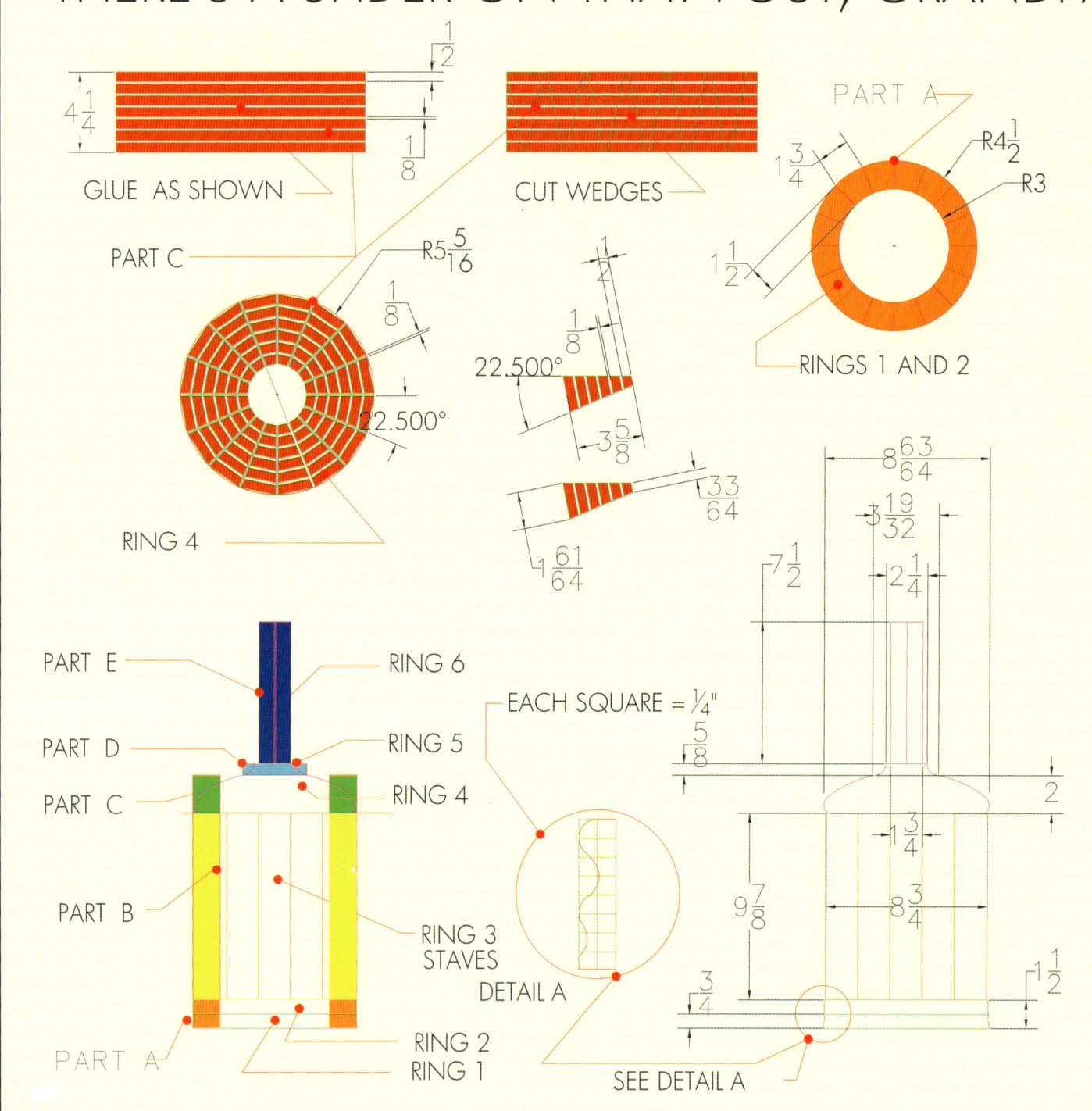

GLUE AS SHOWN — PART C

$4\frac{1}{4}$, $\frac{1}{2}$, $\frac{1}{8}$

CUT WEDGES

PART A — RINGS 1 AND 2

$R4\frac{1}{2}$, $R3$, $1\frac{3}{4}$, $1\frac{1}{2}$

RING 4

$R5\frac{5}{16}$, $\frac{1}{8}$, $22.500°$

$22.500°$, $\frac{1}{2}$, $\frac{1}{8}$, $3\frac{5}{8}$

$\frac{33}{64}$, $1\frac{61}{64}$

PART E — RING 6
PART D — RING 5
PART C — RING 4
PART B — RING 3 STAVES
PART A — RING 2, RING 1

EACH SQUARE = $\frac{1}{4}$"

DETAIL A

SEE DETAIL A

$8\frac{63}{64}$, $3\frac{19}{32}$, $2\frac{1}{4}$, $7\frac{1}{2}$, $\frac{5}{8}$, 2 , $1\frac{3}{4}$, $9\frac{7}{8}$, $8\frac{3}{4}$, $\frac{3}{4}$, $1\frac{1}{2}$

Diag. 39

74 *Segmented Lamp Projects*

THERE'S A SPIDER ON THAT POST, GRANDPA!

PART B

$1\frac{3}{4}$
$R4\frac{1}{2}$
$R3$
$1\frac{1}{2}$

RING 3

The stave should be cut about 10 1/2" long
Finish cut to 9 1/2"

22.500°
$1\frac{11}{64}$

RING 5

PART D

3

BIRCH

COCO BOLO ROSEWOOD

2" sq.–dados are 1/8 x 1" deep

Turn to 1 7/8 dia.

ENLARGED VIEW.

1
$7\frac{1}{2}$
$1\frac{7}{8}$
1

PART E RING 6

PART E is 7-1/2" long with a 1" dia. end to insert into Part D

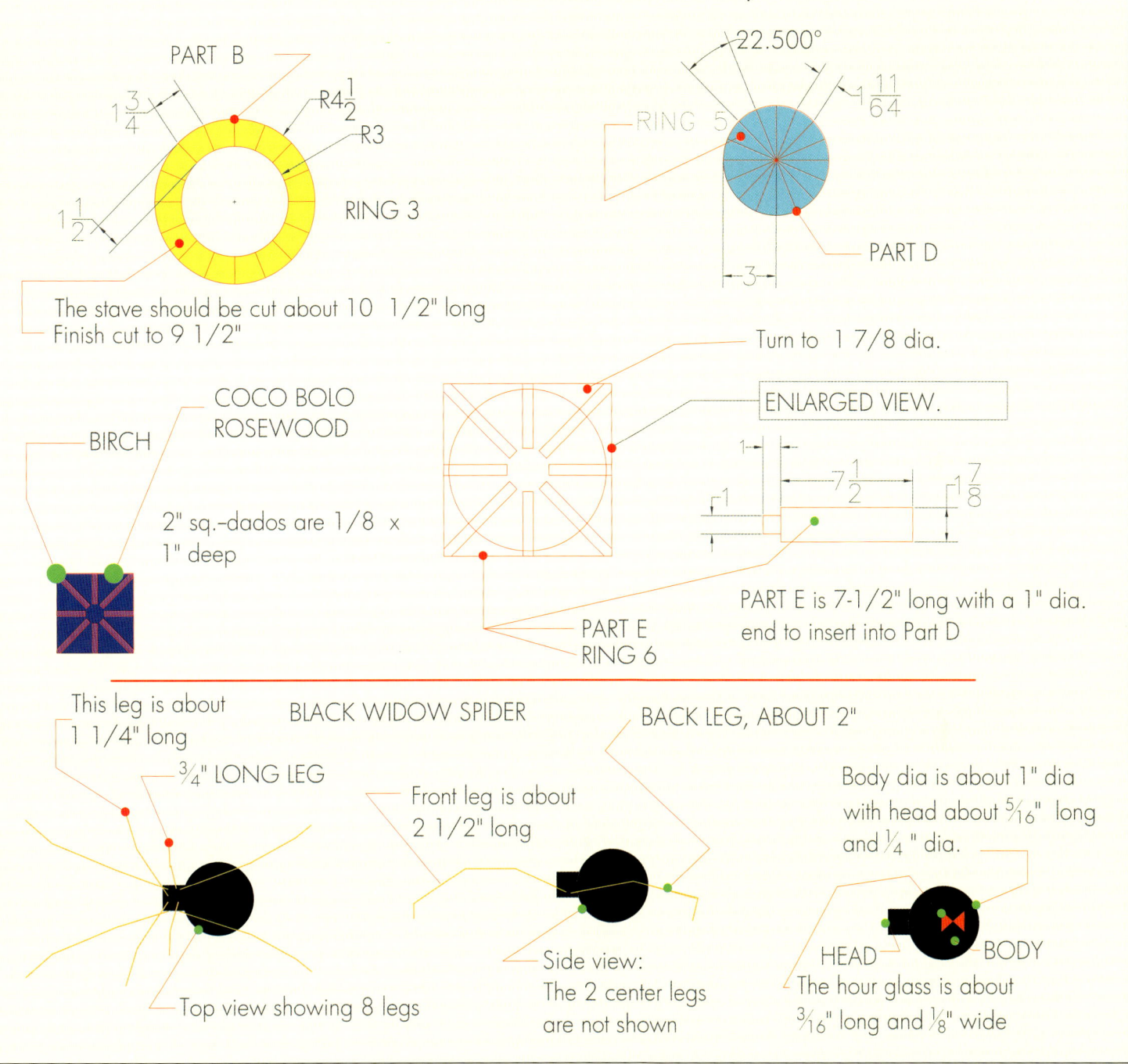

This leg is about 1 1/4" long

BLACK WIDOW SPIDER

BACK LEG, ABOUT 2"

3/4" LONG LEG

Front leg is about 2 1/2" long

Body dia is about 1" dia with head about 5/16" long and 1/4 " dia.

Top view showing 8 legs

Side view:
The 2 center legs are not shown

HEAD   BODY
The hour glass is about 3/16" long and 1/8" wide

Diag. 40

There's a Spider on That Post, Grandpa! **75**

- To construct the staves, I set my table saw to 11 1/4° and make one stave 15" or 16" long out of a piece of scrap wood (see Fig. 72). Once this one stave is made I cut it into 16 segments.

Fig. 72: Cut a practice stave to test for a proper fit.

- Clamp these together to form a ring. Usually the first time you do this, you will have to make some adjustment to the angle of your saw. Then make a second practice piece and clamp these in a circle (see Fig. 73). You may have to do this several times to get the exact angle. But once the exact angle is achieved, cut the 16 staves for the lamp. It is best to make these staves one or two inches longer than what you need. Try to keep one end of Part B as flat as you can so you can attach it to your faceplate and put it on your lathe (see Fig. 74).

- After Part B is made, you can start Part A by gluing up Rings 1 and 2. First, drill four holes in Ring 1 close to the inner edge for attaching the piece to the lathe. Turn Ring 1 on both sides. Then turn Ring 2 on one side only.
- Glue Rings 1 and 2 together and turn them on the lathe to the contour shown in Diag. 39. I use lignum vita for the Part A since it has a green color to represent the grass.

Fig. 74: The stave section after it is attached to a plywood disk and faceplate. It is ready to be turned. If you encounter vibrations, you may want to place a disk on the tailstock end and use it for support.

- For Part C, the brown part is made of coco bolo rosewood and the white wood is birch (see Fig. 75). Cut the wedges as shown in Diag. 40 and glue the ring. Glue part C to a plywood disk so it can be turned. Turn one side flat and smooth—this will become the bottom of the piece.

Fig. 73: Cut this stave into 16 segments and assemble into a trial ring to test the angles. This ring needs a lot of angle adjustments, try again.

Fig. 75: Parts C, D, and E.

Segmented Lamp Projects

• Take Part C off the faceplate, turn it over and use screws to reattach it to the faceplate, making sure your screws will not show on the outside edges. Also, you may want to predrill holes for the screws to be sure you don't break a wedge. Turn the shape of Part C and make it flat on top to accept Part D.

• Turn Part D flat on one side, glue it using your press or using the tailstock of your lathe to hold it in place. Then finish turning Parts C and D to their final shape. Drill a hole in Part D for Part E.

• Next, make Part E, which is not segmented. See the drawings for Part E (Diag. 40) and notice that the birch is inlayed into a groove while Part E is still square. These grooves can be cut on the table saw, then the birch can be inlayed. Then turn Part E.

• Use the same drill bit that was used on Part D to make a pattern (see Fig. 76) to use when turning Part E. Turn the dowel section, which fits into Part D, so it fits snuggly into the pattern as shown.

• Drill a 3/8" hole into Part E on the lathe using a chuck and the tailstock, or use a drill press. At this point, I place a scrap piece of wood into Part B. This is used to attach Part C, D, and E to part B. Place Parts C, D and E (the web) on top of part B. If you have a small gap where these fit together, you may want to sand the top of the scrap board down 1/8" or so and possibly touch up the inner edge of Part B to get a more exact fit.

• Then use a long threaded pipe, approximately 14" to 16" long. This goes down through Part E and down through the scrap board.

• Attach the pipe at the top with a bolt and leave about about 1/4" out for the socket. Then reach up from the bottom of the lamp and tighten up a nut on the threaded pipe which holds Parts C, D, and E to part B. At this point the lamp can be sprayed and the finish applied.

• Turn the body of the spider (see Fig. 77), which is made of black ebony. Inlay the red hour glass, made of bloodwood, into the spider's abdomen using a Dremel tool (see Fig. 78).

Fig. 77: Turning the body of a black ebony spider.

Fig. 76: Using a pattern to insure a snug fit.

Fig. 78: Insert the head of the spider into a scrap board and finish turning the abdomen. The bloodwood hourglass was inlayed using a Dremel tool.

There's a Spider on That Post, Grandpa!

- Turn the head end of the spider and sand while it is on the lathe. This end can be touched up using the Sand-O-Flex sander after taking it off the lathe.
- The legs are made of 14-gauge electrical wire. Strip the plastic off the wire and bend the wire as shown in the drawing. Notice there's a small section at each end of the leg that is inserted in the spider or the web.
- Next drill a 1/8" hole in the spider's body. Then drill a 1/8" hole in the area of part C, the web, that you want to place the spider. Using CA glue, glue the body to the web using a 1/8" diameter dowel rod. The dowel rod should go up into the spider and down into the web about 1/4".
- At this point the legs should all be bent but not yet glued in. Paint them with a black spray lacquer then carefully glue them into the spider and the web using an eensy–weensy bit of glue in each hole. After you have put the legs in, you may have to touch up the legs a little bit since bending them may crack the paint. Do this by spraying some paint in a puddle on a scrap piece of paper and use a brush with a 1/16" tip.
- Wire the lamp.

Kokopelli Lamp

Materials: The Kokopelli Lamp is made of spalted maple and coco bolo rosewood. The figures are made with Inlace and there are also river stones inlayed in the piece.

Refer to Diags. 41 and 42 when working on this lamp:

Images of Kokopelli first appear in Hohokam pottery around 750 A.D. to 850 A.D. Kokopelli is a pictograph (a drawing) often found in the American Southwest. Early pictographs date back as early as 1000 A.D.

Usually Kokopelli is seen bending over, humpbacked playing what might appear as a musical instrument, usually thought to be some type of flute. Today, Kokopelli images are seen on T-shirts, jewelry, baseball caps, key chains, and more. He is often thought of as a man of music, an entertainer and a partier.

Segmented Lamp Projects

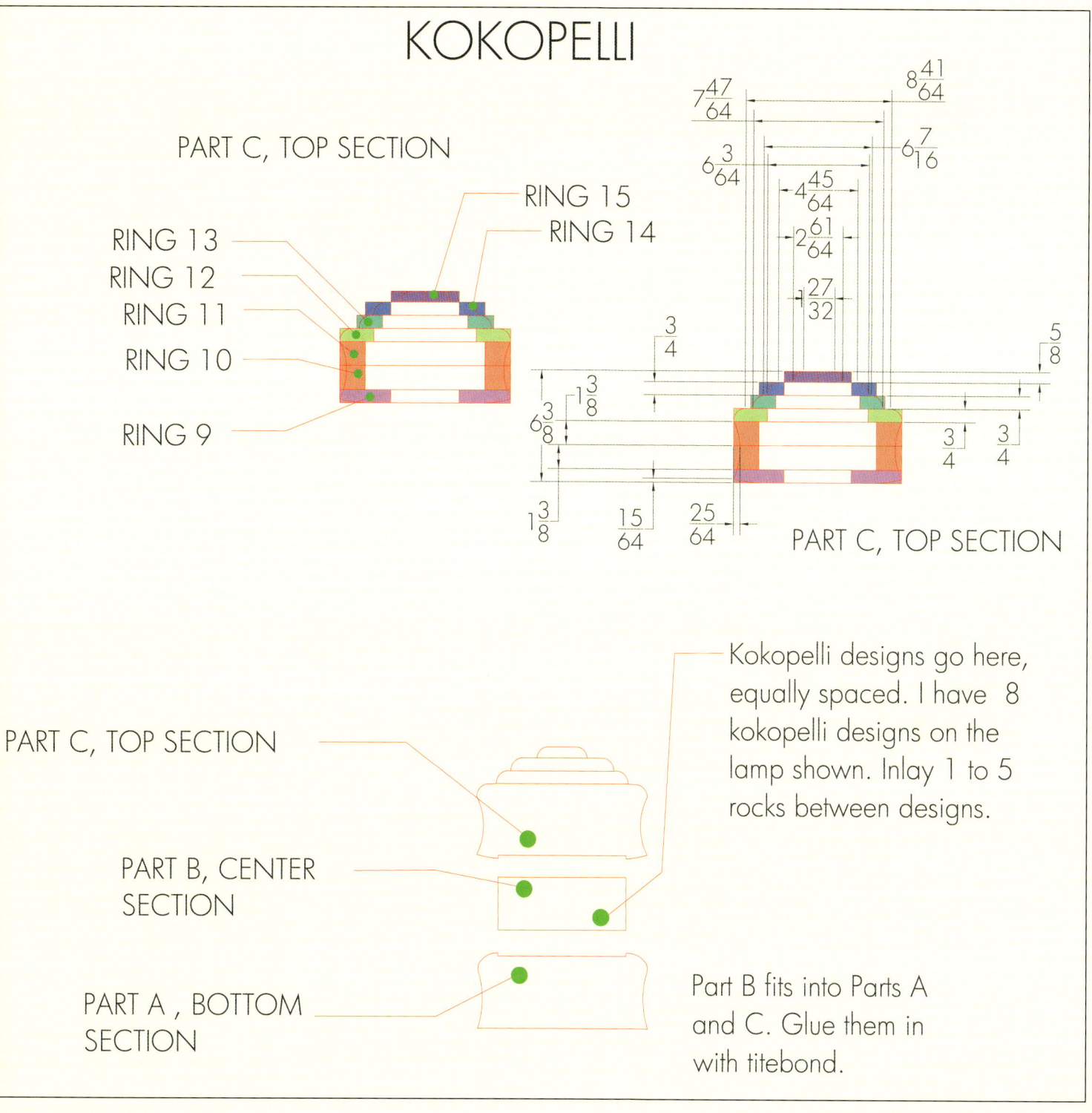

KOKOPELLI

PART C, TOP SECTION

- RING 15
- RING 14
- RING 13
- RING 12
- RING 11
- RING 10
- RING 9

$7\frac{47}{64}$ $8\frac{41}{64}$

$6\frac{3}{64}$ $6\frac{7}{16}$

$4\frac{45}{64}$

$2\frac{61}{64}$

$\frac{27}{32}$

$\frac{3}{4}$ $\frac{5}{8}$

$1\frac{3}{8}$

$6\frac{3}{8}$

$\frac{3}{4}$ $\frac{3}{4}$

$1\frac{3}{8}$ $\frac{15}{64}$ $\frac{25}{64}$

PART C, TOP SECTION

PART C, TOP SECTION

PART B, CENTER SECTION

PART A, BOTTOM SECTION

Kokopelli designs go here, equally spaced. I have 8 kokopelli designs on the lamp shown. Inlay 1 to 5 rocks between designs.

Part B fits into Parts A and C. Glue them in with titebond.

Diag. 41

Kokopelli Lamp **79**

KOKOPELLI

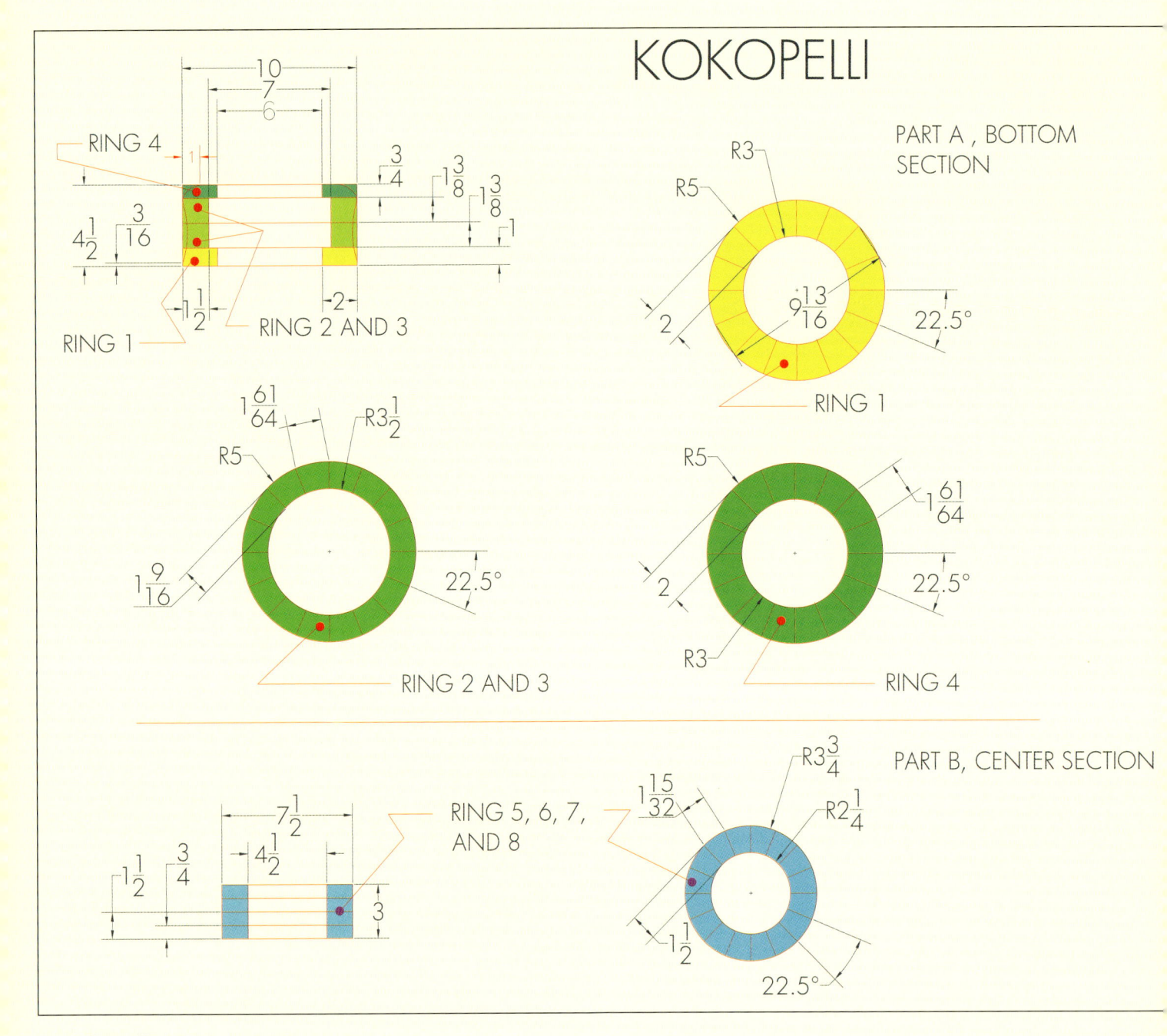

PART A, BOTTOM SECTION

RING 2 AND 3

RING 4

PART B, CENTER SECTION

RING 5, 6, 7, AND 8

Diag. 42

80 Segmented Lamp Projects

- Start the Kokopelli Lamp by gluing up the four center rings (Part B). Turn them so they are straight. Leave them on the faceplate and draw the Kokopelli figures, about 2 1/2 to 3" apart (see Fig. 79).

Fig. 79: Drawing the Kokopelli design, which will be routed out.

- Rout the Kokopelli drawings out using a power carving tool (see Fig. 80). These should be routed out to about 3/32" or 1/8" deep. After routing, pour a puddle of black Inlace into the cavity of the figures. Instruction for Inlace should come with the product.

NOTE: Inlace is a liquid inlay. It comes in a variety of colors. Woodturners commonly use it to fill voids in the wood or sections that have been carved out.

- Next, put the faceplate with the Kokopelli figures back on the lathe. With a sharp scraping tool, scrape the excess Inlace off very, very lightly, leaving the Kokopelli figures. If needed, re-rout and fill any void left without Inlace. Sand Part B.
- Now inlay the stone. I usually use three stones between each figure. These are flat river stones, I collected myself. Glue the stones in with clear CA glue. Then finish Part B with a spray lacquer.
- Assemble Rings 1 to 4 to make the bottom section, Part A. After turning the profile turn the top part, Ring 4, flat to accept Part B. Try to get a snug fit. Sand part A so it is ready to finish.

Fig. 80: Routing Kokopelli figure out with Dremel tool.

- To make Part C, start with Ring 9 and turn the bottom first. After it is turned, glue it to Ring 10 (Fig. 82).
- Once these are dry, make sure Ring 9 fits onto the top of Part B snuggly. Then turn Ring 9 upside down so the bottom part is in contact with the faceplate. Bolt these to the faceplate. Finish gluing the remaining rings and sand.
- Loosen the nut from outside of the faceplate and take Part C off the faceplate. Part A, B, and C are ready to be assembled. Be sure to glue in such a manner that the excess runs into the lamp and not outside on Part B.
- Finish and wire the lamp.

Fig. 82: Notice the recessed cut on Part C for Part B to fit into.

Kokopelli Lamp **81**

Lady Bug Stump Lamp

Materials: Ring 1 is yellowheart, Rings 2 to 5 are lingnum vita. The ladybug bodies are made out of bloodwood or paduak, their heads are made out of black ebony, and the dots on their wings are made out of Inlace.

Refer to Diag. 43 when working on this project:
• Use yellowheart for the first ring, Part A. Drill four holes, and countersink, on the inner edge of the ring and attach to a faceplate with a round plywood disk marked with concentric circles.
• Turn it on one side flat and smooth then turn the other side flat and smooth. Once it is flat and smooth, put four screws from the backside of the plywood to hold the ring in place. Take off the four screws that were countersunk.
• Leave Ring 1 on the faceplate and use a different faceplate with a plywood disk to turn Rings 2, 3, and 4. Use the same process of attaching with screws and turn one side flat and smooth.
• Use a press to glue Ring 2 to Ring 1. Once these have dried, flatten the outside part of Ring 2, turn Ring 3 and 4 and repeat the process.
• The wood used for Rings 2 to 5 is lignum vita, ranked the world's hardest wood by the Janka Scale (see topic VII on page 28).

NOTE: Due to its hardness and the oily nature of the wood, lignum vita was once used for bearings that held propeller shafts on ships. It is also used for cricket balls, croquet mallets, and mallets used in woodworking. Lignum vita is also referred to as a green wood.

Segmented Lamp Projects

LADY BUG STUMP

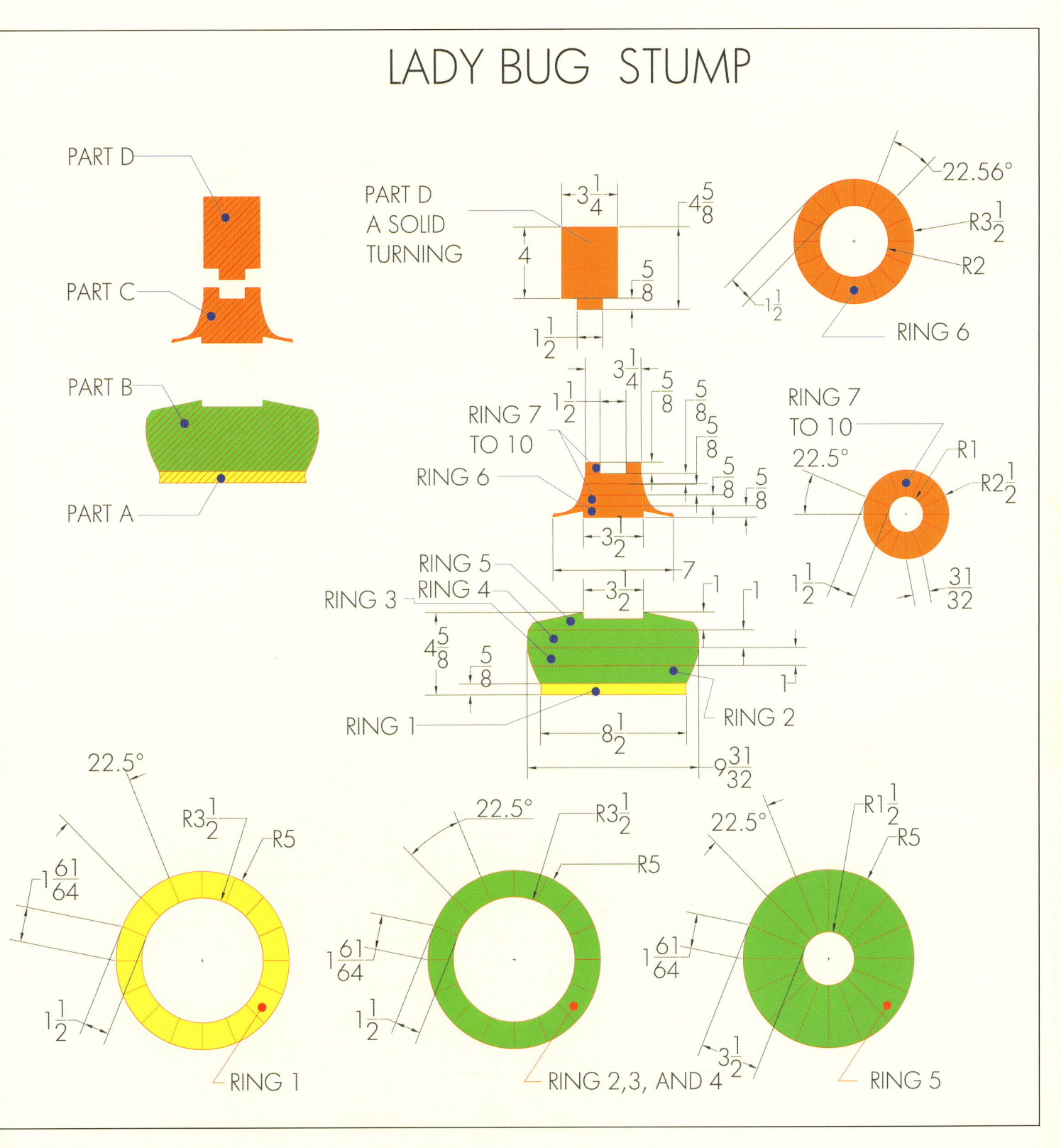

Diag. 43

Lady Bug Stump Lamp 83

- After Rings 1 through 5 are glued, Part A and B can be turned and sanded to a point where this section is ready to be finished (see Fig. 83).

Fig. 83: Notice recess in Part B for Part C to fit into.

- To make Part C, turn Ring 6 on both ends. Next, lay out the shapes for Ring 6, leaving a raised section in the center (see Fig. 84). This raised section will serve as a plug so that Ring 6 (Part C) has a snug fit in the bottom section of the lamp (Part A and B) as in Fig. 85.
- At this point you can attach Ring 6 to the face plate using a plywood disk and turn Rings 7 to 10.

Fig. 84: The contour shown on Ring 6 was cut out to match the recess in Part B before Rings 7 and 10 were glued on. The scroll saw cut section makes it easy to see how well it fits over and onto Part B.

Fig. 85: Placing Part C into Part B.

- Cut the stump out using a table jig saw or scroll saw (see Fig. 86).

Fig. 86: Cutting the stump out with the scroll saw. Notice that Ring 6 is cut fairly thin on the outside edge. This makes it easier to cut.

- Turn Part D, insuring a good fit into Part C (see Fig. 87). With Part C still attached to the faceplate, glue Part C and D together.
- Put Parts C and D on the lathe and turn to the appropriate size. Do your finish sanding on Parts C and D.
- I use a carving tool (Dremel tool) to carve the vertical grooves in the tree trunk. Sand this with a Sand-O-Flex sander.
- Attach Parts C and D to Parts A and B with screws from the bottom and inside of Parts A and B.
- Drill the 3/8" hole for the threaded pipe in Part D using a drill press to insure it is vertical. This could also be done on the lathe using a chuck in your tailstock.

Fig. 87: Inserting Part D into Part C.

- The ladybugs are randomly spaced. Notice that I have a couple of the ladybugs on top of the stump. See topic VIII, "Ladybugs," which is the same process I used to make the dots on the dot lamp. D-43

Segmented Lamp Projects

Pink Ivory Lamp

Materials: Spalted maple, purpleheart, and pink ivory are used to make this lamp.

Refer to Diags. 44 to 47 when making this lamp:

• Start Ring 1 by turning it smooth and flat on both sides. Screw it to a scrap board on a faceplate to do this. Remember to countersink the screws so you don't hit them when you are flattening the piece.

Detail of handle.

Pink Ivory Lamp

PINK IVORY VASE

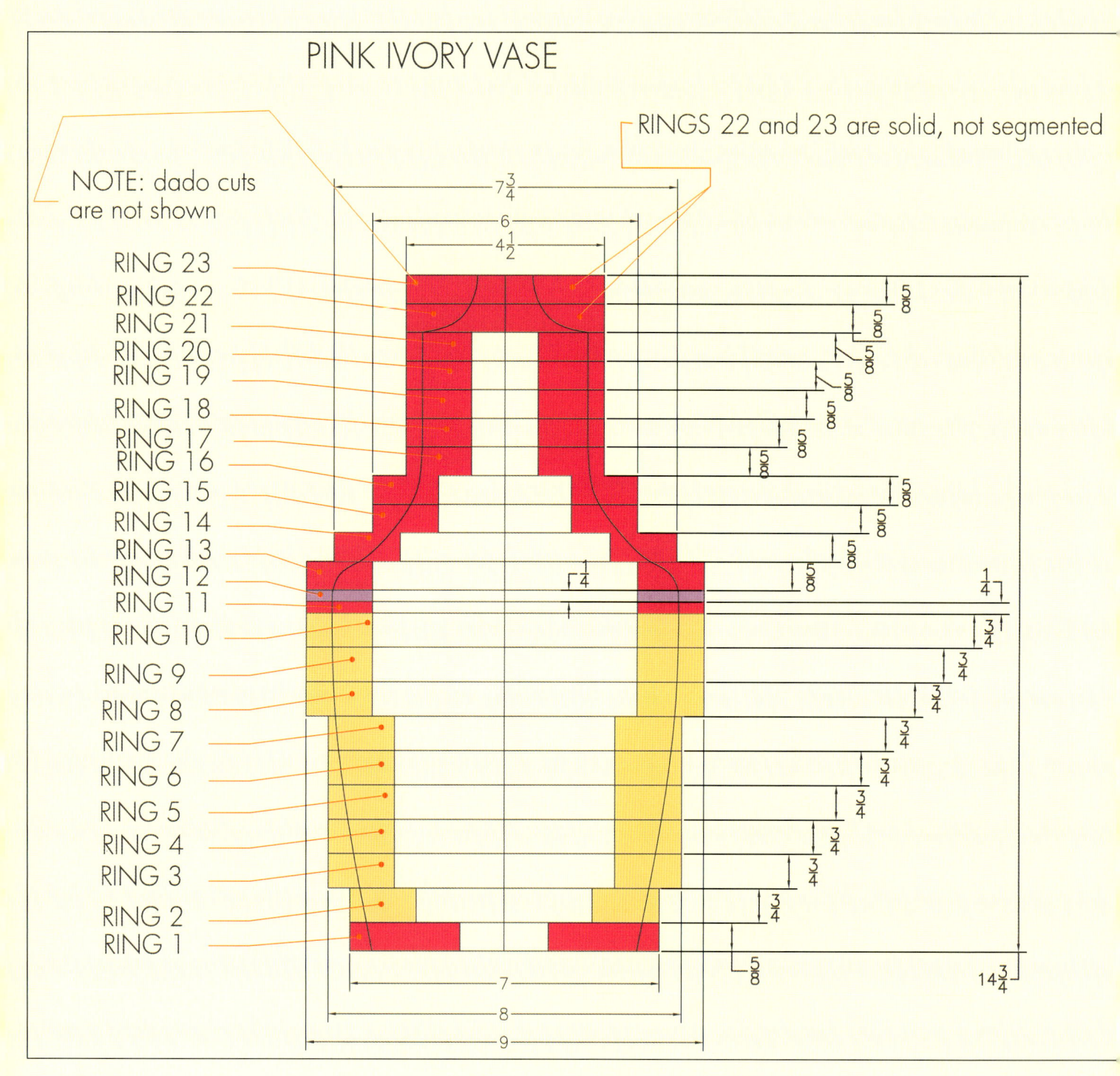

NOTE: dado cuts are not shown

RINGS 22 and 23 are solid, not segmented

- RING 23
- RING 22
- RING 21
- RING 20
- RING 19
- RING 18
- RING 17
- RING 16
- RING 15
- RING 14
- RING 13
- RING 12
- RING 11
- RING 10
- RING 9
- RING 8
- RING 7
- RING 6
- RING 5
- RING 4
- RING 3
- RING 2
- RING 1

Diag. 44

86   *Segmented Lamp Projects*

PINK IVORY VASE

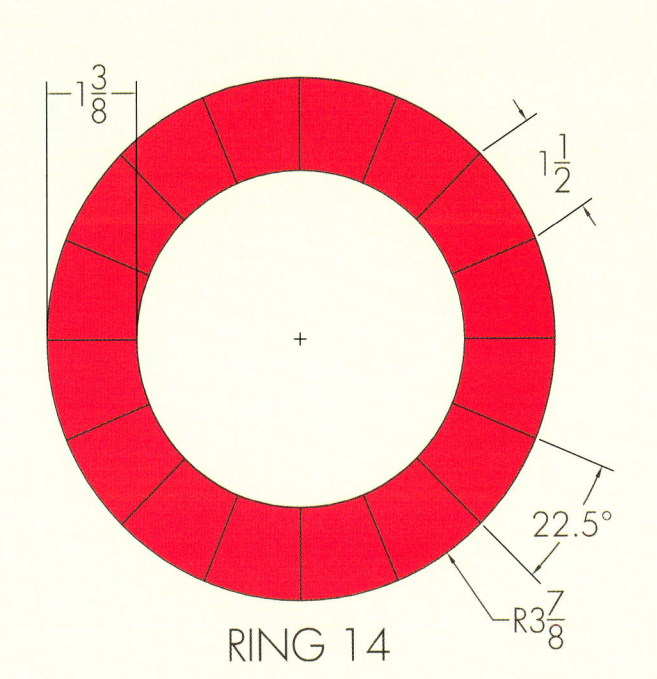

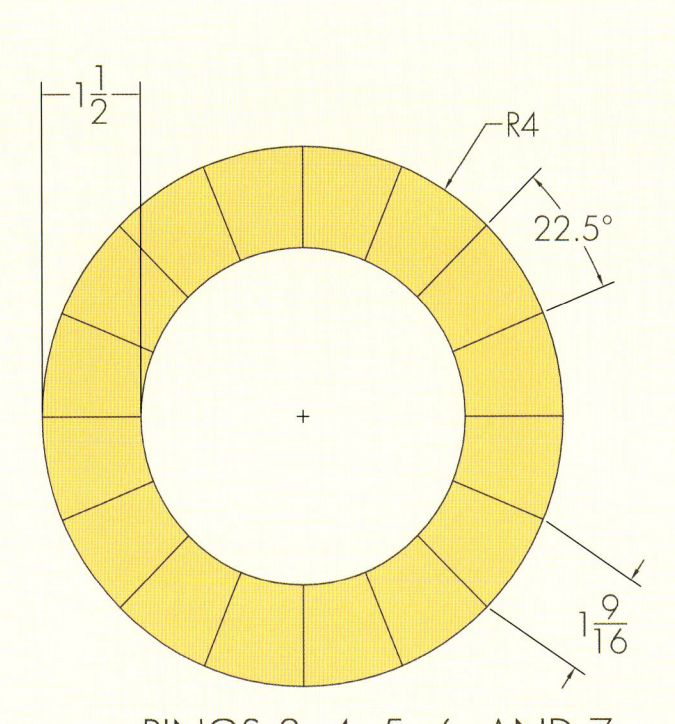

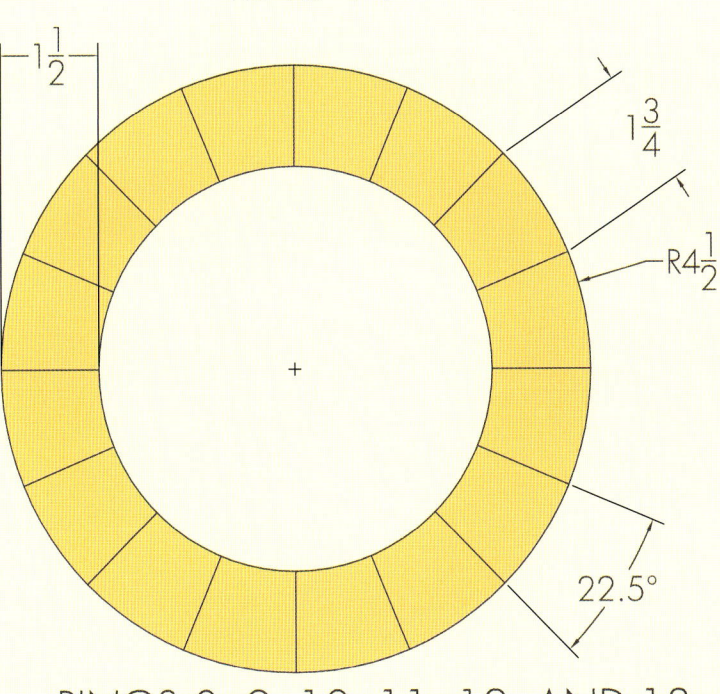

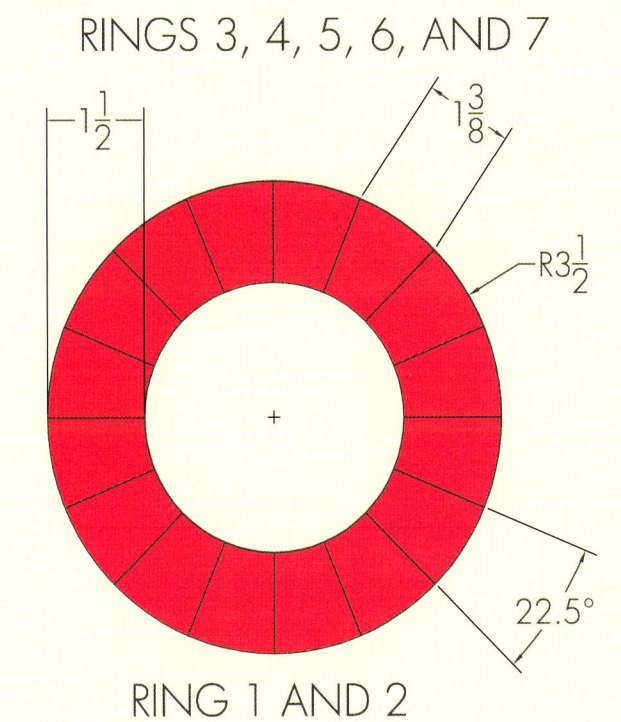

RING 14 — 1 3/8, 1 1/2, 22.5°, R3 7/8

RINGS 3, 4, 5, 6, AND 7 — 1 1/2, R4, 22.5°, 1 9/16

RINGS 8, 9, 10, 11, 12, AND 13 — 1 1/2, 1 3/4, R4 1/2, 22.5°

RING 1 AND 2 — 1 1/2, 1 3/8, R3 1/2, 22.5°

Diag. 45

Pink Ivory Lamp 87

PINK IVORY VASE

RINGS 17, 18, 19, 20, AND 21

RING 15 AND 16

RINGS 22 AND 23, both solid not segmented

HANDLES

NOTE: each square = 1/4"

DETAIL A
RINGS 20 AND 21

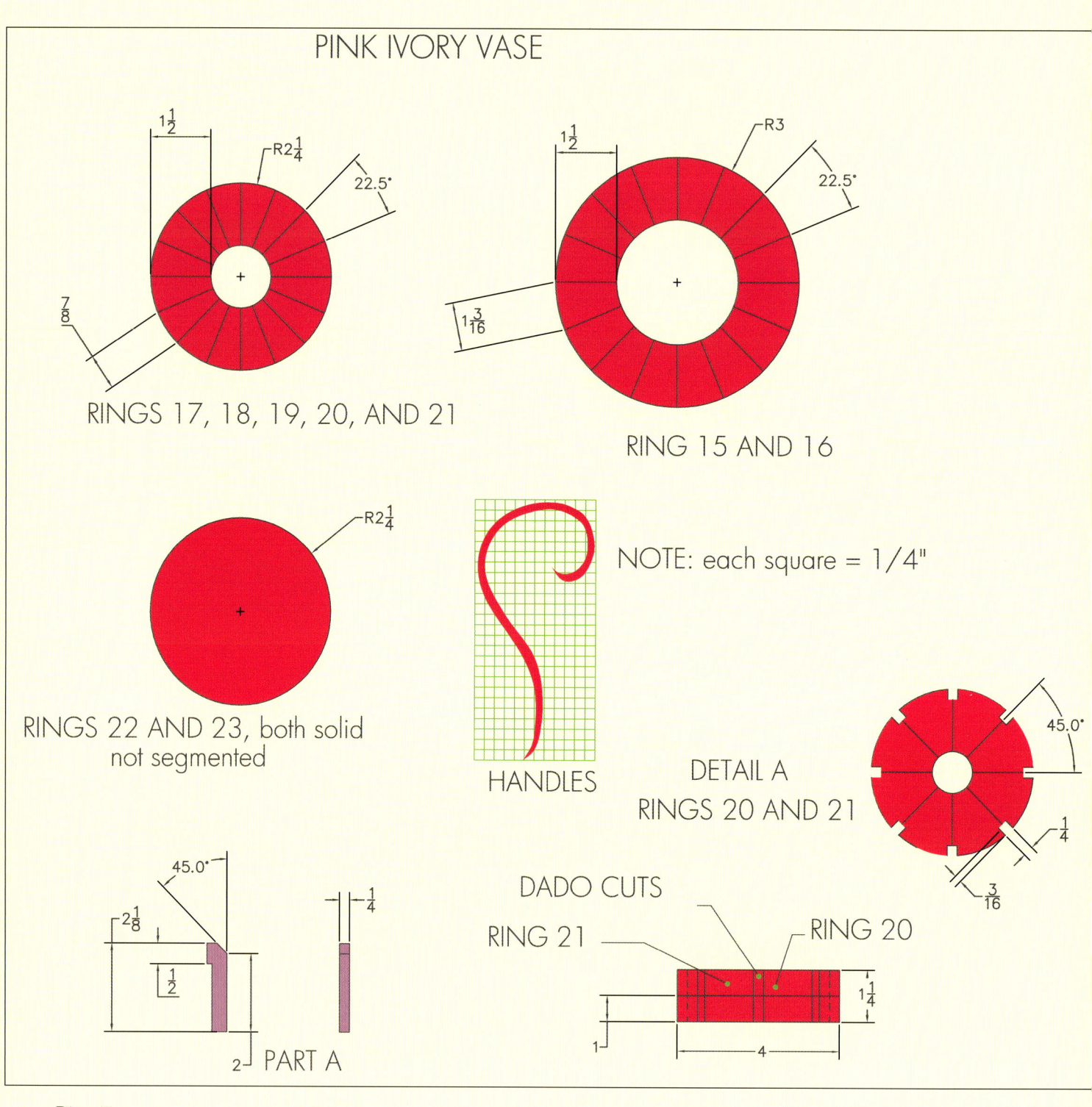

PART A

DADO CUTS
RING 21
RING 20

Diag. 46

88 *Segmented Lamp Projects*

PINK IVORY VASE

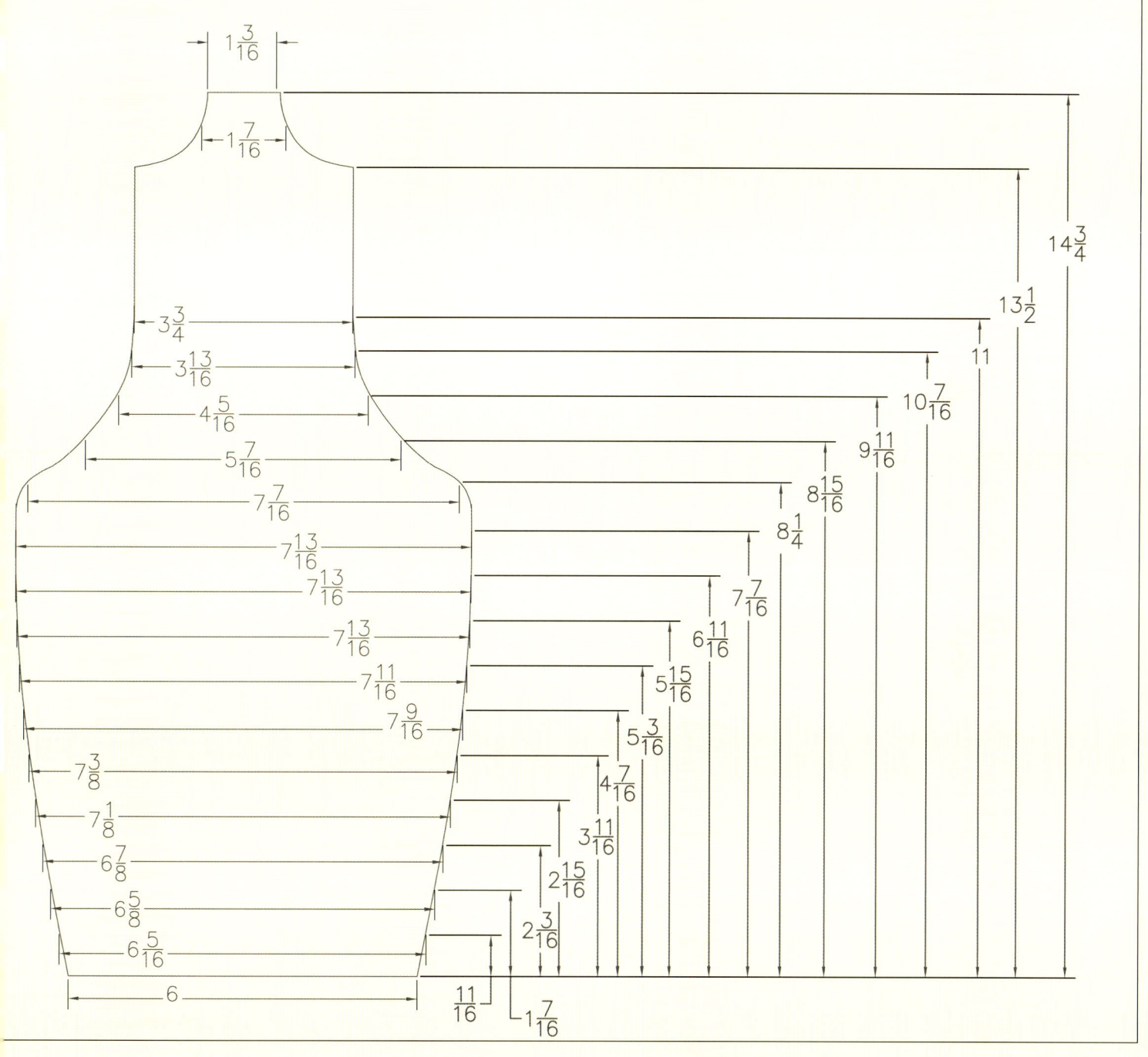

Diag. 47

Pink Ivory Lamp

- Flatten Ring 2 on one side and glue it to Ring 1 using the press. Flatten the outside of ring two. Repeat this process through Ring 19 (see Fig. 88).

Fig. 88: The bottom section has been turned to its finished dimensions. The top section is still being built with rings.

- Flatten Ring 20 on both sides (see Fig. 89), then flatten Ring 21 on one side. Glue these two together and cut the dado (see Fig. 90). Also, see the Dado Jig in topic II on page 20. Once the dados are cut, Rings 20 and 21 can be glued to Ring 19. Continue the process of gluing rings through Ring 23.

Fig. 90: Jig used to cut dado.

- At this point, turn the project on the lathe (see Fig. 91) to its final dimensions and sand. Cut Part A, the pink ivory pieces, and glue them into the dado.
- For the handles, glue up two outside pieces of purpleheart with the grain running vertical. In the center, glue a piece of purpleheart running horizontal, that is at 90 degrees in relation to the outside piece. This will laminate three pieces together and insure strength. Cut these out on a table jig saw and use a Sand-o-flex for sanding.
- Attach the handles with very small 3/8" screws, lightly countersinked into the handles. Fill over the tops of the screws with a mixture of CA glue and fine dust from the purpleheart wood.
- Drill the holes required for the wire and wire the lamp.

Fig. 89: Rings 20 and 21 glued together and mounted on a faceplate. They are turned smooth on the outside.

Fig. 91: Pink ivory lamp ready to be turned to its final dimensions.

Segmented Lamp Projects

Sunbonnet Sue Lamp

Materials: The main areas of the Sunbonnet Sue Lamp are made of curly maple and walnut. The wood in the actual character of Sunbonnet Sue will be described later.

Refer to Diags. 48, 49, and 50 when making this lamp:

Sunbonnet Sue Lamp

92 *Segmented Lamp Projects*

SUNBONNET SUE

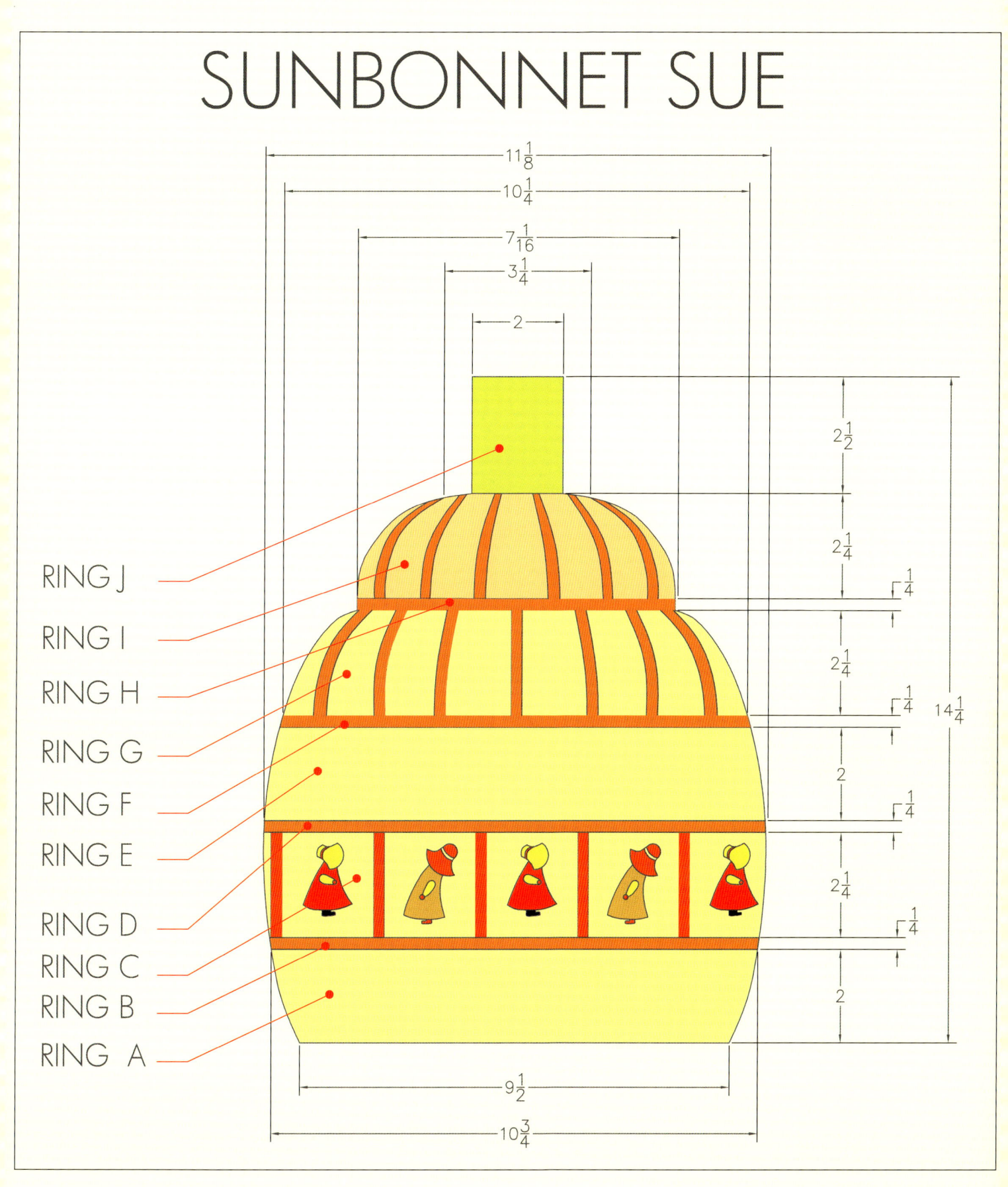

Diag. 48

Sunbonnet Sue Lamp 93

SUNBONNET SUE

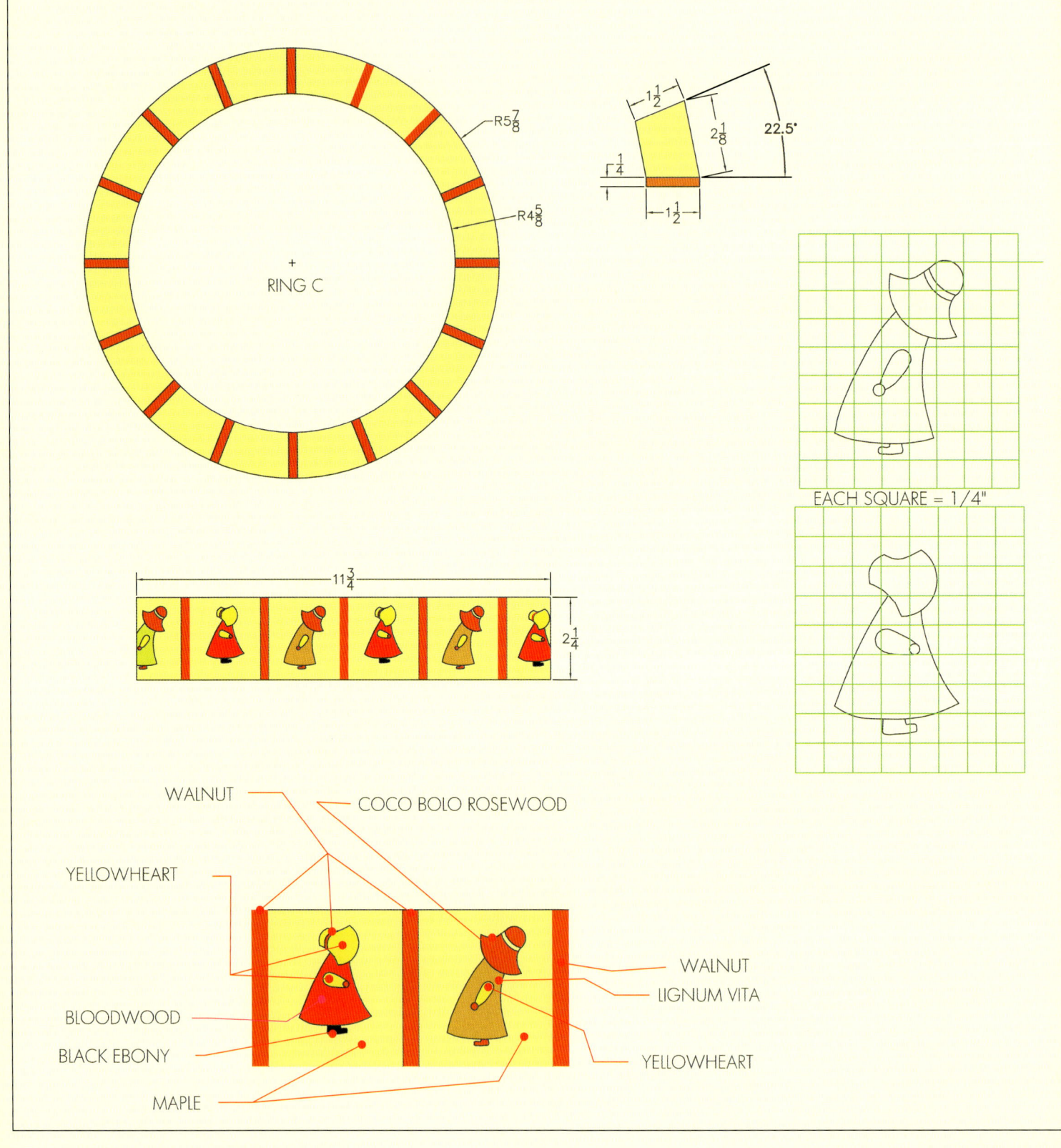

Diag. 49

94 *Segmented Lamp Projects*

SUNBONNET SUE

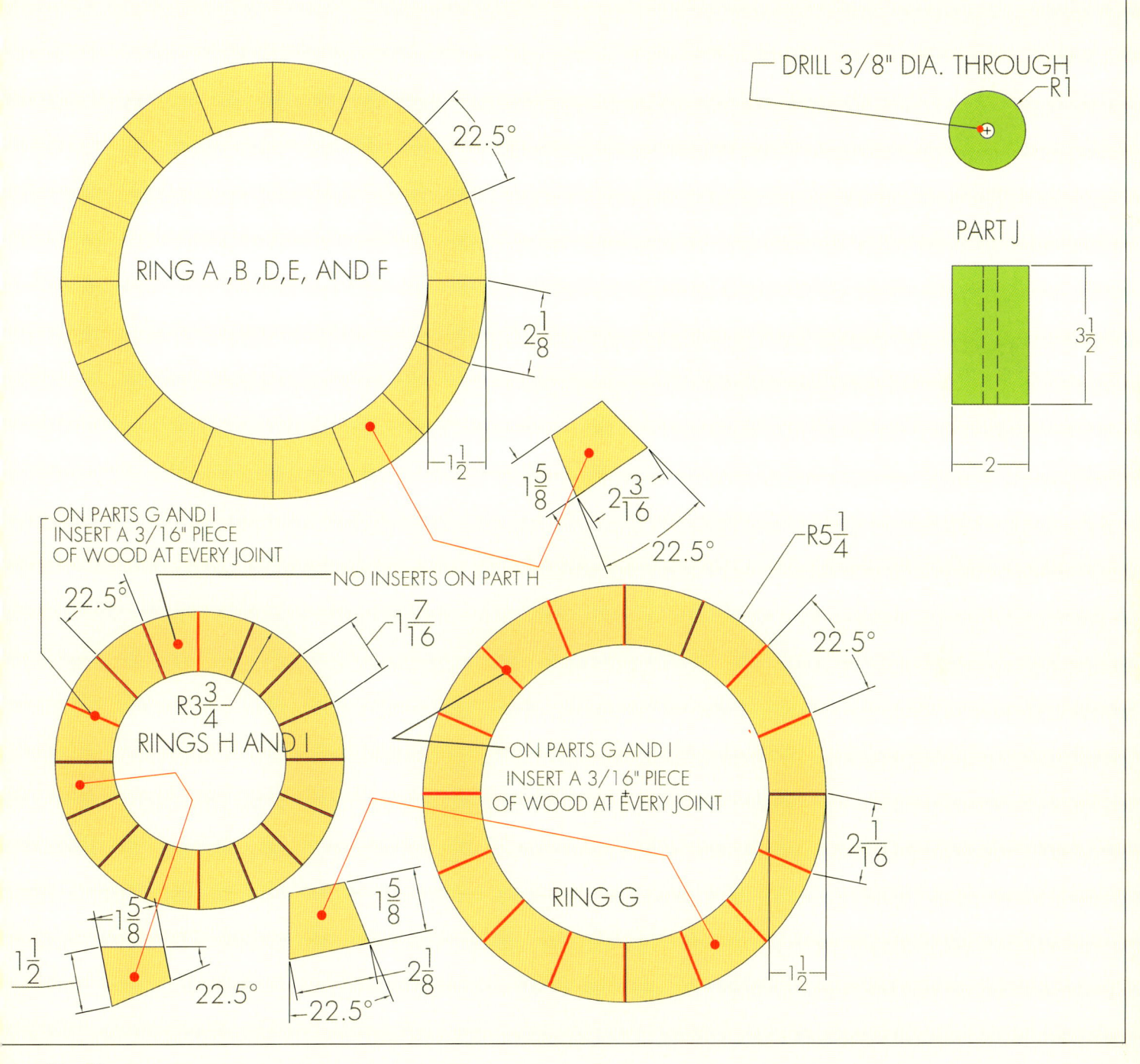

DRILL 3/8" DIA. THROUGH — R1

PART J
$3\frac{1}{2}$
2

RING A, B, D, E, AND F
22.5°
$2\frac{1}{8}$
$1\frac{1}{2}$
$1\frac{5}{8}$
$2\frac{3}{16}$
22.5°

ON PARTS G AND I INSERT A 3/16" PIECE OF WOOD AT EVERY JOINT
NO INSERTS ON PART H
22.5°
$1\frac{7}{16}$
R$3\frac{3}{4}$
RINGS H AND I
$1\frac{5}{8}$
$1\frac{1}{2}$
22.5°

R$5\frac{1}{4}$
22.5°
ON PARTS G AND I INSERT A 3/16" PIECE OF WOOD AT EVERY JOINT
RING G
$2\frac{1}{16}$
$1\frac{1}{2}$
$1\frac{5}{8}$
$2\frac{1}{8}$
22.5°

Diag. 50

Sunbonnet Sue Lamp

• Make and turn Ring C first. Start with Sunbonnet Sue (see Fig. 92) by gluing two pieces of wood together with CA glue (see Fig. 93).

Fig. 92: Ring C after it has been turned

Fig. 93: Notice the spot of CA glue which is used to hold two pieces of wood together.

• Trace the dress as shown in Fig. 94 and cut it out by first drilling a small 1/32" diameter hole and using a .007" jigsaw blade. Cut the dress out, take it out of the wood, and put the red bloodwood dress into the maple (see Fig. 95).

• Glue these together with CA glue. Then, with this piece of maple, with the dress in it, use the same process to make the bonnet and arms from yellowheart.

• Place a piece of black ebony or wenge under the maple with the bonnet and dress. Cut out the shoes and insert them into the maple. After this, use the same process for the hand and the bonnet band. At this point, you may have some small gaps between the colors of wood. These can be filled later.

Segmented Lamp Projects

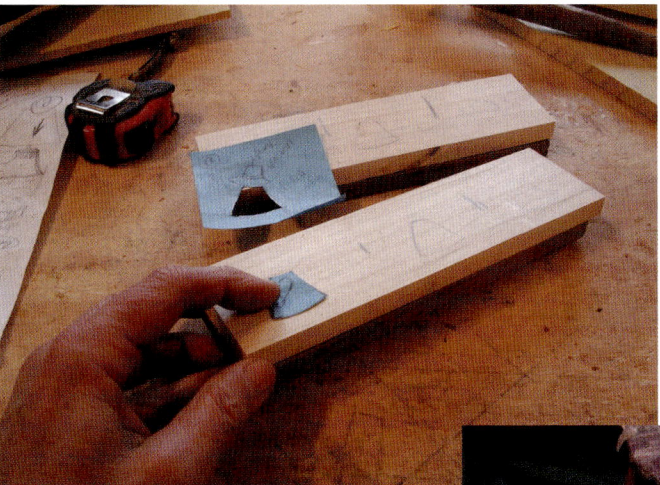

Fig. 94: Tracing the dress.

Fig. 95: Notice the black ebony shoes that have been inlayed using the same method as the dress.

• Finish the second Sunbonnet Sue in a similar fashion (see Fig. 96). Here the dress is made of lignum vita, the hat is coco bolo rosewood, the shoes are walnut, and the hands are round holes with bloodwood plugs.

Fig. 96: This is the second Sunbonnet Sue figure.

Sunbonnet Sue Lamp

- Turn this ring on both sides. Notice the concentric rings used for alignment (see Fig. 97). Also, notice the flat wedges which contain the Sunbonnet Sue panels. Be careful not to turn too deeply into the wood. Sunbonnet Sue is only 5/16" to 3/8" thick. If you turn too deeply, you will turn past the 5/16". For this reason, this ring has to be centered very precisely so it cuts equally on all sides.

Fig. 97: Notice the concentric circles that were used to align Ring C before it was turned.

- Next glue up the rings A, B, D, E, F, and G. Figure 98 shows Ring A. Flatten Ring A on both sides by screwing it to a plywood disk and attaching the disk to a faceplate.

Fig. 98: Ring A, once turned, is glued to Ring B then Rings A and B are glued to Ring C.

- Turn Ring B on one side and glue it to Ring A. Be sure Ring A is screwed from the faceplate side, so you can take it off the lathe later. Leave ring A on the faceplate from this point until you finish the lamp. Turn Ring B flat to the required thickness. Draw concentric circles on Ring B.
- In a press, glue Ring B to Ring C. Make sure Ring C is centered precisely on Ring B. Otherwise, you may turn too deeply and cut past Sunbonnet Sue. Continue the same process with Rings D, E, F and G.
- Add a stabilizer (see Fig. 99) to help reduce vibration. Turn this much of the lamp to its finished dimensions.

Fig. 99: Notice the stabilizer, which helps prevent against vibrations.

- Glue Ring H, turn on one side and glue it to Ring G. Do the same process for Ring I. Notice the tailstock's ball bearing center goes into Rings H and I and presses against the stabilizer (see Fig. 100).
- Finish turning the lamp, sand, and drill the 2" hole at the end of Ring I. I use a Forstner Bit and chuck with a Morse taper in the tailstock of the lathe, this can also be done on the drill press or with a parting tool on the lathe.
- Make Ring J, the stem, and drill a 3/8" hole into it. Insert and glue it into Ring I. Be sure all sanding is done before inserting Ring J. If there are gaps around Sunbonnet Sue, use a clear CA glue and a fine mixture of sawdust to fill the gaps. I use a 220 grit belt to collect saw dust from the same type of wood that I want to match. Make a small puddle of CA glue (1/2 the size of a dime) and mix the glue with the sawdust. Fill the gaps and do the same for any other gaps that may require different colored sawdust. After this dries, I prefer sanding with an orbital sander. Sanding on the lathe can leave glue marks all the way around your project.
- Drill the hole for the cord, finish, and wire the lamp.

Segmented Lamp Projects

Fig. 100: The tailstock goes inside to the stabilizer.

Sunbonnet Sue Lamp

A Bad Day in the Shop

Materials: Lacewood is used for the base and the table saw's throat plate. The table is hackberry wood and the blade is yellowheart. The fingernails are made from pink ivory and a thin piece of hard maple.

Refer to Diags. 51, 52, and 53 when making this lamp:

Segmented Lamp Projects

A Bad Day in the Shop 101

"BAD DAY IN THE SHOP"

PART E
THROAT PLATE

TABLE

FENCE

$11\frac{3}{4}$

$R\frac{5}{16}$

PART A
TABLE

$11\frac{3}{4}$

PART D, FENCE

PART F

2

$8\frac{1}{2}$

15

$\frac{3}{8}$

$2\frac{3}{4}$

PART D , FENCE

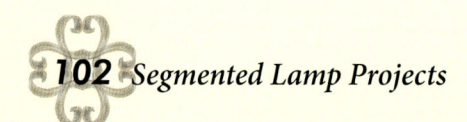

1   $1\frac{1}{8}$ $R\frac{1}{4}$ $1\frac{1}{2}$

1   $\frac{1}{2}$

Diag. 51

102 *Segmented Lamp Projects*

"BAD DAY IN THE SHOP"

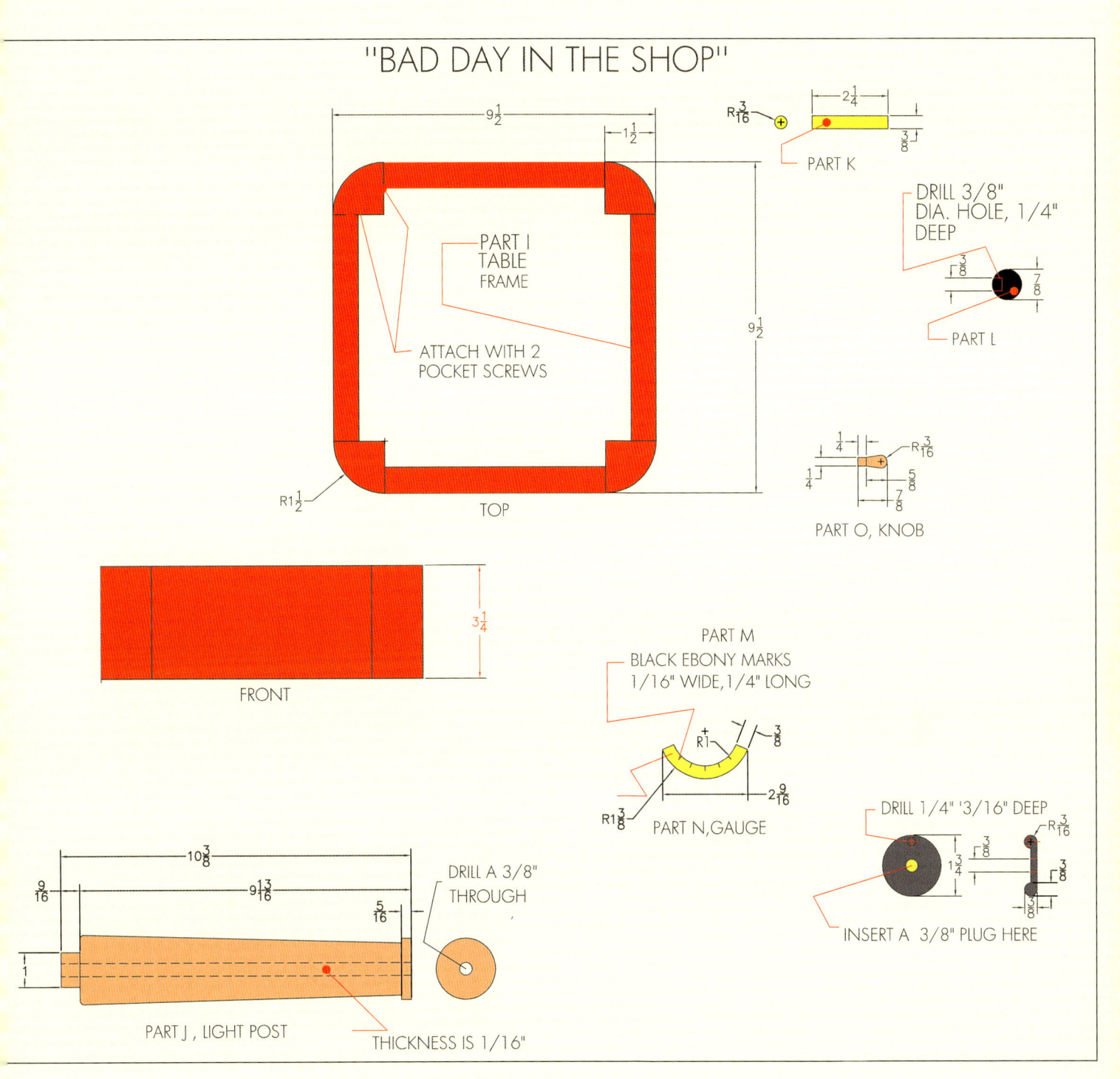

PART I, TABLE FRAME — ATTACH WITH 2 POCKET SCREWS
- $9\frac{1}{2}$ × $9\frac{1}{2}$, corner $1\frac{1}{2}$, R$1\frac{1}{2}$
- TOP
- FRONT: $3\frac{1}{4}$

PART K — $2\frac{1}{4}$ × $\frac{3}{8}$, R$\frac{3}{16}$

PART L — DRILL 3/8" DIA. HOLE, 1/4" DEEP; $\frac{3}{8}$, $\frac{7}{8}$

PART O, KNOB — $\frac{1}{4}$, $\frac{1}{4}$, $\frac{5}{8}$, $\frac{7}{8}$, R$\frac{3}{16}$

PART N, GAUGE — PART M BLACK EBONY MARKS 1/16" WIDE, 1/4" LONG; R1, R$1\frac{3}{8}$, $\frac{3}{8}$, $2\frac{9}{16}$

PART J, LIGHT POST — $10\frac{3}{8}$, $9\frac{13}{16}$, $\frac{9}{16}$, $\frac{5}{16}$, 1, DRILL A 3/8" THROUGH, THICKNESS IS 1/16"

DRILL 1/4" 3/16" DEEP; INSERT A 3/8" PLUG HERE; $\frac{3}{8}$, $1\frac{3}{4}$, R$\frac{3}{16}$

Diag. 52

A Bad Day in the Shop 103

"BAD DAY IN THE SHOP"

FINGER

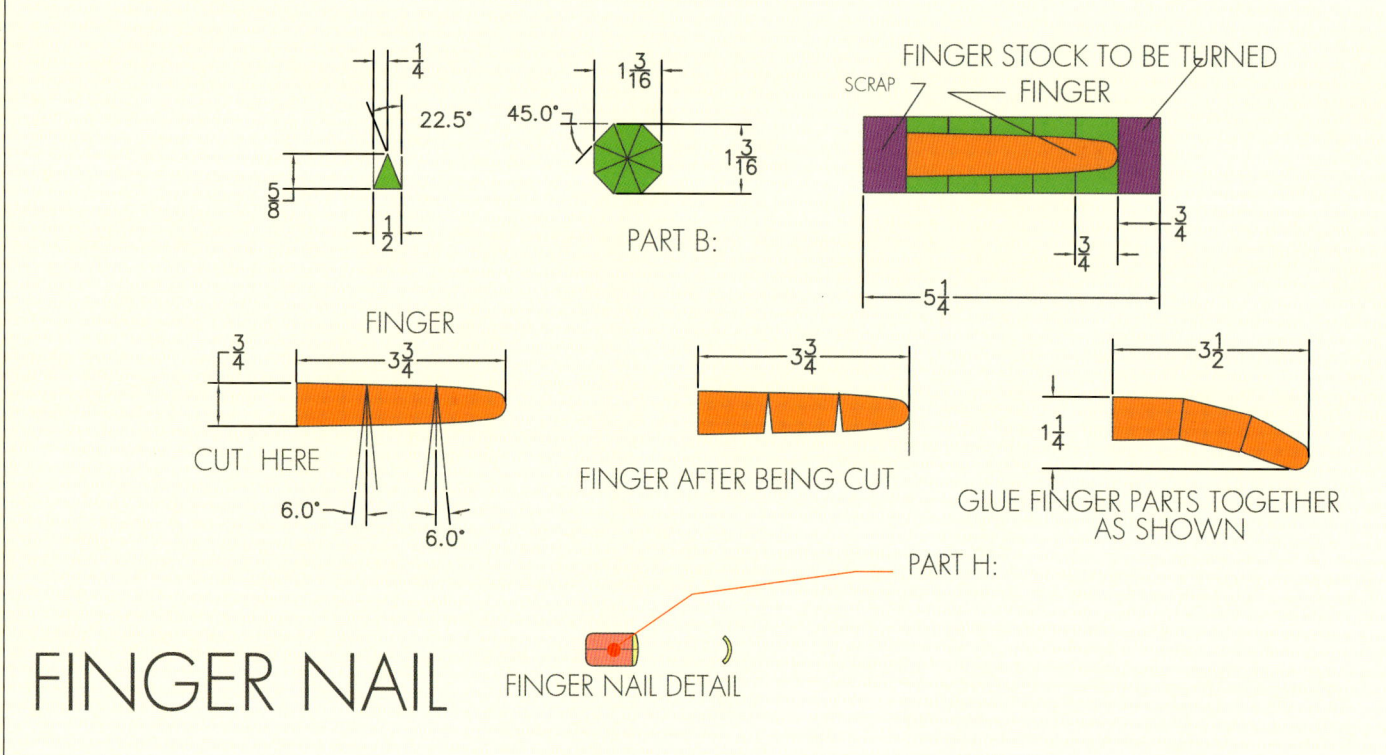

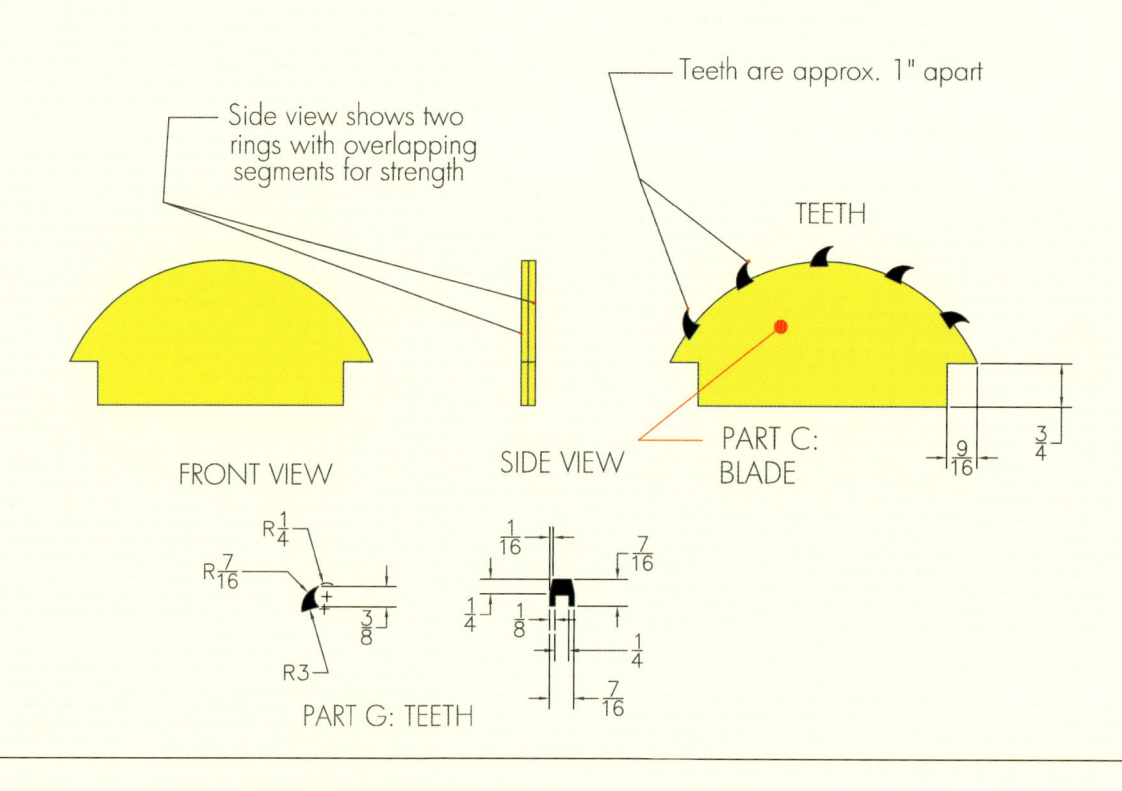

PART B:

FINGER STOCK TO BE TURNED
SCRAP — FINGER

CUT HERE — FINGER

FINGER AFTER BEING CUT

GLUE FINGER PARTS TOGETHER AS SHOWN

PART H:
FINGER NAIL DETAIL

FINGER NAIL

Side view shows two rings with overlapping segments for strength

FRONT VIEW

SIDE VIEW

Teeth are approx. 1" apart

TEETH

PART C: BLADE

PART G: TEETH

Diag. 53

104 Segmented Lamp Projects

• Start the base, lacewood, by gluing the four corners as shown in Fig. 101. Use a piece of manila folder and glue two pieces of wood together with the paper in between them. After this dries, cut the piece perpendicular to the paper and glue paper in between these two sections.

Fig. 101: Gluing paper between the four parts for the corners of the base.

• Put the piece made up of four separate corners on the lathe and turn it round making sure that the drive center does not split the paper (see Fig. 102).

• After the corner pieces are turned, use a parting tool to make both ends square and take the piece off the lathe.

Fig. 102: The four corners turned round.

• Use a chisel and split the four parts (see Figs. 103 and 104). You will need to sand the end of each part to make it perfectly flat. After cutting the sides, attach them to the corners using pocket screws.

• Glue the wood for the table saw's table. Use a router and a sleeve (these sleeves are for making male and female parts) to make the table saw's table and throat plate. Inlay the throat plate. The table is hackberry wood and the throat plate is lacewood.

Fig. 103: Using a chisel to separate the four corner pieces.

Fig. 104: The four corners after they have been split.

A Bad Day in the Shop

- The blade (yellowheart) can be made by gluing one circle. After it is dried, cut it in half. Glue these two halves together alternating the joints. Cut to the correct thickness on the bandsaw (see Fig. 105) . Then sand (see Fig. 106).

Fig. 105: When you get almost to the end, as shown, turn the piece around to finish the cut. This prevents binding.

Fig. 106: Sanding the blade flat on a belt sander.

106 Segmented Lamp Projects

- To make the teeth for the saw blade, cut a dado as shown in Fig. 107. Cut the teeth out on the jigsaw (see Fig. 108). I use CA glue to glue these on, in addition to the blood dripping from them.

Fig. 107: Notice the dado cut made before cutting the teeth out on the scroll saw.

Fig. 108: Cutting teeth for the blade on the scroll saw.

A Bad Day in the Shop 107

• Notice when I cut the blood drips I use a piece of scrap wood laying on the jigsaw so these small pieces don't fall through the throat of the jigsaw (see Fig. 109). Make the throat plate using a router template guide. I use a Freud FT 1500 Inlay Template Guide Set with Router Bit. This set will insure that the throat plate will fit exactly into the required hole. Directions are included with the kit. Glue the blade into the throat plate as in Fig. 110.

Fig. 109: Cutting out blood drippings for the blade.

Fig. 110: The blade is ready to be glued into the throat plate.

• The fingers are made out of several small segmented rings (see Fig. 111). Turn them and then cut as shown in Fig. 112.

Fig. 111: The finger after it has been turned.

Segmented Lamp Projects

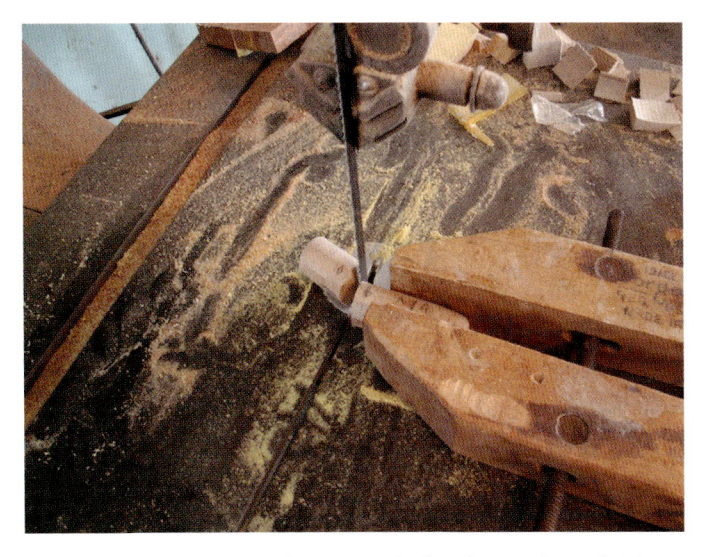

Fig. 112: When cutting small pieces on the band saw, I always hold them with a clamp for safety.

• After you cut them, use a disk sander to sand a slight angle so the finger looks bent (see Fig. 113). Glue the segments back together.

Fig. 113: Bent finger after gluing.

• The fingernails are made by gluing a piece of pink ivory to a thin piece of hard maple (see Fig. 114). Notice the thin strip of hard maple wood on the bottom.

Fig. 114: Making the fingernail.

A Bad Day in the Shop

- Drill a hole in the corner of the pink ivory block. Sand the outside, so it leaves about 1/16" thickness (see Fig. 115), then cut the fingernail out.

Fig. 115: Showing the thickness of the fingernail.

- Now sand the front edge of the fingernail and the back round (see Fig. 116).

Fig. 116: Sanding the fingernail tip.

- Use a Dremel tool to rout out a space for the fingernail on the finger and inlay the fingernail (see Figs. 117 and 118). Glue the fingernails with clear, thick CA glue.
- Cut the puddles of blood for underneath the fingers out of bloodwood. This bloodwood is only 1/16" thick. Use a clear CA glue to glue them down.
- Sand the fingers so they have a small flat area on them and place them as shown in the lamp photo.

- Make the fence support rods, Part F, of yellowheart. Turn them and attach to the table with 1/4" dowel rods. You must drill corresponding holes in the support rods and the table.
- Attach the fence (coconut palm) with two screws from the bottom. Turn the fence lock, Part K, with yellowheart and the ball with black ebony.

Fig. 117: Routing the fingertip out for the nail using a Dremel tool.

Fig. 118: Checking the fit of the nail on the finger tip.

- The adjustment wheel is not segmented and should be turned. Drill the hole on the lathe, for the yellowheart, Part M, to be inserted (see Fig. 119). Make the yellowheart plug on the lathe and glue it into the wheel. When it is dry, turn

110 *Segmented Lamp Projects*

it down to a smooth state. Remove the adjustment wheel from the lathe with a chisel, this process is shown in Figs. 13 and 13A on page 11.

• Drill and insert the knob, Part O, into the adjustment wheel. Glue the adjustment wheel to the table, Part I, as seen in the photograph.

• Part N, the gauge, requires several small black ebony marks. To make these marks, cut a black ebony strip on the saw about 1/16" thick, then use a razor blade knife to cut a real small mark about 1/16" wide and about 1/4" long. Glue these marks to Part N, spacing them equally so they appear as a scale.

• Turn the lamp's light post, Part J, on the lathe and drill out the 3/8" hole. This hole can be drilled on the lathe using a chuck and a tailstock, or it can be done on a drill press. The light post should be glued in the right hand corner of the table. The hole in the table is not shown in the drawing. At this point all the parts should be glued.

• Now you can apply the finish and wire the lamp.

Fig. 119: Using the lathe to drill the hole in one of the two adjustment wheels.

A Bad Day in the Shop

The Quilted Milk Can Lamp

Materials: The red wood on this lamp is bloodwood, including the rivets on the handle. The handles are made of yellowheart. The door and windows in the pattern are made of a dark wenge. Lignum vita is used for the ground below the schoolhouses. Around the door I use bloodwood and around the windows and the gable I use yellowheart. The roof and chimney are coco bolo. The top section above the roof and chimney is made of birch. Above each ring of schoolhouses the thin dark ring is made of walnut. Notice that there is a strip between each schoolhouse and the adjoining segment with a diamond shape. This piece is walnut and should be glued between the segments.

Refer to Diags. 54, 55, 56, and 57 when making this lamp:

- Cut the segments for Rings 1, 2, and 3. Turn the first ring flat on both sides so the bottom of the lamp has a smooth surface. Notice that Ring 1 is deeper than Ring 2 and 3. Turn Rings 2 and 3 down, glue up the first three rings, and then turn to approximately 1/8" of the finished size.

Segmented Lamp Projects

QUILTED MILK CAN LAMP: HOUSE DESIGN

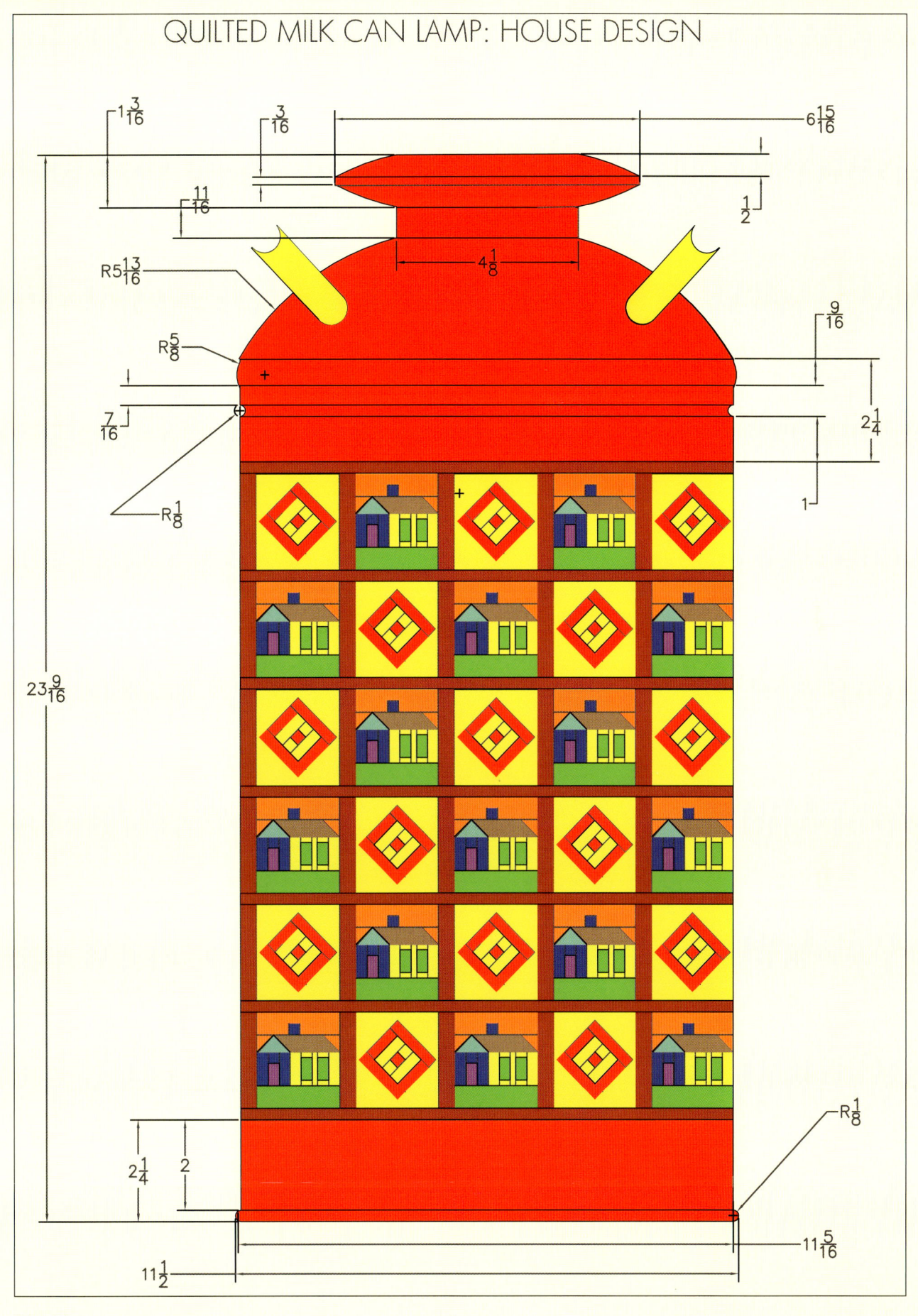

Diag. 54

The Quilted Milk Can Lamp 113

QUILTED MILK CAN LAMP: HOUSE DESIGN

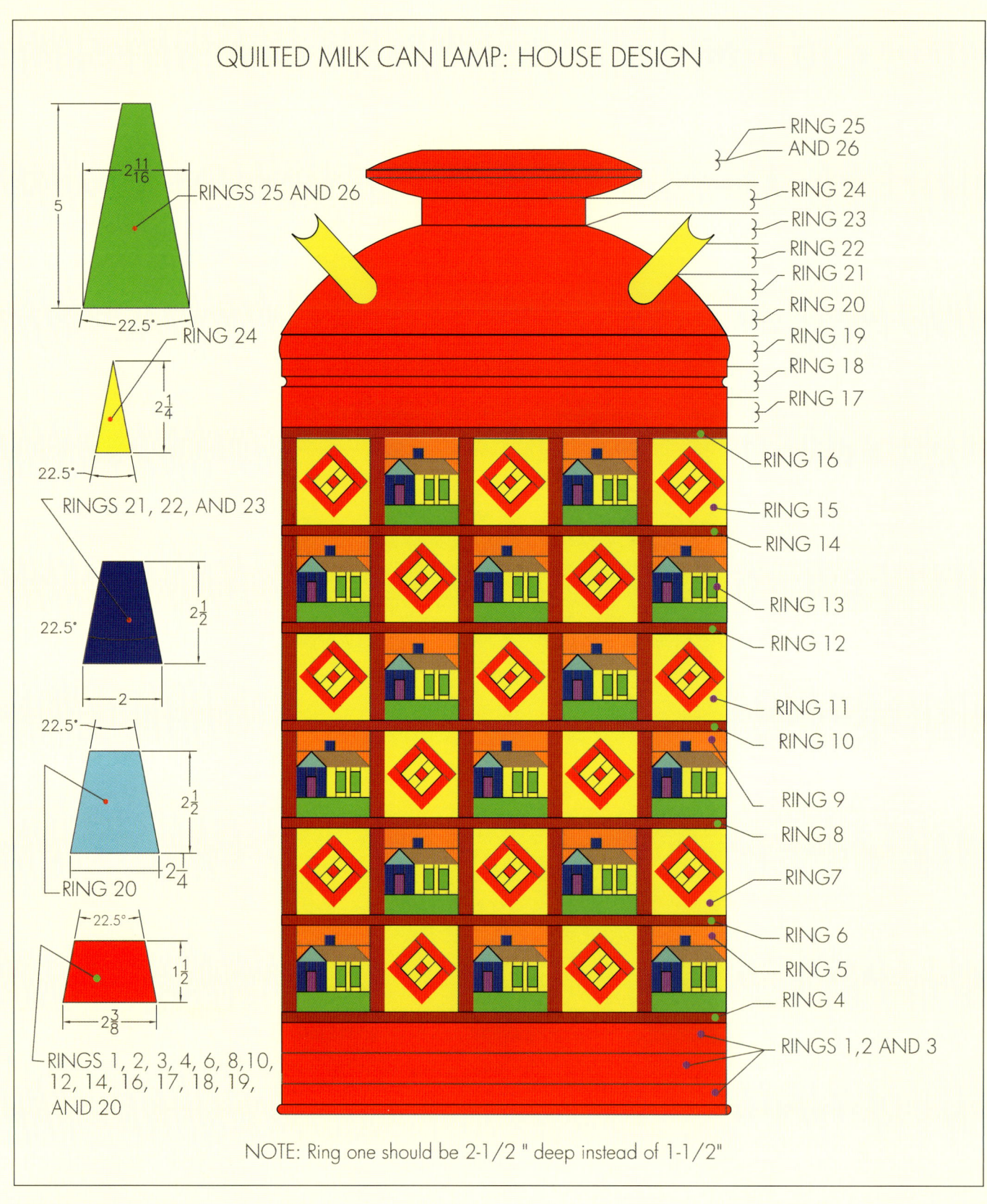

RINGS 25 AND 26 — $2\frac{11}{16}$, 5, 22.5°

RING 24 — $2\frac{1}{4}$, 22.5°

RINGS 21, 22, AND 23 — 22.5°, $2\frac{1}{2}$, 2

RING 20 — 22.5°, $2\frac{1}{2}$, $2\frac{1}{4}$

RINGS 1, 2, 3, 4, 6, 8, 10, 12, 14, 16, 17, 18, 19, AND 20 — 22.5°, $1\frac{1}{2}$, $2\frac{3}{8}$

RING 25 AND 26
RING 24
RING 23
RING 22
RING 21
RING 20
RING 19
RING 18
RING 17
RING 16
RING 15
RING 14
RING 13
RING 12
RING 11
RING 10
RING 9
RING 8
RING7
RING 6
RING 5
RING 4
RINGS 1, 2 AND 3

NOTE: Ring one should be 2-1/2" deep instead of 1-1/2"

Diag. 55

114 *Segmented Lamp Projects*

QUILTED MILK CAN LAMP: HOUSE DESIGN

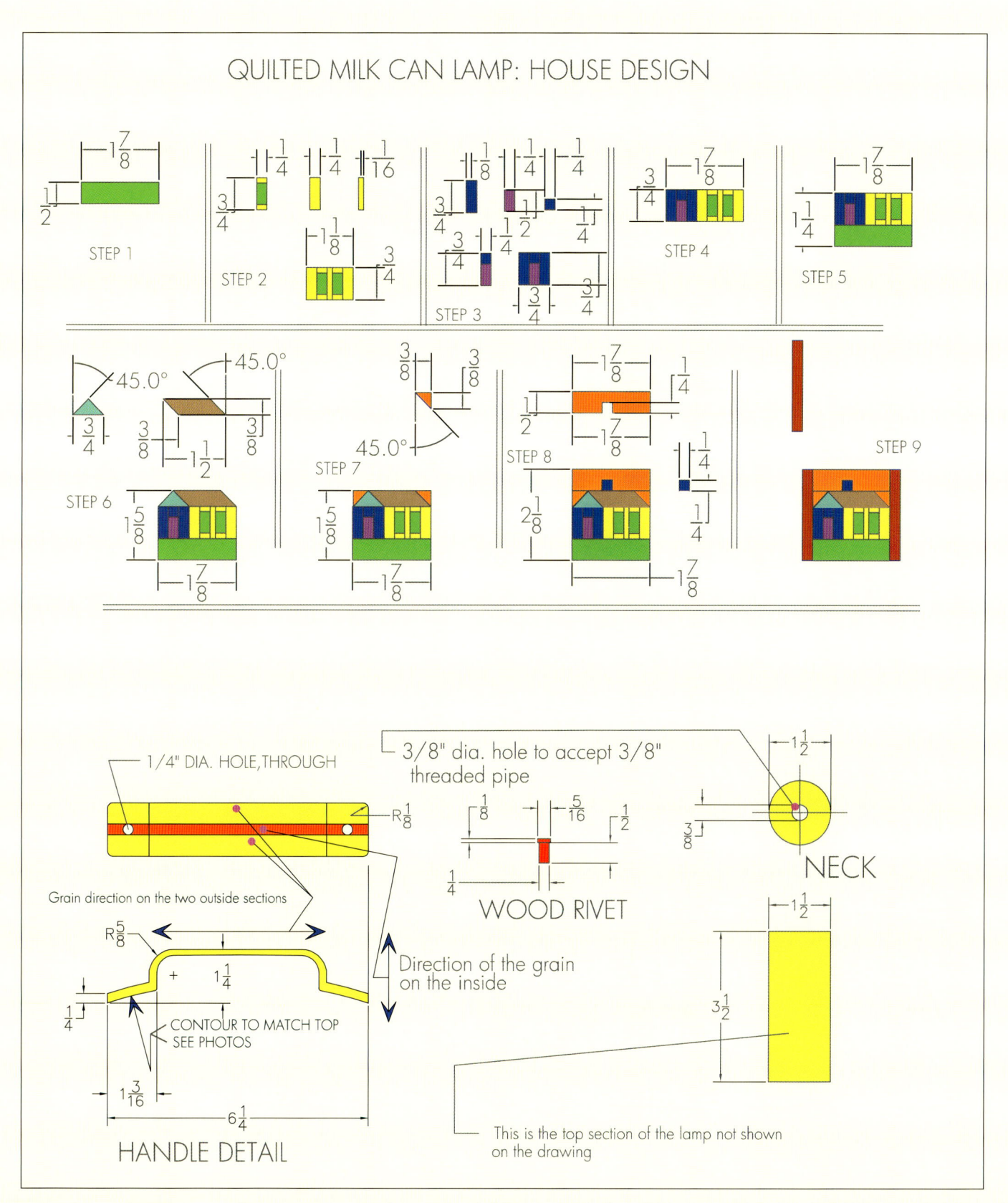

STEP 1

STEP 2

STEP 3

STEP 4

STEP 5

STEP 6

STEP 7

STEP 8

STEP 9

1/4" DIA. HOLE, THROUGH

3/8" dia. hole to accept 3/8" threaded pipe

NECK

Grain direction on the two outside sections

Direction of the grain on the inside

CONTOUR TO MATCH TOP SEE PHOTOS

WOOD RIVET

This is the top section of the lamp not shown on the drawing

HANDLE DETAIL

Diag. 56

The Quilted Milk Can Lamp 115

QUILTED MILK CAN LAMP: HOUSE DESIGN

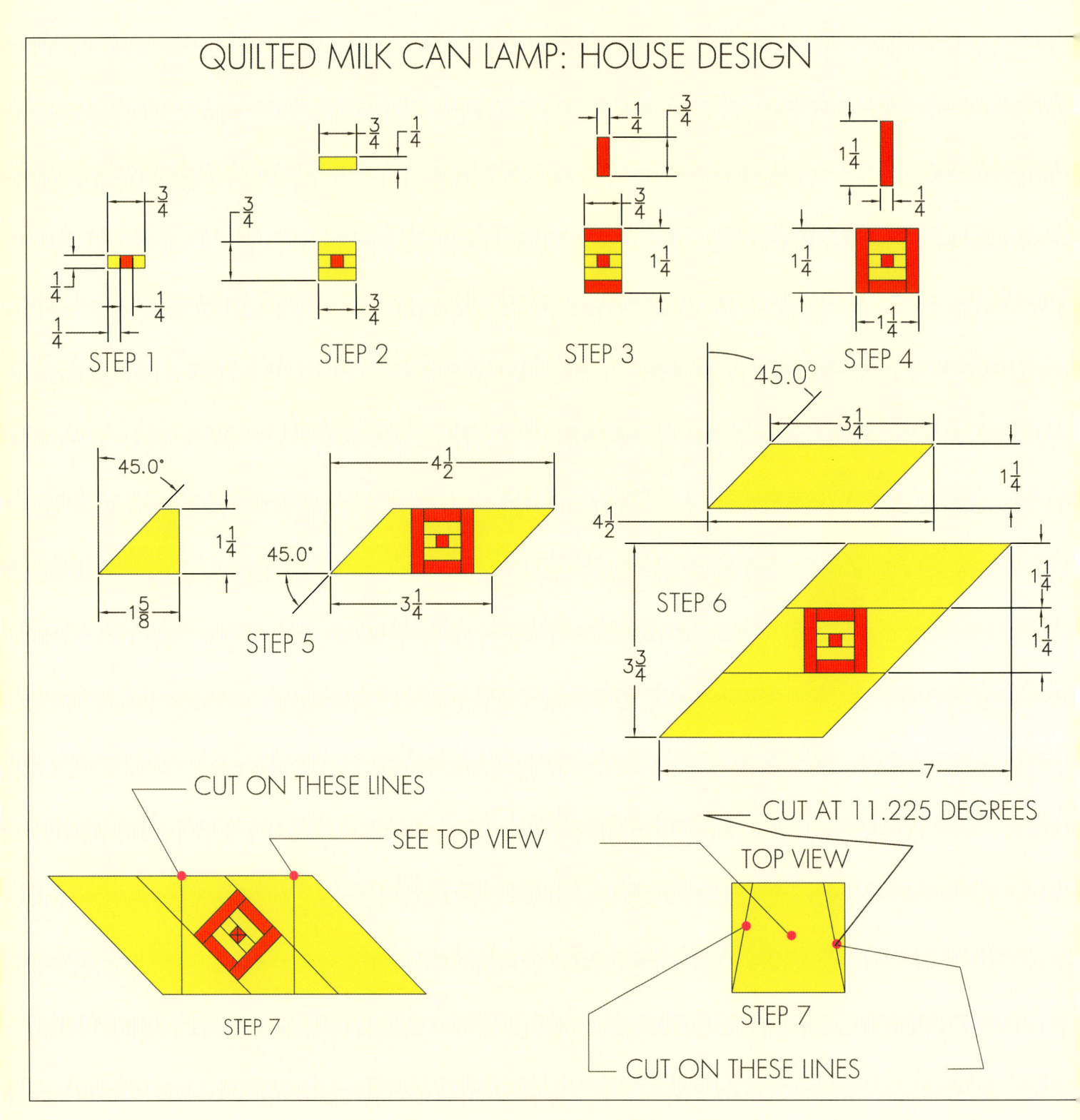

STEP 1

STEP 2

STEP 3

STEP 4

STEP 5

STEP 6

STEP 7 — CUT ON THESE LINES — SEE TOP VIEW

STEP 7 — TOP VIEW — CUT AT 11.225 DEGREES — CUT ON THESE LINES

Diag. 57

116 *Segmented Lamp Projects*

- Next, make the schoolhouses and diamond shapes as shown in Diag. 56. I use a small piece of lignum vita and oak on the back part of the wedge to make the bottom part of the schoolhouse (see Fig. 120). This is an economical way to get the appearance of the lignam vita on the outside of the lamp, but use the oak for most of the substance.

Fig. 120: Making segments using a small section of lingnum vita backed by a larger section of oak is more economical.

- Cut the windows next (see Fig. 121).

Fig. 121: Cutting the schoolhouse windows.

- Then start assembling the schoolhouse. Glue the door and windows as in Fig. 122 . Attach the roof with CA glue (see Fig. 123). Then make the dado for the chimney (see Fig. 124).
- Next, assemble and glue up Rings 4 through 16, turn them, and attach them to each other. I use a stabilizer inside the lamp around Ring 12 or 13 to cut down on vibrations. Turn this part of the lamp to its finished size and sand.
- Turn Ring 17 flat on both sides. Then attach it to the lathe faceplate with a plywood disk and screws from the outside.
- Attach Rings 18 to 25 to each other using normal segmented methods. Once assembled, turn these to the finished size for the lamp and do the final sanding.

Fig. 122: Gluing up the schoolhouse windows, door, and base.

Fig. 123: Gluing the roof onto the schoolhouse with a thick CA glue.

Fig. 124: Gluing the chimney into the dado.

The Quilted Milk Can Lamp **117**

- Drill a 1 1/2" hole about 1" deep into the top of the lamp (see Fig. 125).

Fig. 125: This hole is for the neck of the lamp.

- This section, Rings 17 to 25, can now be glued to the bottom section (see Fig. 126).

Fig. 126: Preparing to glue the top section to the bottom.

- Next, make the neck and glue it into the top of the lamp (see Fig. 127).
- Moving on to the handles, match the contour of the handles to the contour of the milk can (see Fig. 128). I use a Dremel tool for this. The handles should be laminated, by this I mean you should have the grain going in two directions as shown in Diag. 56.

Fig. 127: I use this pattern to turn the neck to the exact size.

Fig. 128: Matching the contour of the handle to the contour of the milk can.

The Quilted Milk Can Lamp

• Fig. 129 shows the finished handle being sanded. Cut the rest of the handle out on the jig saw. Notice the top of the handle is concave to look like a metal handle—use the Dremel tool to sand the concave section on the top of the handle.

Fig. 129: My wife helps out, sanding the handle on a Sand-O-Flex.

• Turn the small rivet (see Fig. 130) and attach the handle to the milk can by inserting the 1/4" rivet through a hole and into the lamp.
• Finish and wire the lamp.

Fig. 130: The 1/4", turned wood rivet with one of the concave handles.

The Pagoda Lamp

Materials: Walnut is the dark wood and maple is the light wood. In some cases spalted maple was used. Rosewood is used for the roofs.

Refer to Diags. 58 through 72 when making this lamp:
• Start the Pagoda Lamp by cutting the segments for Section 1. NOTE: For this project I leave my miter box saw set to 11 1/4°.

Segmented Lamp Projects

The Pagoda Lamp

PAGODA

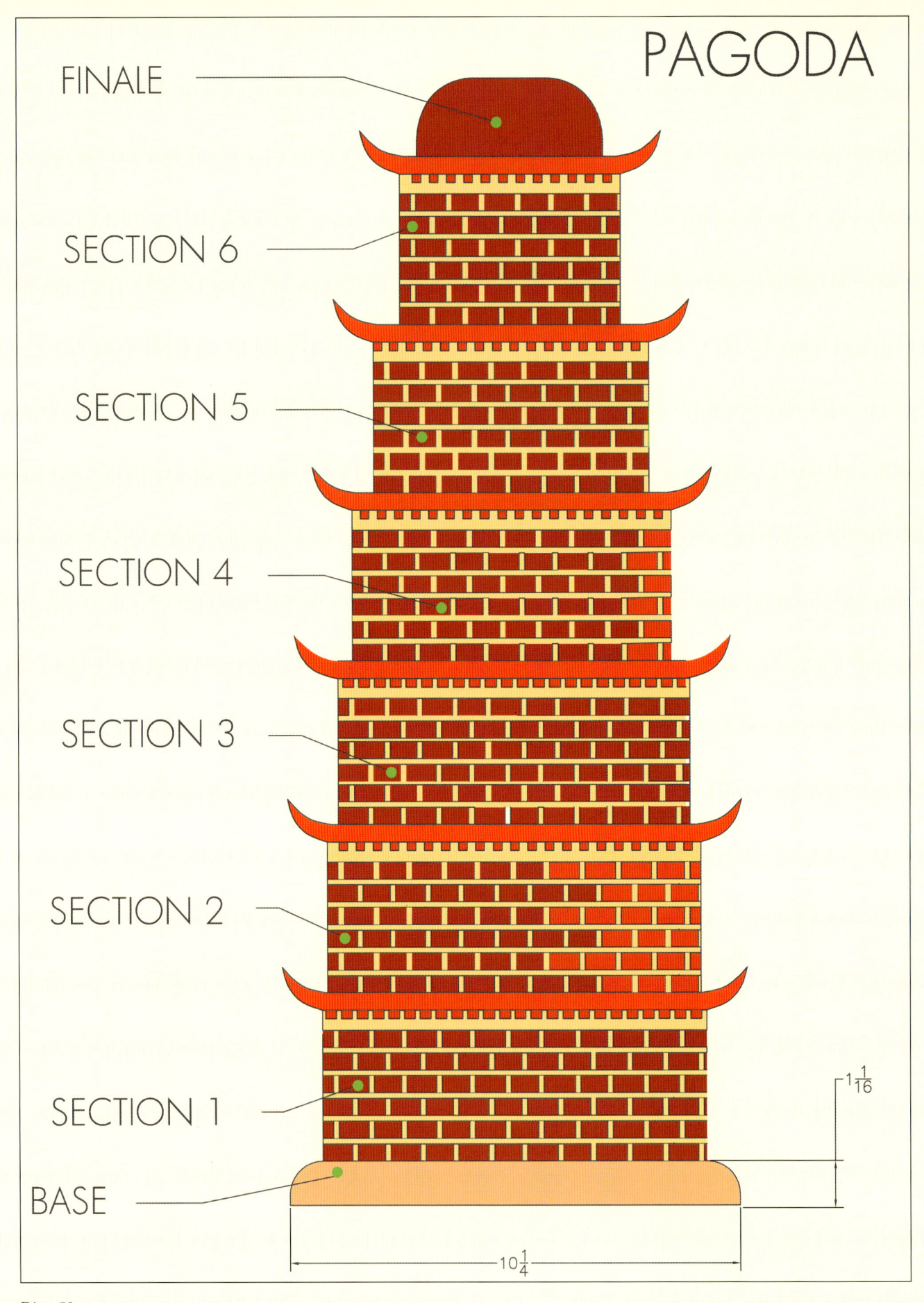

- FINALE
- SECTION 6
- SECTION 5
- SECTION 4
- SECTION 3
- SECTION 2
- SECTION 1
- BASE

$1\frac{1}{16}$

$10\frac{1}{4}$

Diag. 58

122 *Segmented Lamp Projects*

PAGODA

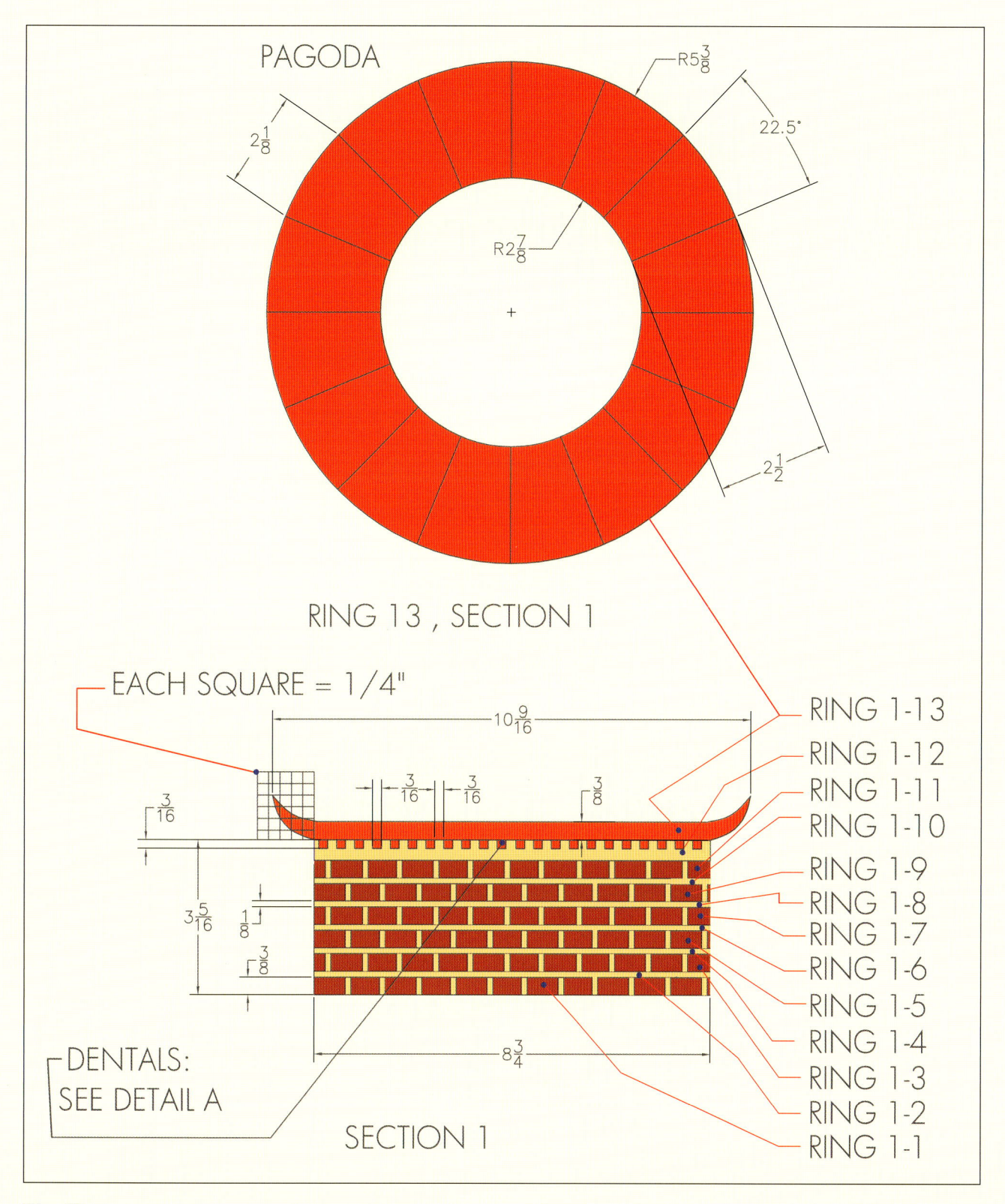

R$5\frac{3}{8}$

$2\frac{1}{8}$

22.5°

R$2\frac{7}{8}$

$2\frac{1}{2}$

RING 13, SECTION 1

EACH SQUARE = 1/4"

$10\frac{9}{16}$

$\frac{3}{16}$ $\frac{3}{16}$

$\frac{3}{8}$

$\frac{3}{16}$

$3\frac{5}{16}$

$\frac{1}{8}$

$\frac{3}{8}$

$8\frac{3}{4}$

DENTALS: SEE DETAIL A

SECTION 1

- RING 1-13
- RING 1-12
- RING 1-11
- RING 1-10
- RING 1-9
- RING 1-8
- RING 1-7
- RING 1-6
- RING 1-5
- RING 1-4
- RING 1-3
- RING 1-2
- RING 1-1

Diag. 59

The Pagoda Lamp **123**

PAGODA

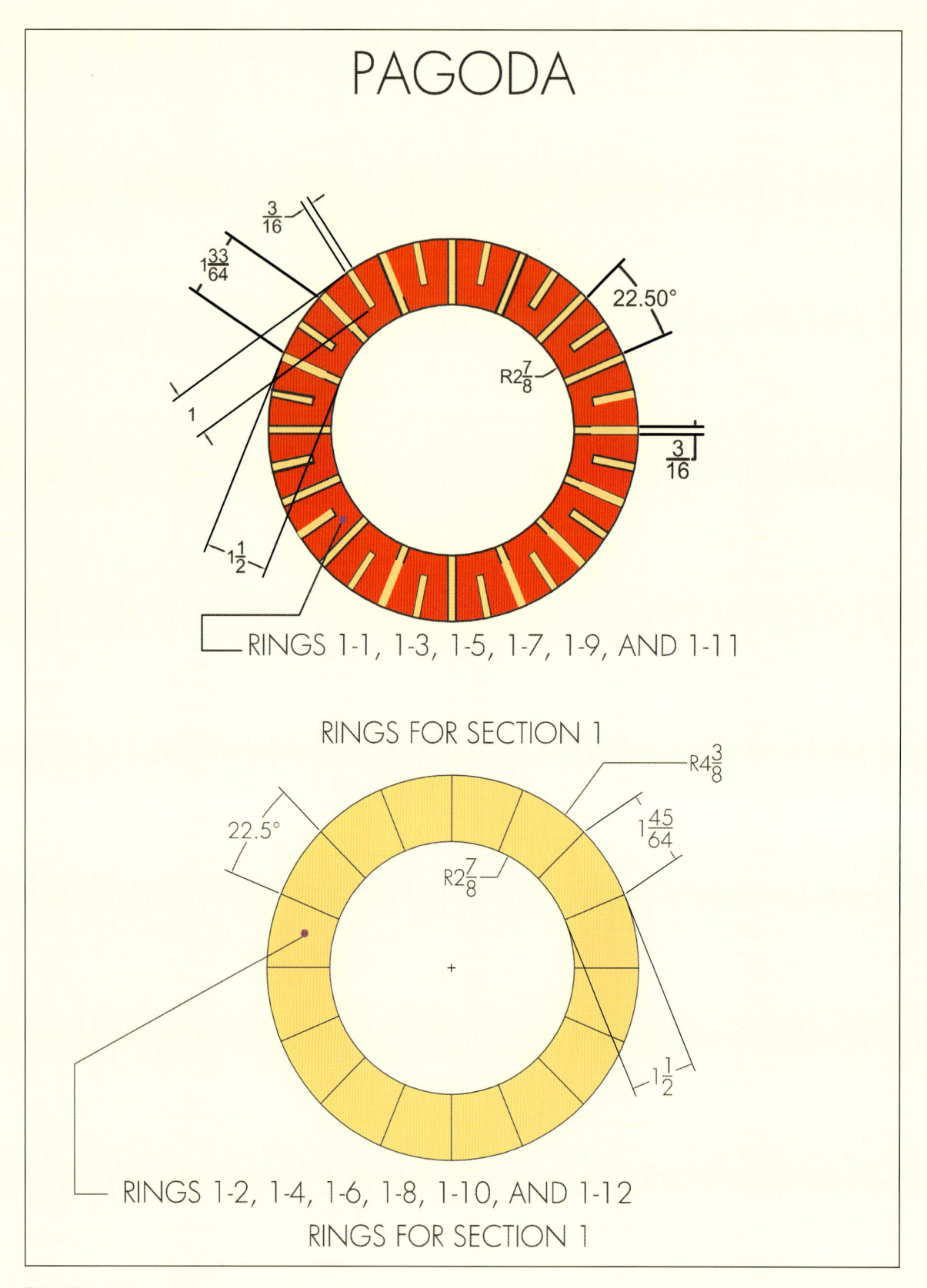

RINGS 1-1, 1-3, 1-5, 1-7, 1-9, AND 1-11

RINGS FOR SECTION 1

RINGS 1-2, 1-4, 1-6, 1-8, 1-10, AND 1-12
RINGS FOR SECTION 1

Diag. 60

SECTION 2

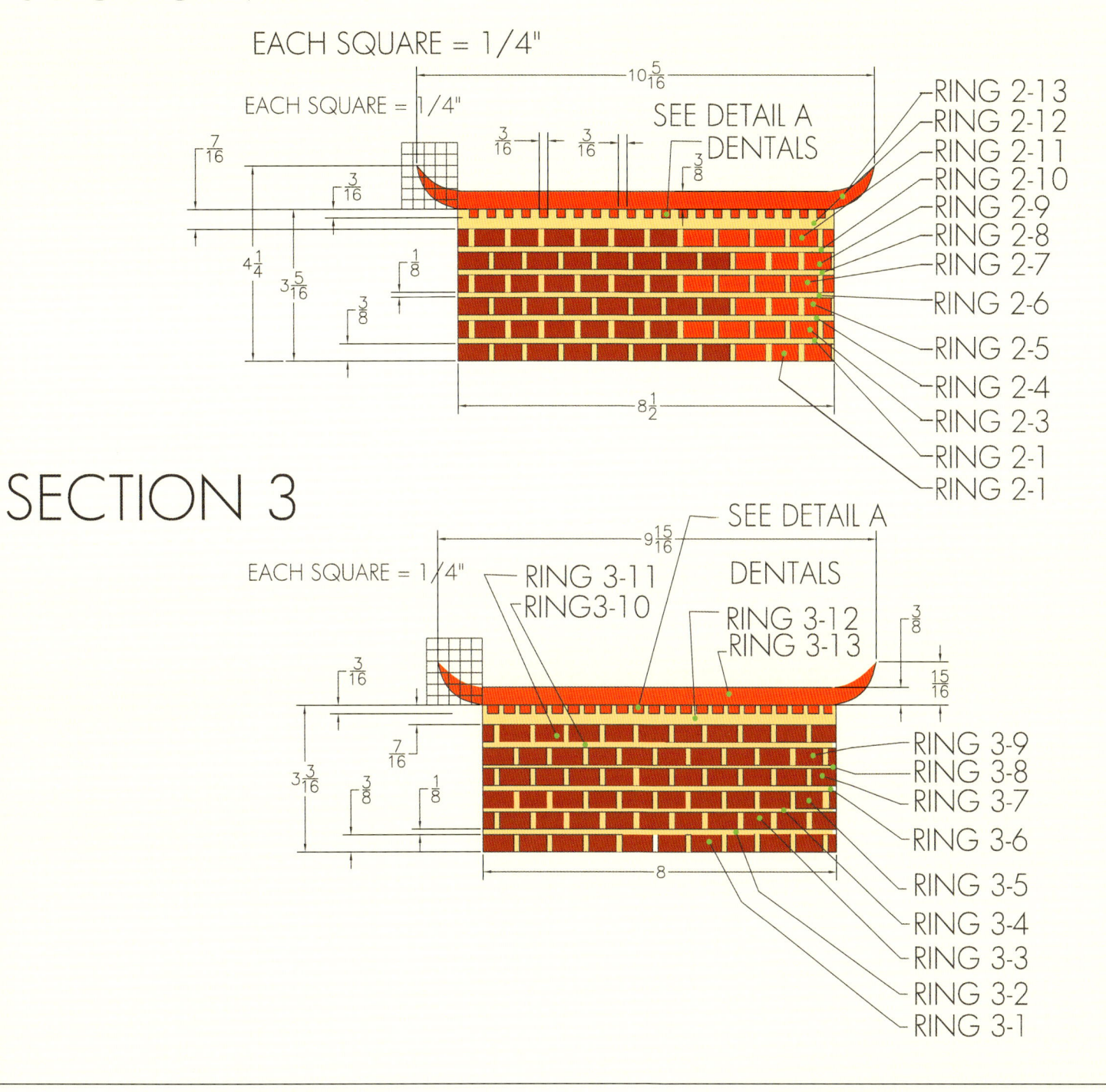

EACH SQUARE = 1/4"
EACH SQUARE = 1/4"

- $10\frac{5}{16}$
- $\frac{7}{16}$
- $\frac{3}{16}$
- $4\frac{1}{4}$
- $3\frac{5}{16}$
- $\frac{1}{8}$
- $\frac{3}{8}$
- $\frac{3}{16}$
- $\frac{3}{16}$
- $\frac{3}{8}$
- $8\frac{1}{2}$

SEE DETAIL A
DENTALS

- RING 2-13
- RING 2-12
- RING 2-11
- RING 2-10
- RING 2-9
- RING 2-8
- RING 2-7
- RING 2-6
- RING 2-5
- RING 2-4
- RING 2-3
- RING 2-1
- RING 2-1

SECTION 3

EACH SQUARE = 1/4"

- $9\frac{15}{16}$
- $\frac{3}{16}$
- $3\frac{3}{16}$
- $\frac{7}{16}$
- $\frac{3}{8}$
- $\frac{1}{8}$
- $\frac{3}{8}$
- $\frac{15}{16}$
- 8

SEE DETAIL A
DENTALS

- RING 3-11
- RING 3-10
- RING 3-12
- RING 3-13
- RING 3-9
- RING 3-8
- RING 3-7
- RING 3-6
- RING 3-5
- RING 3-4
- RING 3-3
- RING 3-2
- RING 3-1

Diag. 61

The Pagoda Lamp 125

PAGODA

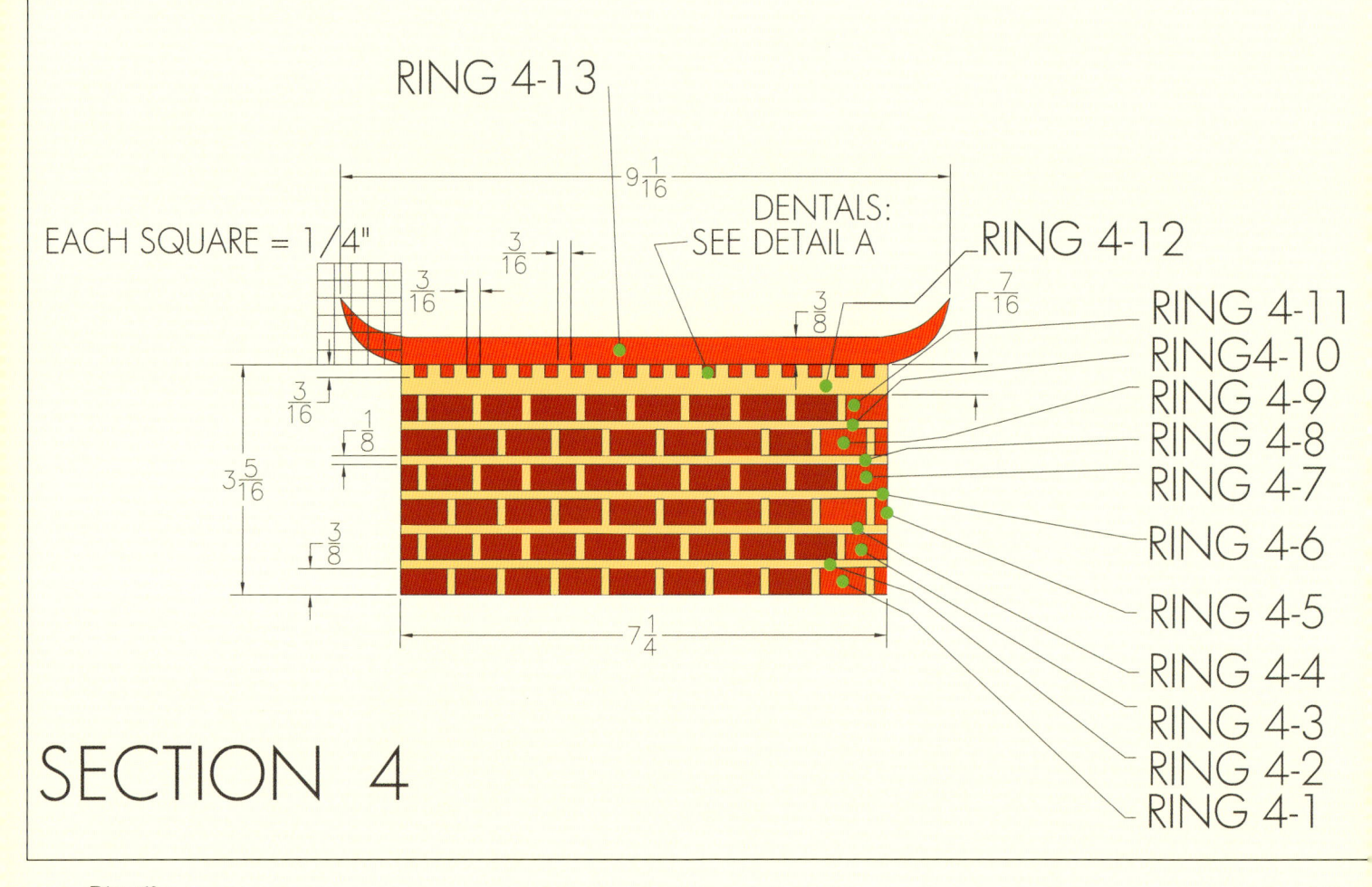

RING 4-13

$9\frac{1}{16}$

DENTALS: SEE DETAIL A

RING 4-12

EACH SQUARE = 1/4"

$\frac{3}{16}$

$\frac{3}{16}$

$\frac{3}{8}$

$\frac{7}{16}$

RING 4-11
RING 4-10
RING 4-9
RING 4-8
RING 4-7
RING 4-6
RING 4-5
RING 4-4
RING 4-3
RING 4-2
RING 4-1

$\frac{3}{16}$

$\frac{1}{8}$

$3\frac{5}{16}$

$\frac{3}{8}$

$7\frac{1}{4}$

SECTION 4

Diag. 62

126 *Segmented Lamp Projects*

PAGODA

RINGS 2-1, 2-3, 2-5, 2-7, 2-9, AND 2-11

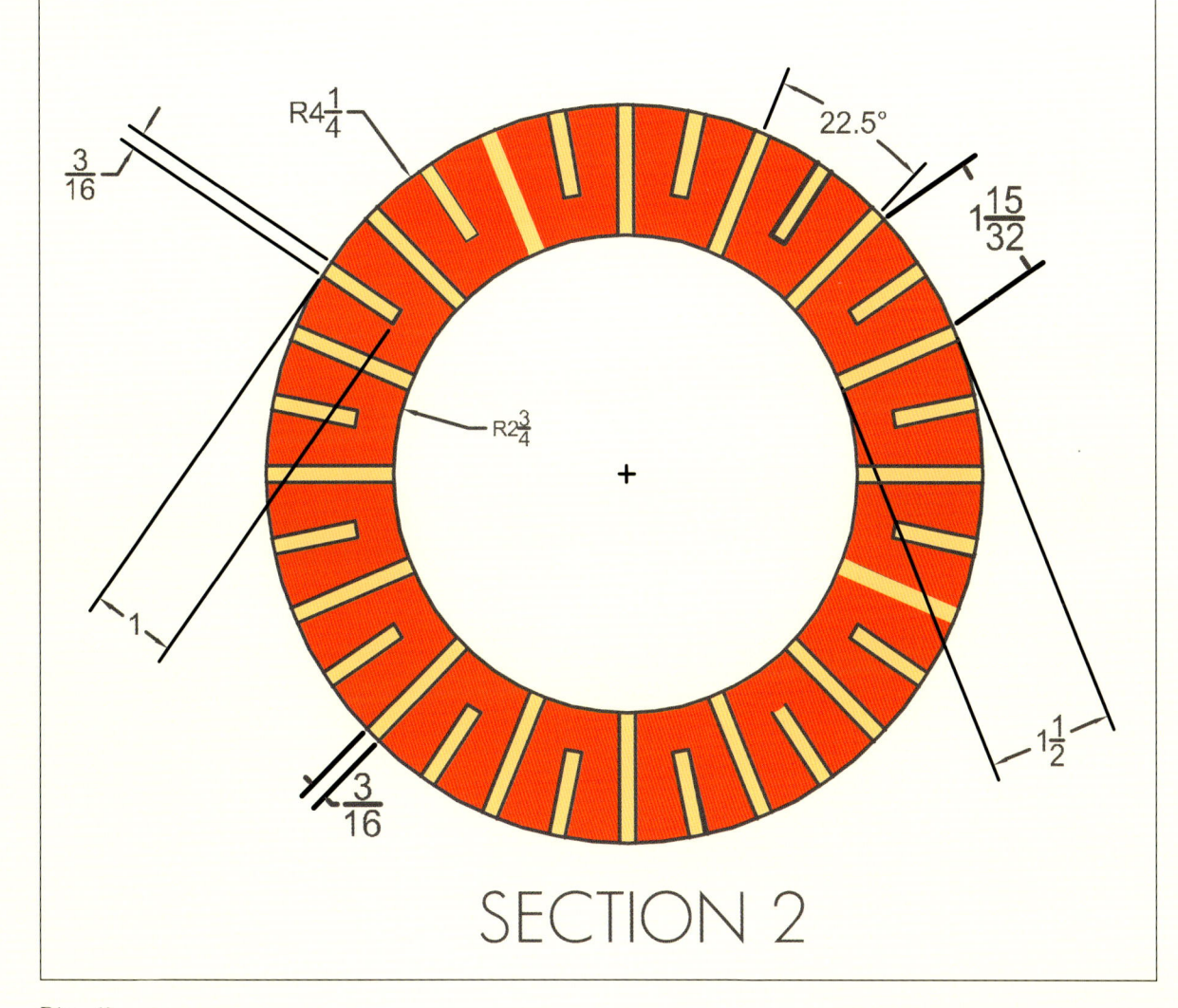

SECTION 2

Diag. 63

PAGODA

RING 2-13
SECTION 2

RINGS 2-2, 2-3, 2-5, 2-7, 2-9, AND 2-11

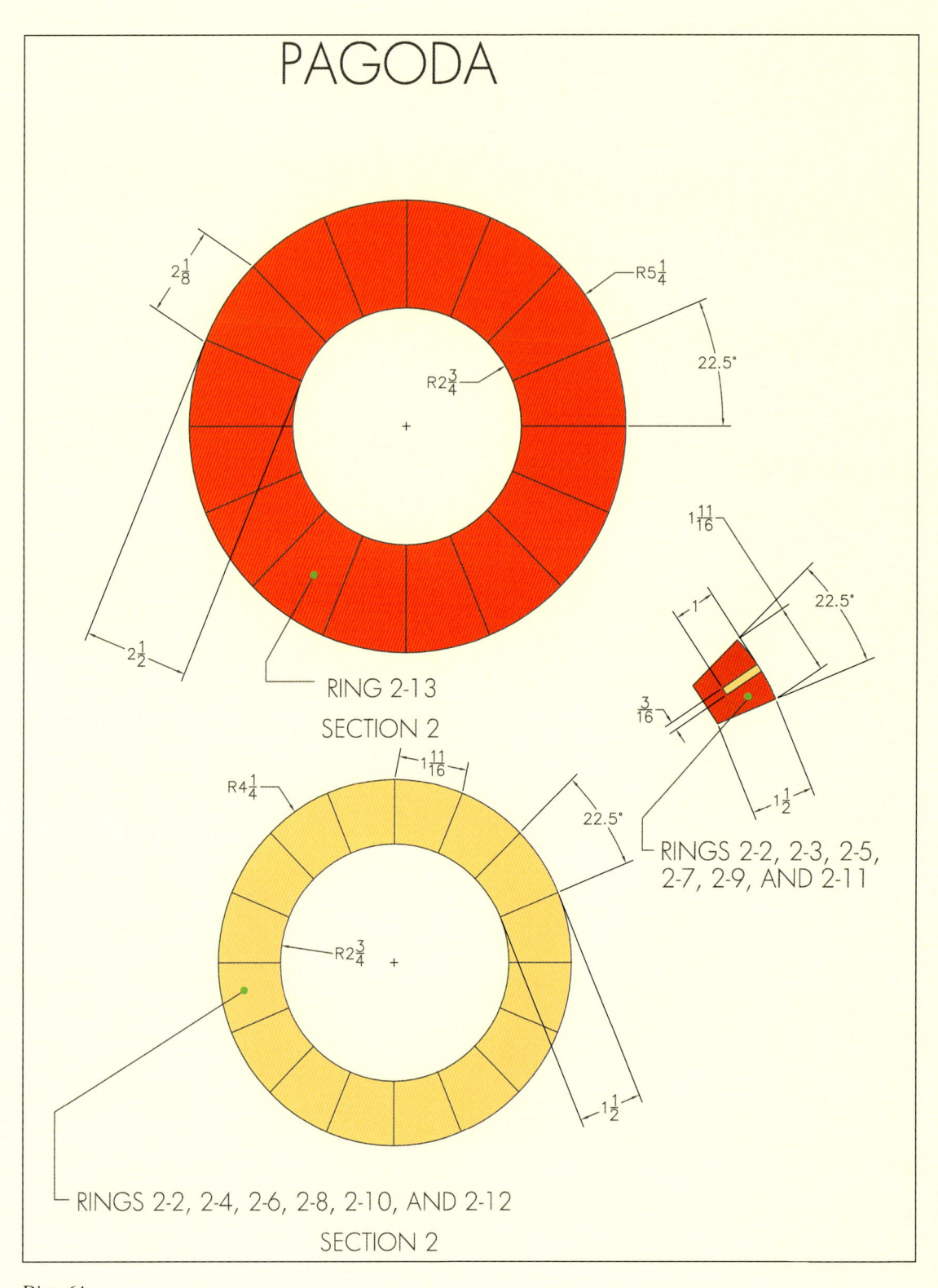

RINGS 2-2, 2-4, 2-6, 2-8, 2-10, AND 2-12
SECTION 2

Diag. 64

128 *Segmented Lamp Projects*

PAGODA SECTION 3

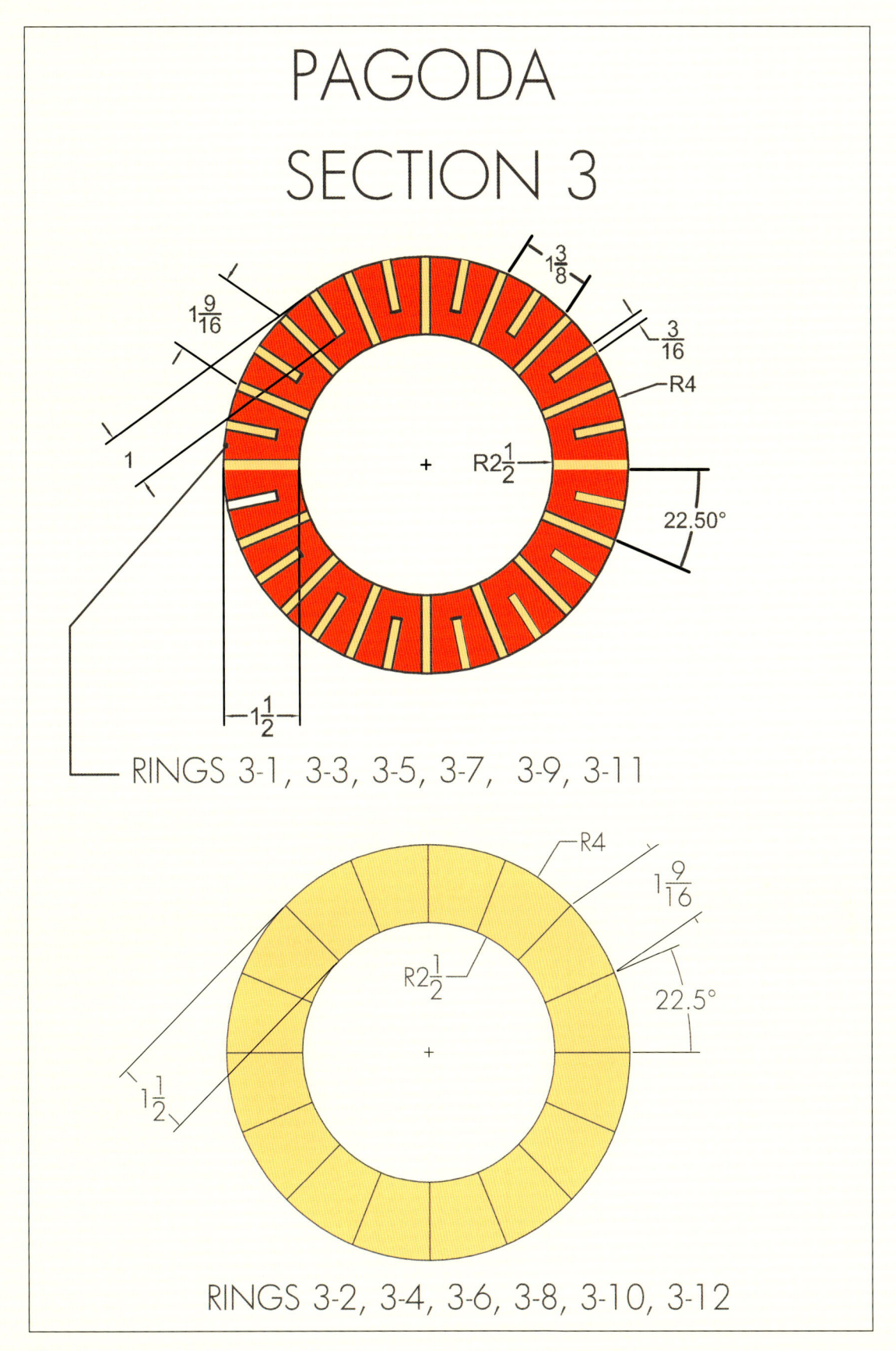

RINGS 3-1, 3-3, 3-5, 3-7, 3-9, 3-11

RINGS 3-2, 3-4, 3-6, 3-8, 3-10, 3-12

Diag. 65

The Pagoda Lamp

PAGODA

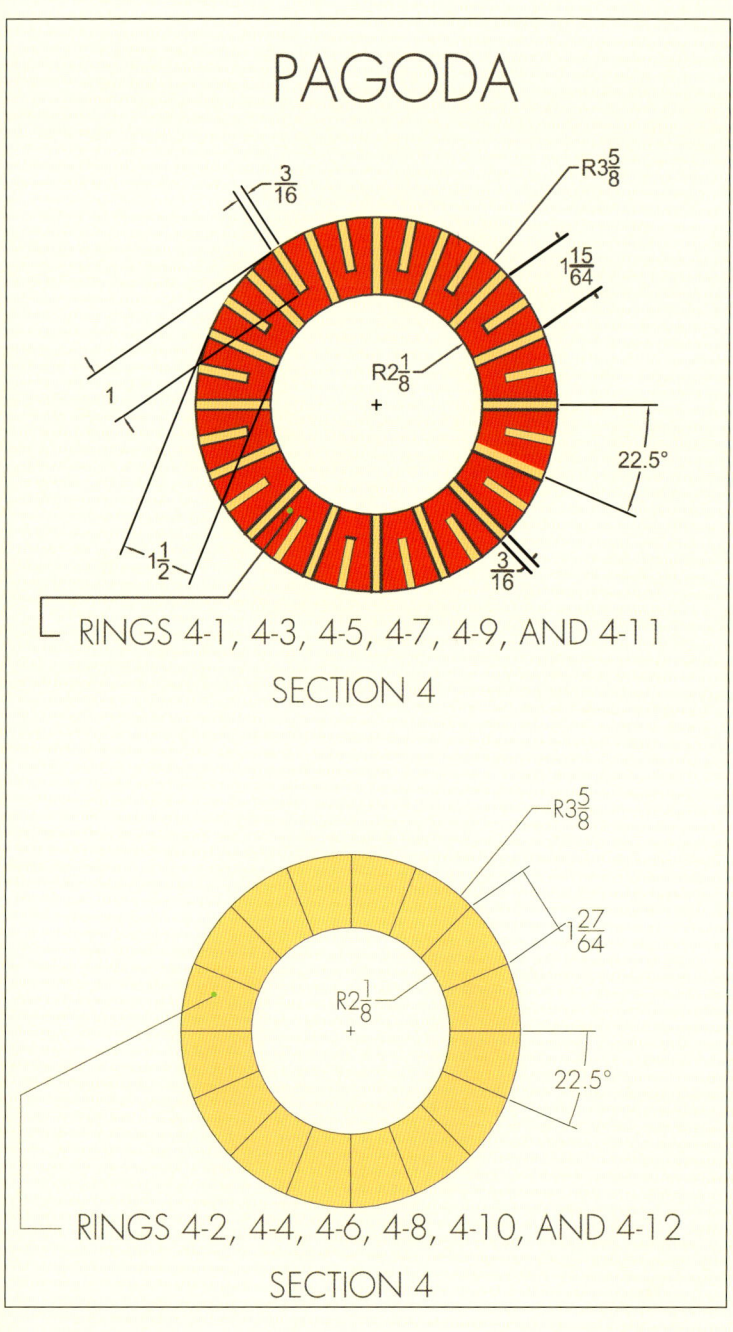

RINGS 4-1, 4-3, 4-5, 4-7, 4-9, AND 4-11
SECTION 4

RINGS 4-2, 4-4, 4-6, 4-8, 4-10, AND 4-12
SECTION 4

Diag. 66

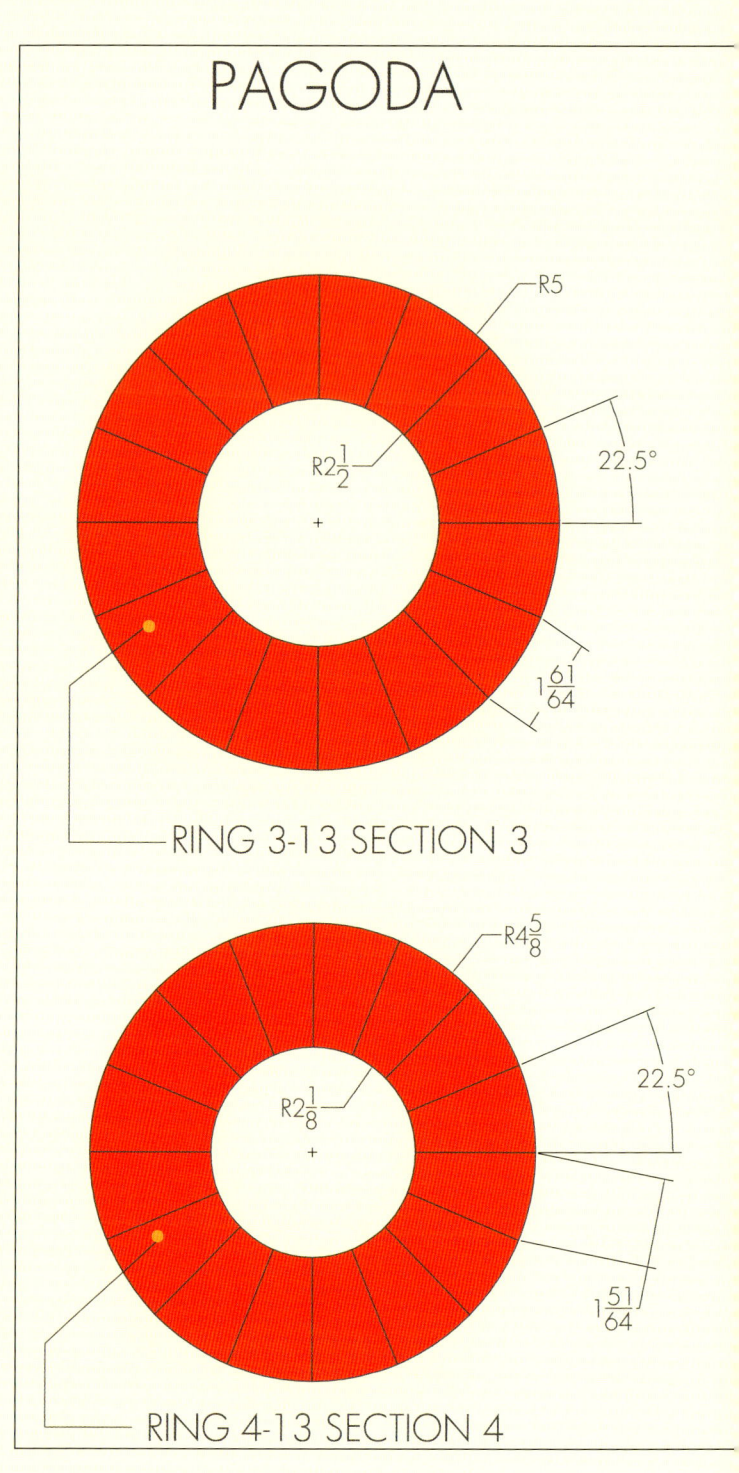

PAGODA

RING 3-13 SECTION 3

RING 4-13 SECTION 4

Diag. 67

130 *Segmented Lamp Projects*

PAGODA

SECTION 5

DETAIL A

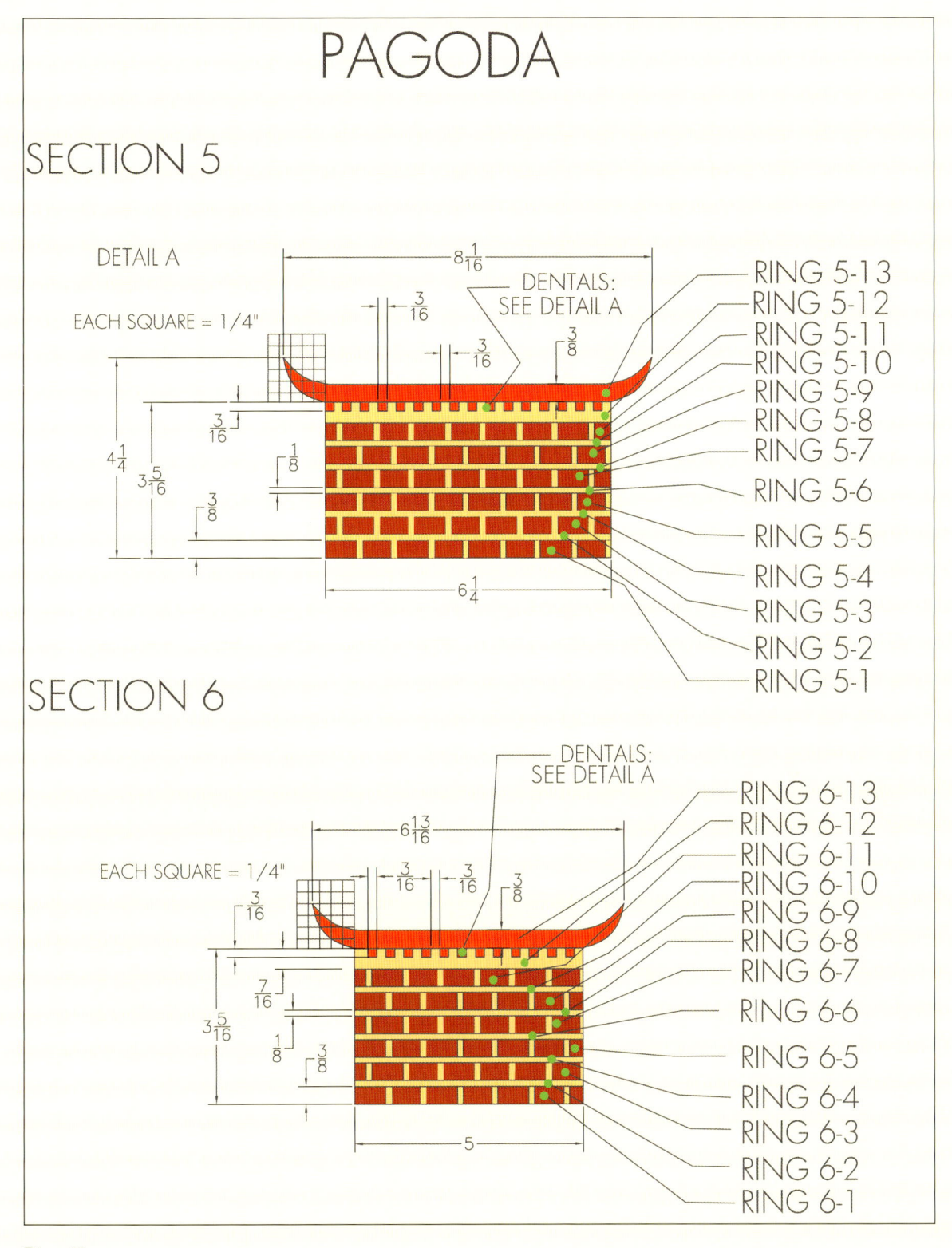

EACH SQUARE = 1/4"

- RING 5-13
- RING 5-12
- RING 5-11
- RING 5-10
- RING 5-9
- RING 5-8
- RING 5-7
- RING 5-6
- RING 5-5
- RING 5-4
- RING 5-3
- RING 5-2
- RING 5-1

DENTALS: SEE DETAIL A

$8\frac{1}{16}$
$\frac{3}{16}$
$\frac{3}{16}$
$\frac{3}{8}$
$4\frac{1}{4}$
$3\frac{5}{16}$
$\frac{3}{16}$
$\frac{1}{8}$
$\frac{3}{8}$
$6\frac{1}{4}$

SECTION 6

EACH SQUARE = 1/4"

DENTALS: SEE DETAIL A

- RING 6-13
- RING 6-12
- RING 6-11
- RING 6-10
- RING 6-9
- RING 6-8
- RING 6-7
- RING 6-6
- RING 6-5
- RING 6-4
- RING 6-3
- RING 6-2
- RING 6-1

$6\frac{13}{16}$
$\frac{3}{16}$
$\frac{3}{16}$
$\frac{3}{8}$
$\frac{3}{16}$
$3\frac{5}{16}$
$\frac{7}{16}$
$\frac{1}{8}$
$\frac{3}{8}$
5

Diag. 68

The Pagoda Lamp 131

PAGODA

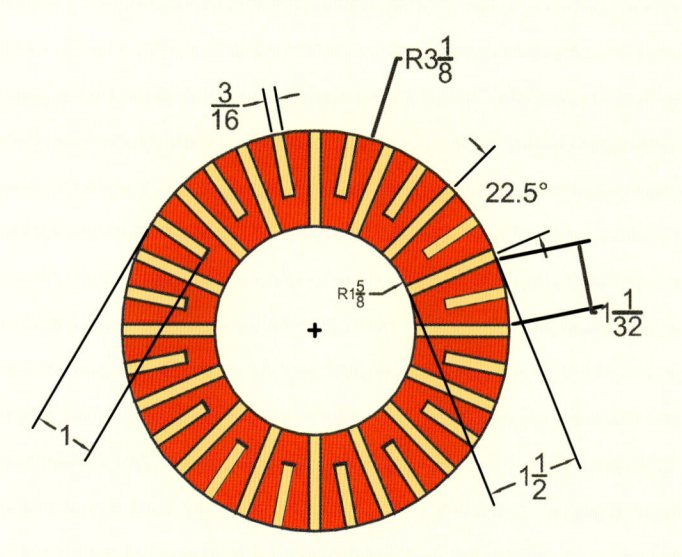

RINGS 5-1, 5-3, 5-5, 5-7, 5-9, AND 5-11
RINGS FOR SECTION 5

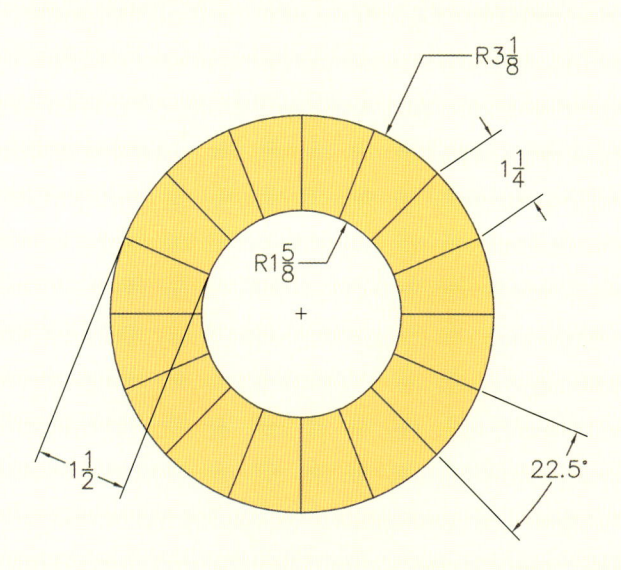

RINGS 5-2, 5-4, 5-6, 5-8, 5-10, AND 1-12
RINGS FOR SECTION 5

Diag. 69

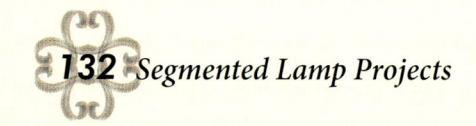

PAGODA

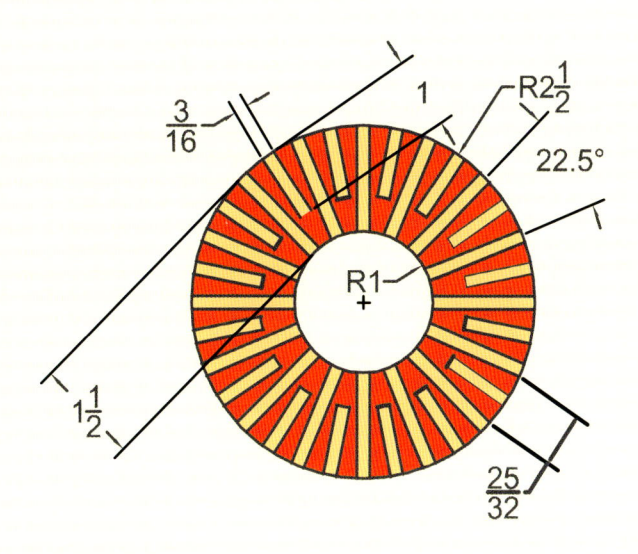

RINGS 6-1, 6-3, 6-5, 6-7, 6-9, and 6-11
RINGS FOR SECTION 6

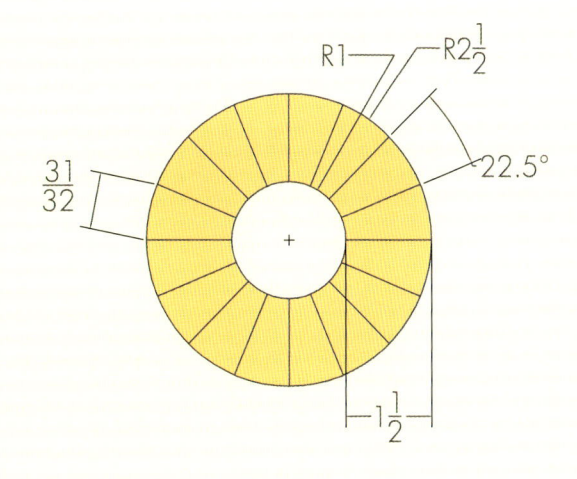

RINGS 6-2, 6-4, 6-6, 6-8, 6-10, AND 6-12
RINGS FOR SECTION 6

Diag. 69a

The Pagoda Lamp

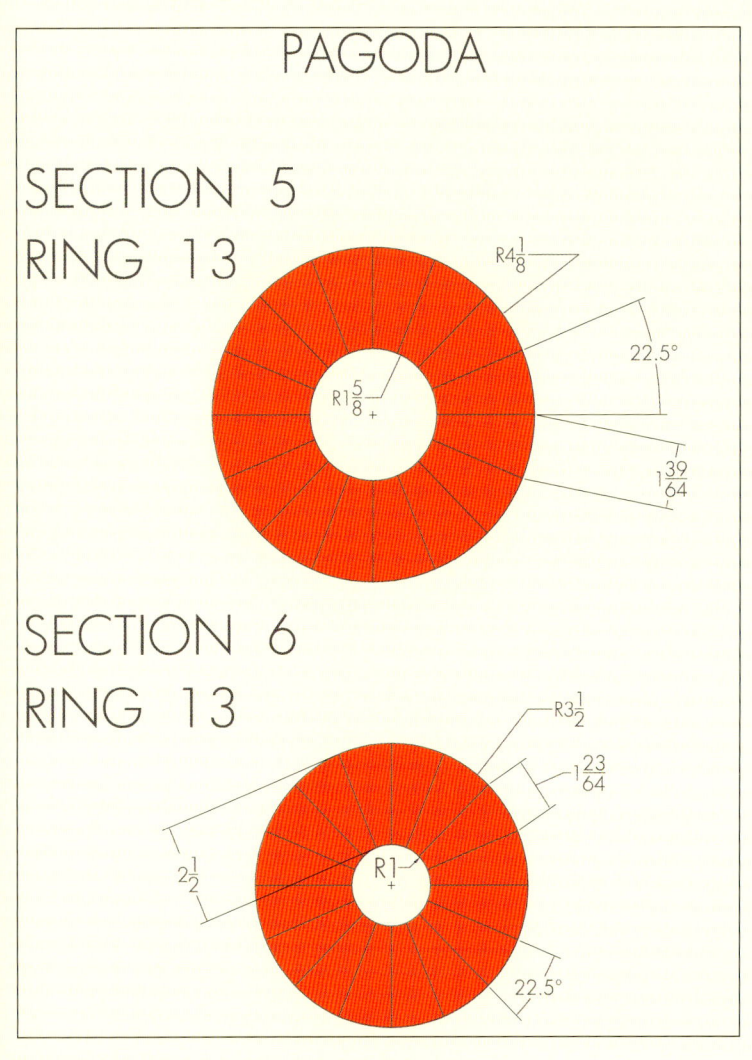

Diag. 70

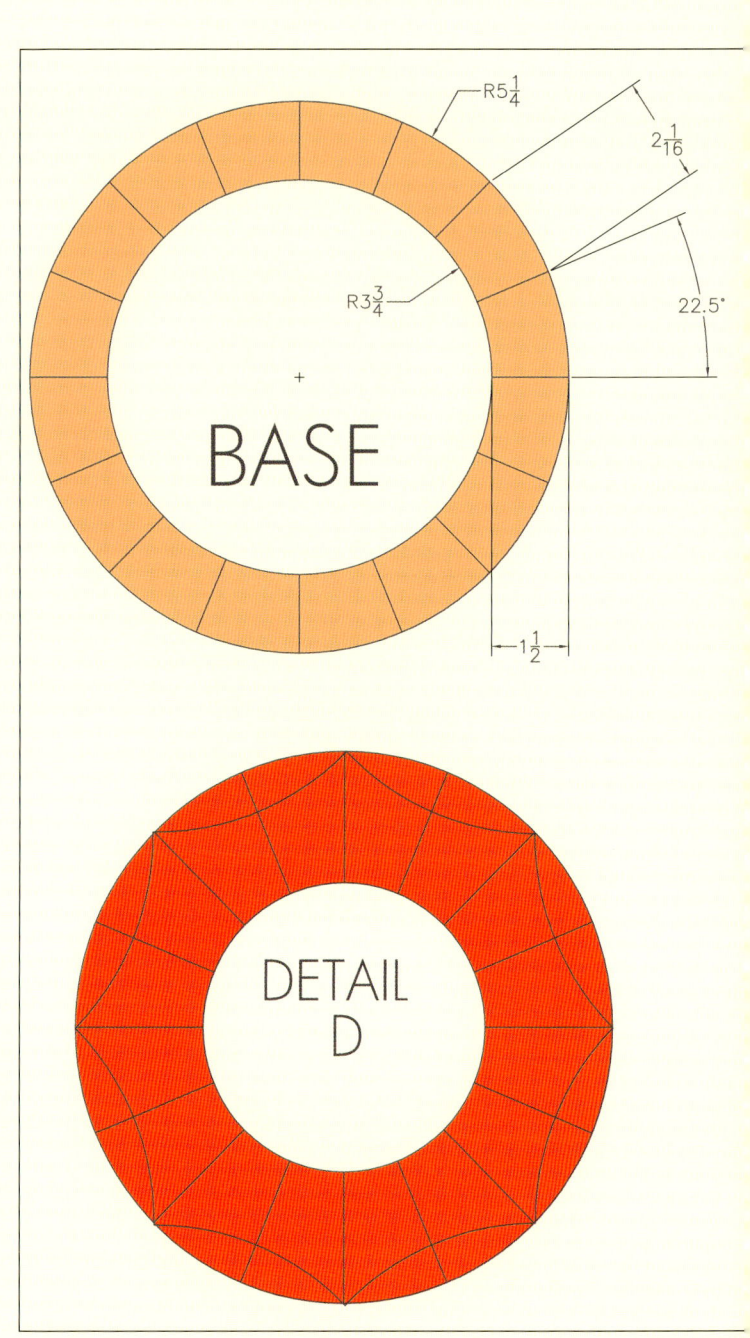

Diag. 71

134 *Segmented Lamp Projects*

FINALE

The total thickness of the Finale is 2"

R$2\frac{1}{8}$

22.5°

$\frac{13}{16}$

$2\frac{1}{8}$

R$2\frac{1}{8}$

DETAIL A

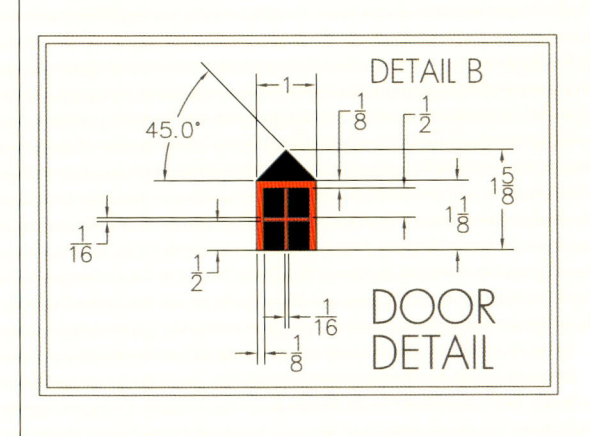

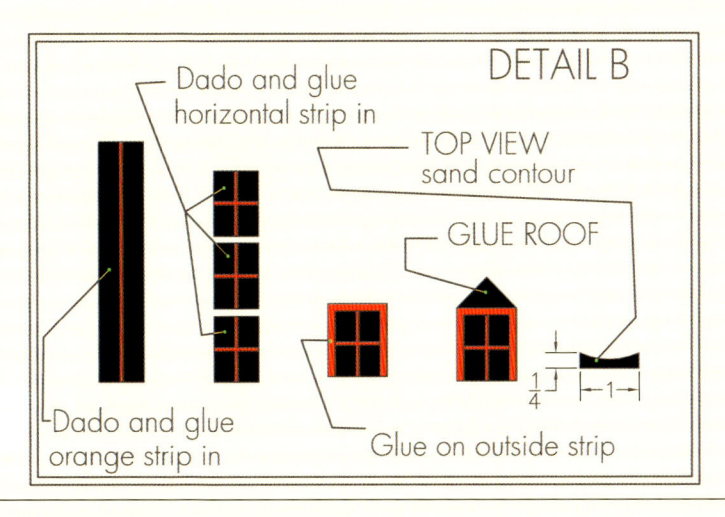

$\frac{3}{16}$ | 1 | $\frac{3}{16}$

OR

$1\frac{1}{16}$ | $\frac{3}{16}$ | $\frac{5}{16}$ | $\frac{5}{16}$

DOOR DETAIL

DETAIL B

45.0°

1

$\frac{1}{8}$ | $\frac{1}{2}$

$1\frac{5}{8}$

$1\frac{1}{8}$

$\frac{1}{16}$

$\frac{1}{2}$

$\frac{1}{16}$

$\frac{1}{8}$

DETAIL B

Dado and glue horizontal strip in

TOP VIEW sand contour

GLUE ROOF

Dado and glue orange strip in

Glue on outside strip

$\frac{1}{4}$ | 1

Diag. 72

- Section 1 contains twelve rings, and each ring has 16 segments. Using a radial arm saw, make a jig (see Fig. 131) and cut the groove that you will later use to insert the lighter colored maple pieces into the walnut (see Fig. 132). In some cases I used spalted maple.

- Using the jig shown in Fig. 131, you can cut the groove, or dado cut, for eight or more segments at the same time. Notice I have two strips of wood holding the segments. Use thicker strips as the segments get smaller. Doing this on the radial arm saw, which in most cases will have a wooden table, the jig can be screwed to the table using square headed screws. Once you have the jig set up to cut exactly in the center you can use this same jig and setup for all six sections of the lamp. I use a thick blade from a dado set to cut this groove.

Fig. 131: I use two thin strips on the side of the wedge for stability. As the wedges get smaller from Section 1 to Section 6, the width of the strips increases.

Fig. 132: Walnut wedges with maple inserts.

Segmented Lamp Projects

• Ring 1 in each section should be turned flat and smooth on both sides (see Fig. 133). Use a plywood disk marked with concentric circles to insure the rings are centered on the lathe before turning. With Ring 1 turned and screwed securely from the back, turn Ring 2 then glue Ring 2 onto Ring 1. Repeat this process until Section 1 is completed. Then repeat to make all six sections individually.

Fig. 133: Turning a ring to its correct thickness.

• With the twelve rings assembled (sec Fig. 134), each section can now be turned to the required diameter. Sand each section on the lathe to its finished state.

Fig. 134: Clamping the top maple ring, Ring 12, to Ring 11.

The Pagoda Lamp

- Cut a groove in ring twelve using a radial arm saw. Notice that a "V" block is used for holding and centering each section (see Fig. 135). The "V" block can be screwed to the table. I use a holding device (see Fig. 136) to hold each section, which keeps your hands in a safer position. This jig can be used for all six sections.

Fig. 135: The "V" block, which is screwed to the radial arm saw table, will properly align all six sections when cutting the dado.

Fig. 136: Using an easy, and quickly made, holding device insures a safer operation.

138 *Segmented Lamp Projects*

• Once the dados are cut (see Fig. 137), cut the dentals. In Diag. 72 you will see that you can make either a square dental, as shown on the left, or a dental with a design, as shown on the right. On the lamp shown, I used the pattern on the right. Sand these small pieces on a Sand-O-Flex, holding them with a pair of pliers (see Fig. 138).

Fig. 137: A section with newly cut dados.

• Glue the dentals into the dados on Ring 12 of each section. Clear CA glue does a good job. Watch for squeeze out as you press the dental into the dado. Be sure to wipe any excess glue off. After the glue has dried, sand each section with its dentals in place on a large belt sander or disk sander so it is flat and ready to accept the roof section.

Fig. 138: Sanding a dental on a Sand-O-Flex.

Fig. 139: Laying out a curve on the roof using a template made of lauan plywood.

The Pagoda Lamp **139**

• In the diagrams the roofs are shown in orange. Turn the roof sections on both sides and cut the shape as shown in Detail D of Diag. 71. First, draw the curve for the roofs as in Fig. 139. I attach these rings to the lathe by drilling a hole and countersinking the screw to hold it. Be sure to drill very close to the inside of the ring so the hole will not be seen later.

• Once the roofs are turned and sanded, use a table jig saw (scroll saw) to cut the roofs to shape (see Fig. 140). Once this curve is cut, sand with a Sand-O-Flex Flip Sander (see Fig. 141).

Fig. 140: Cutting the shape of the roof using a table scroll saw.

140 *Segmented Lamp Projects*

Fig. 141: Sanding the cut portion of a roof.

• Glue the roof sections on with CA glue (see Fig. 142), making sure each section and the roof are line up with each other. Glue all six sections individually.

• Now you will make the base (see Diag. 71). I use two, 3/4" thick rings glued together then turned to 1". Before I assemble these two rings the bottom ring should be turned on both sides. To avoid holes in the bottom of your lamp, attach these rings to the faceplate of your lathe with CA glue. Once this section is turned, it can be glued with CA glue to Section 1. Again, be sure these two pieces are lined up with each other.

• After assembling Sections 1 through 6 and the base, next you can turn the finale. The finale is made in three sections. The bottom section is segmented and the top two sections are solid wood. I do this because I feel that solid wood has less chance of breaking as you insert the 3/8" threaded pipe into the top of the lamp.

• Drill the 3/8" hole for the threaded pipe using the drill press to assure it is vertical. Then glue the finale to the top of the lamp. Drill a 3/8" hole for the cord in the lower part of Section 1 or the base.

• Make the doors as shown in the step by step drawing labeled "Detail B" in Diag. 72 and Fig. 143. Glue these parts together with CA glue.

Fig. 142: Gluing the next section to a roof with CA glue.

Fig. 143: Doors under construction.

Segmented Lamp Projects

- After the door is made, use the round wheel of a belt sander to sand a curve on the back of the door (see Fig. 144). This curve will allow you to fit the doors snuggly on each section of the lamp. NOTE: The curve will vary as the diameter of each section gets smaller. Once the door fits snuggly with no gaps, glue it to the lamp, making sure that all doors align vertically (see Figs. 145 and 146).

- Finish the project with spray lacquer and wire the lamp.

Fig. 144: Sanding the contour of the door to match the curve of the each section.

Fig. 145: Glue the doors to the lamp with CA glue. The contour of each doors will differ slightly.

The Pagoda Lamp **143**

Fig. 146: Align the doors vertically along the length of the lamp.